Federal Job Dispute Procedures

From the Editors of the

FEDERAL EMPLOYEES NEWS DIGEST

Federal Employees
News Digest
INC.

Published by:
Federal Employees News Digest, Inc.
1850 Centennial Park Drive, Suite 520
Reston, VA 20191
Printed in the United States of America

ISBN 0-910582-52-1

Contents

PART 1: TYPES OF DISPUTES

CH. 4: DISCIPLINE

CH. 5:DISCRIMINATION

CH. 6: SEXUAL HARASSMENT

CH. 10: SECURITY CLEARANCES

CH. 11: REDUCTIONS-IN-FORCE

CH. 12: VETERANS PROTECTIONS

PART 2: DISPUTE AND APPEAL PROCESSES

CH. 13: GRIEVANCES

Foreword

"Dispute"—look up the term in a dictionary and you'll find definitions ranging from an "argument" or "debate" to a "spirited" discussion or "vehement" quarrel or contest.

Truth be told, in the federal workplace, job disputes can—and usually do—include all these aspects. What starts as a spirited discussion—perhaps even an argument—often ends up as a "vehement quarrel," which all too frequently boils over into a legal challenge. The causes or roots of these problems are varied, stemming from employee unhappiness over a disciplinary proposal to worker disgruntlement over a job classification or pay action.

What's important for employees—and their managers—to remember is that federal employment, unlike many private-sector jobs, provides workers with avenues of redress and potential remedies for many, if not most, job disputes. The problem is that while many federal workers may be aware of their general rights to file complaints or pursue remedies, depending on the type of dispute encountered, they can quickly get bogged down or bewildered by the array of procedural options and remedial paths that seem open to them.

That's where *Federal Job Dispute Procedures* can save the day—and perhaps an employee's (or manager's) career. In clear, understandable language, *Federal Job Dispute Procedures* identifies and explains the overlapping, and seemingly conflicting, remedial routes available for federal workers who become embroiled in workplace problems and legal squabbles. Building on the strengths of its predecessor volume *Your Job Rights*, this book describes, in accessible, easy-to-understand terms, the major appeals and dispute-resolution channels established by federal agencies to address and resolve employee complaints and concerns about a wide range of management decisions and actions. Not only are the major appeals channels identified and discussed, but *Federal Job Dispute Procedures* also includes focused explanations of the most common types of disputes and challenges that federal workers are apt to file or face. Throughout this volume, readers should find helpful tips, suggestions, reminders, and lists of resources (and case citations) that will help them figure out what their response could (or should) be, as well as what alternative avenues might be open in dealing with the most frequently encountered disputes or problems.

Along with a tip of our hat to all the readers of *Your Job Rights*, whose calls and questions through the years have made this new (and greatly expanded) volume possible, the editors at FEND wish to express our thanks to the attorneys at the Washington, D.C., firm of Kator, Scott & Parks, whose suggestions and legal review helped sharpen and improve a number of chapters in this brand new edition of *Federal Job Dispute Procedures*.

CHAPTER ONE

Introduction

The federal personnel system has been called both too protective of employees and tilted in favor of agencies—depending on the point of view of whoever is doing the assessment. Undeniably, federal employees have rights uncommon in other workplaces. But also undeniably, they work in a special environment in which the public interest is at stake and that interest must be protected from abuses for partisan, personal, or other reasons.

Employee rights are protected under a complex, layered, and duplicative system of laws, rules, and procedures. Employees might end up having their workplace disputes resolved within their employing agency, at adjudicatory agencies, by the federal courts, or through some combination of those three levels. Employees who belong to collective bargaining units—which cover about 60 percent of the non-postal work force and about 90 percent of postal employees—have additional rights granted by contracts, rights that are enforceable through the arbitration process.

Complaints stemming from a particular dispute usually can be submitted to more than one of the various routes. Matters are further complicated by the fact that each of the adjudicatory agencies has its own procedures and precedents. These agencies also vary in their authority to order corrective actions and enforce their decisions.

One reaction to dissatisfaction with the government's complex dispute-resolution system has been a stronger emphasis in recent years on resolving workplace issues in less formal ways. Agencies are doing this by stressing counseling and other efforts to correct problems in their early stages. They also are making available the services of facilitators, mediators, and other professional problem-solvers to address problems early and save the time, effort, and ill feelings that often are expended in the formal appeals processes.

Rights, Processes, and Agencies

Employee Rights in Context

For its first century, the federal government operated under a spoils system, meaning the party in power could hire and fire government employees as it pleased. It took the 1881 assassination of President Garfield by a disgruntled job seeker to spur the first move toward a merit system, the 1883 Civil Service Act. Passage of that law meant that some federal workers would be hired on the basis of competitive examinations—only a few at first, but Congress and the White House steadily increased their numbers. Also, a Civil Service Commission was created to enforce the merit system.

Another breakthrough came in 1944, with the Veterans Preference Act. That law said veterans could not be fired, suspended for more than 30 days, or reduced in rank or pay, "except for such cause as will promote the efficiency of the service." Veterans could demand written notice of an adverse personnel action and appeal to the Civil Service Commission. Since veterans made up more than half of the postwar civil service, this was a dramatic change in workers' rights. For the first time, federal managers would have to justify their personnel actions to an impartial third party and their actions might be overruled.

Pressures arose to grant the same rights to non-veterans, and this was done by a 1962 executive order on labor-management relations issued by President Kennedy. The order further allowed employees to appeal an adverse personnel action within their agency, and, if unsuccessful, to take their appeal to the Commission. It also formally recognized employee unions for the first time. Another executive order, issued in 1969 by President Nixon, solidified labor unions' rights to arbitration and to bargain on operational issues that adversely affect employees.

Three years later, the Equal Employment Opportunity Act of 1972 extended the protections of the Civil Rights Act of 1964 to federal workers and gave the Civil Service Commission enforcement powers.

In the 1970s, critics charged that the government's employment dispute system suffered from a conflict of interest, in that the Civil Service Commission was responsible both for regulating employees' conduct and for deciding employees' appeals from disciplinary actions. These concerns were addressed in the Civil Service Reform Act of 1978, which eliminated the Commission and assigned its powers to five agencies, four of them newly created: the Merit Systems Protection Board, the Office of Special Counsel, the Federal Labor Relations Authority, the Equal Employment Opportunity Commission, and the Office of Personnel Management.

Another major reform, the 1989 Whistleblower Protection Act, arose out of concerns that the 1978 Reform Act did not adequately prevent retaliation against employees who make disclosures of wrongdoing by agency officials.

Meanwhile, quasi-judicial appeals agencies and federal courts over the years have issued important precedential decisions interpreting the various laws, and, in the process, defining who is covered by which protections and what types of personnel actions are or aren't allowed in various situations.

Thus, employee rights arise from a mixture of actions by all three branches of government—legislation, executive orders, and court rulings. This contributes to the overlap and confusion. But there is a basic structure.

A Quick Tour of the Options

On serious personnel matters, such as being fired, laid off, or demoted, you may appeal to the Merit Systems Protection Board or use your agency's negotiated grievance system if you are a member of a bargaining unit.

On less serious matters not appealable to MSPB, you can use your agency's negotiated grievance system if you are in a bargaining unit or the administrative dispute resolution process set up by your agency if you are not in a bargaining unit.

If you think you have been discriminated against because of your race, color, sex, religion, national origin, age, or disability, or you believe you have been subjected to sexual harassment, go to your agency's EEO counselor.

If you are in a union bargaining unit, your union can push a grievance to arbitration and can appeal arbitration decisions to the Federal Labor Relations Authority. The union also can go to FLRA to resolve disputes over employee rights granted by contract, as well as employee rights to join, form, or assist a union.

If you believe your agency has taken reprisals against you because you disclosed evidence of gross mismanagement or violations of the law—that is, you are a whistleblower—or you want to report an alleged prohibited personnel practice, you may go to the Office of Special Counsel or, if the actions are the type ordinarily appealable to MSPB, directly to that agency.

The Office of Personnel Management will consider your complaints about your agency's decisions on your job classification, your coverage or pay under the Federal Labor Standards Act, and monetary claims arising out of leave or compensation disputes.

Also available at many agencies are alternative dispute resolution channels, which—depending on their design and scope—can be used as a substitute for many of the formal routes.

Grievances— Negotiated and Administrative

The Reform Act requires that collective bargaining agreements between agencies and unions establish a negotiated grievance procedure that bargaining unit members can use to pursue a workplace grievance. Grievable issues are broadly defined,

ranging from complaints about the office environment and shift assignments to appeals of major adverse actions, such as dismissals or demotions. In cases of major adverse actions, employees can appeal either through the negotiated process or to MSPB, but they cannot pursue both.

Agencies and unions have great flexibility in designing their negotiated grievance procedures. These procedures typically provide for a grievance to be reviewed by two or three levels of management and then, if not resolved, to be submitted to binding arbitration by a private-sector arbitrator. Except for major adverse actions, which can only be appealed to the courts, either side can appeal an arbitrator's decision to the FLRA. The Authority can affirm, modify, or reverse an arbitrator's decision. Unless an unfair labor practice is involved, the Authority's decision is final.

In non-union settings, administrative grievance processes are generally available for matters not ordinarily appealable elsewhere, such as suspensions of under 14 days. Agencies have a great deal of latitude in designing such programs, but in general the administrative procedures are intended to provide a route to present a complaint and receive fair consideration, which may or may not involve hearings, fact-finding, and other information gathering techniques.

Union-represented employees also may use administrative grievance processes if there is no negotiated grievance procedure or where such a procedure excludes the matter at issue. Decisions on administrative grievances are final.

ADR and Settlements

The government in recent years has increasingly made available alternative dispute resolution channels, seeking to save the time and money

Merit System Principles

Merit system principles applicable to federal employment are found in Section 2301 of Title 5, United States Code. Under the law, executive agencies and the Government Printing Office are to assure that their personnel management is consistent with these principles:

(1) Recruitment should be from qualified individuals from appropriate sources in an endeavor to achieve a work force from all segments of society, and selection and advancement should be determined solely on the basis of relative ability, knowledge, and skills, after fair and open competition which assures that all receive equal opportunity.

(2) All employees and applicants for employment should receive fair and equitable treatment in all aspects of personnel management without regard to political affiliation, race, color, religion, national origin, sex, marital status, age, or handicapping condition, and with proper regard for their privacy and constitutional rights.

(3) Equal pay should be provided for work of equal value, with appropriate consideration of both national and local rates paid by employers in the private sector, and appropriate incentives and recognition should be provided for excellence in performance.

(4) All employees should maintain high standards of integrity, conduct, and concern for the public interest.

(5) The federal work force should be used efficiently and effectively.

(6) Employees should be retained on the basis of adequacy of their performance, inadequate performance should be corrected, and employees should be separated who cannot or will not improve their performance to meet required standards.

(7) Employees should be provided effective education and training in cases in which such education and training would result in better organizational and individual performance.

(8) Employees should be—

(A) protected against arbitrary action, personal favoritism, or coercion for partisan political purposes, and

(B) prohibited from using their official authority or influence for the purpose of interfering with or affecting the result of an election or a nomination for election.

(9) Employees should be protected against reprisal for the lawful disclosure of information which the employees reasonably believe evidences—

(A) a violation of any law, rule, or regulation, or

(B) mismanagement, a gross waste of funds, an abuse of authority, or a substantial and specific danger to public health or safety.

It is a prohibited personnel practice to take or fail to take any personnel action if the taking or failure to take the action violates any law, rule or regulation implementing or directly concerning these principles.

invested in, and the ill feelings that are often generated through, the formal appeals channels. In some cases, such options are triggered after a formal personnel action is taken, but they frequently are also available to address and resolve earlier issues that arise between employees and their agencies.

These channels may include the use of mediators, arbitrators, fact-finders, ombudsmen, peer review panels, and a variety of similar programs that agencies have designed, often with input from individual employees and/or employee unions.

In addition, each of the major appeals agencies—MSPB, FLRA, and EEOC—has developed its own programs for resolving formal appeals in a less structured way, emphasizing in particular the use of settlement agreements that strike a compromise between the two sides in which each promises to do something. For example, in a case involving discipline for charges of excessive absenteeism, the agency might agree to reduce the penalty and expunge certain records from the employee's file in exchange for the worker's commitment to meet attendance standards in the future.

In general, such agreements are viewed as binding contracts between the two sides, and alleged violations are reviewed under standards that govern breaches of contract.

Merit Systems Protection Board

MSPB functions much like a court, hearing appeals from agency personnel actions and cases brought by the Office of Special Counsel. Most federal employees have the right to appeal major personnel actions to MSPB. For example, if you are fired or demoted for misconduct or poor performance, suspended for more than 14 days, furloughed, or laid off or demoted during a reduction in force (RIF), you can appeal to MSPB.

If you claim that an adverse personnel action was the result of illegal discrimination, MSPB can decide both the merits of the case and whether the discrimination claim is valid. In these "mixed cases," after the MSPB decision, you can ask the Equal Employment Opportunity Commission (EEOC) to review the discrimination aspect of the decision or you can appeal to a federal district court. The EEOC's review is only "on the record"—you are not entitled to a new hearing.

When an MSPB office receives an appeal, it is assigned to an administrative judge. The agency must provide its file on the case to both the employee and the judge. Both the worker and the agency can present new information to the judge.

You have the right to a hearing on the merits once jurisdiction and timeliness are established. The administrative judge will hold at least one prehearing conference to define the issues and seek a settlement. If the case proceeds to a hearing, both sides can present evidence, make arguments to the judge, and call witnesses, after which the judge issues an initial decision.

Either you or the agency can ask the three-member Board to review an administrative judge's decision. A final MSPB decision is the end of the administrative review process for all except mixed cases. However, the worker (but not the agency) can seek judicial review at the U.S. Court of Appeals for the Federal Circuit.

In cases brought by the Office of Special Counsel, OSC acts as the investigator and prosecutor, while the MSPB acts as a court. Most OSC cases are based on employees' charges of prohibited personnel practices.

Equal Employment Opportunity Commission

If you are a federal worker and believe you have been discriminated against, you can seek assistance within your agency and you also can appeal to EEOC.

The five-member EEOC has primary responsibility for enforcing the laws prohibiting discrimination in the federal workplace. It advises other agencies on EEO issues, directs a nationwide staff of administrative judges who hear discrimination cases, and resolves appeals of discrimination cases. Almost all federal employees can file appeals with the EEOC, as can job applicants who think they have been discriminated against.

Discrimination arises when an employee has been denied a promotion, downgraded, dismissed, or been subjected to some other adverse personnel action because of race, color, sex, religion, national origin, age, or disability. Discrimination does not have to involve a personnel action. For example, if an agency fails to accommodate your physical or mental disability, that could be discrimination. It could also involve an agency paying unequal wages for the same work, or having a workplace environment marked by sexually harassing behavior.

If you think you have been discriminated against and want to take action, you must first talk with an EEO counselor at your agency. The counselor will gather facts about your case and try to resolve it informally. If your complaint cannot be resolved informally, the counselor will explain the EEO process and give you written notice of your right to file an EEO complaint with your agency.

If your complaint is accepted, the agency must conduct a full investigation of the alleged discrimination. This can include interviewing you and others, and obtaining documentary evidence. When the agency completes its investigation, it must give you a copy of its investigatory file.

If the agency rejects your complaint, you have the right to appeal to EEOC for review.

When you receive the copy of your investigation file, you have a choice. You can request an immediate final decision from the agency, based on the evidence it has compiled. Or, you can request a hearing before an EEOC administrative judge. At these hearings, both sides can introduce new evidence and call witnesses. The administrative judge then issues a decision.

If EEOC finds that you were discriminated against, it can issue binding orders for corrective action by your agency. This can include a promotion, back pay, compensatory damages, or attorney's fees for you, or recommendations for disciplinary action against those who discriminated against you, or changes in the system that permitted the discrimination to exist.

EEOC also can review the discrimination portion of "mixed" cases decided by MSPB, as well as discrimination issues that arise under negotiated grievance procedures.

Federal Labor Relations Authority

FLRA administers the labor-management relations program for over 1.9 million non-postal federal employees, more than 1.3 million of whom are represented by unions. (The National Labor Relations Board has jurisdiction over postal union matters.) The 1978 Civil Service Reform Act guaranteed federal employees the right to form, join, or assist a union—or to refrain from doing so—and to engage in collective bargaining through representatives of their own choosing without fear of reprisal.

FLRA has three main components: the Authority, a three-member, quasi-judicial panel that, along with its administrative law judges, functions much like a court in deciding cases; the Office of the General Counsel, which investigates and prosecutes cases before the Authority; and the Federal Service Impasses Panel, which can impose binding settlements on unions and agencies when they fail to reach agreement through collective bargaining.

The law creates rights and obligations on the part of unions, management, and employees in a workplace represented by a union. If either labor or management fails to perform its obligations to the other, or interferes with the other's rights, an unfair labor practice (ULP) charge can be filed with one of the FLRA's regional offices.

For example, it is illegal for management to threaten or retaliate against workers for seeking union representation, and neither an agency nor a union can refuse to bargain in good faith.

FLRA's Office of the General Counsel investigates ULP charges through its regional offices, which settle many disputes short of litigation. When charges have merit and are not resolved informally, the general counsel prosecutes the case before one of FLRA's administrative law judges, who decides whether a ULP was committed. These decisions can be appealed to the Authority, and its decisions in turn can be appealed to federal appeals courts.

FLRA also resolves representation issues, sometimes by conducting and supervising secret-ballot union elections and also by deciding who can be in a bargaining unit. These cases begin when an agency or union (or, in rare cases, an individual) files a representation petition with one of FLRA's regional offices.

When an agency and a union cannot reach agreement through collective bargaining, they can seek help from FLRA's Federal Service Impasses Panel. The panel will help the parties try to reach an informal agreement; if that isn't possible, FSIP has the authority to impose settlement terms that are binding on both parties and cannot be appealed to the courts.

When an agency refuses to bargain over a proposal it considers non-negotiable, the union can appeal to the Authority.

Office of Personnel Management

OPM has jurisdiction to hear complaints from workers who believe they have been denied overtime pay because it was improperly calculated or because their agency has improperly excluded them from FLSA coverage. If you are not covered by a negotiated grievance procedure, you can appeal an agency decision on these FLSA issues to OPM. If OPM rules against you, you have the right to appeal to the federal courts.

If you are covered by a negotiated grievance procedure, you must use that procedure, and OPM is not involved.

OPM also has authority to review complaints that a job classification does not accurately reflect the work the employee is performing. OPM will examine the facts, compare your duties to official criteria for the positions in question, and issue a decision. OPM's classification decisions cannot be appealed.

Further, OPM decides certain claims on leave and compensation issues (other monetary claims, involving travel and transportation allowances and transportation rates are under the General Services

Administration's authority). Monetary claims must be first brought before the employing agency, and then may be appealed to OPM or GSA, as appropriate.

OPM may intervene in cases before MSPB when its director believes a decision involves a misinterpretation of a civil service law or regulation and will have a substantial impact on the civil service. OPM also can seek the reconsideration of arbitration awards involving firings, demotions, and suspensions in cases of poor performance or misconduct. It can appeal adverse rulings to the federal courts.

Office of Special Counsel

OSC is an independent investigative and prosecutorial agency with three main areas of responsibility:

Prohibited Personnel Practices—You can request OSC's assistance if you believe an agency has committed a prohibited personnel practice, especially taking, threatening, or failing to take a personnel action in reprisal for whistleblowing. Other prohibited practices include reprisal for exercising an appeal right, grant-

ing an unauthorized preference to a job candidate, and nepotism. OSC investigates reports of such violations. It may negotiate with the agency for voluntary corrective action and, if necessary, will petition the MSPB to stay a personnel action and order corrective action or disciplinary action against those charged with committing the prohibited practice.

The Hatch Act—The Hatch Act restricts some political activities by federal employees, such as running for public office and soliciting political donations. OSC provides guidance on what is permitted under the Act, investigates alleged violations, and, if necessary, seeks disciplinary action by MSPB.

Whistleblower Disclosures—Federal employees sometimes see fellow workers breaking the law, wasting money, abusing their authority, endangering public health or safety, yet fear retaliation if they speak out. OSC provides a channel for such disclosures and also investigates and may prosecute allegations of retaliation for whistleblowing.

Prohibited Personnel Practices

The law on prohibited personnel practices is found in Section 2302 of Title 5, United States Code. Under the law, a "personnel action" means: an appointment; a promotion; a disciplinary or corrective action; a detail, transfer, or reassignment; a reinstatement; a restoration; a reemployment; a performance evaluation; a decision concerning pay, benefits, or awards concerning education or training if the education or training may reasonably be expected to lead to an appointment, promotion, performance evaluation, or other action described in the section; a decision to order psychiatric testing or examination; or any other significant change in duties, responsibilities, or working conditions.

Covered positions are those in the competitive service, career appointee positions in the Senior Executive Service, or positions in the excepted service. Non-covered positions are those excepted from the competitive service because of their confidential, policy-determining, policy-making, or policy-advocating character; or those exempted by the President based on a determination by the President that such action is necessary and warranted by conditions of good administration.

Covered agencies are executive agencies and the Government Printing Office, but not: a government corporation, except for practices under (8) below; the Federal Bureau of Investigation, Central Intelligence Agency, Defense Intelligence Agency, Central Imagery Office, National Security Agency, and, as determined by the President, any executive agency or unit whose principal function is the conduct of foreign intelligence or counterintelligence activities; or the General Accounting Office.

The law says any employee who has authority to take, direct others to take, recommend, or approve any personnel action, shall not:

(1) discriminate for or against any employee or applicant for employment—

   (A) on the basis of race, color, religion, sex, or national origin, as prohibited under section 717 of the Civil Rights Act of 1964 (42 U.S.C. 2000e-16);

   (B) on the basis of age, as prohibited under sections 12 and 15 of the Age Discrimination in Employment Act of 1967 (29 U.S.C. 631, 633a);

   (C) on the basis of sex, as prohibited under section 6(d) of the Fair Labor Standards Act of 1938 (29 U.S.C. 206(d));

   (D) on the basis of handicapping condition, as prohibited under section 501 of the Rehabilitation Act of 1973 (29 U.S.C. 791); or

   (E) on the basis of marital status or political affiliation, as prohibited under any law, rule, or regulation;

(2) solicit or consider any recommendation or statement, oral or written, with respect to any individual who requests or is under consideration for any personnel action except as provided under section 3303(f);

(3) coerce the political activity of any person (including the providing of any political contribution or service), or take any action against any employee of applicant for employment as a reprisal for the refusal of any person to engage in such political activity;

(4) deceive or willfully obstruct any person with respect to such person's right to compete for employment;

(5) influence any person to withdraw from competition for any position for the purpose of improving or injuring the prospects of any other person for employment;

Prohibited Personnel Practices (continued)

(6) grant any preference or advantage not authorized by law, rule, or regulation to any employee or applicant for employment (including defining the scope or manner of competition or the requirements for any position) for the purpose of improving or injuring the prospects of any particular person for employment;

(7) appoint, employ, promote, advance, or advocate for appointment, employment, promotion, or advancement in or to a civilian position any individual who is a relative (as defined in section 3110(a)(3) of this title) of such employee if such position is in the agency in which such employee is serving as a public official (as defined in section 3110(a)(2) of this title) or over which such employee exercises jurisdiction or control as such an official;

(8) take or fail to take, or threaten to take or fail to take, a personnel action with respect to any employee or applicant for employment because of—

    (A) any disclosure of information by an employee or applicant which the employee or applicant reasonably believes evidences — (i) a violation of any law, rule or regulation, or (ii) gross mismanagement, a gross waste of funds, an abuse of authority, or a substantial and specific danger to public health or safety, if such disclosure is not specifically prohibited by law and if such information is not specifically required by Executive order to be kept secret in the interest of national defense or the conduct of foreign affairs; or

    (B) any disclosure to the Special Counsel, or to the Inspector General of an agency or another employee designated by the head of the agency to receive such disclosures, of information which the employee or applicant reasonably believes evidences — (i) a violation of any law, rule, or regulation, or (ii) gross mismanagement, a gross waste of funds, an abuse of authority, or a substantial and specific danger to public health or safety;

(9) take or fail to take, or threaten to take or fail to take, any personnel action against any employee or applicant for employment because of—

    (A) the exercise of any appeal, complaint, or grievance right granted by any law, rule, or regulation;

    (B) testifying for or otherwise lawfully assisting any individual in the exercise of any right referred to in subparagraph (A);

    (C) cooperating with or disclosing information to the Inspector General of an agency, or the Special Counsel, in accordance with applicable provisions of law; or

    (D) refusing to obey an order that would require the individual to violate a law.

(10) discriminate for or against any employee or applicant for employment on the basis of conduct which does not adversely affect the performance of the employee or applicant or the performance of others; except that nothing in this paragraph shall prohibit an agency from taking into account in determining suitability or fitness any conviction of the employee or applicant for any crime under the laws of any State, of the District of Columbia,

(11) take or fail to take any other personnel action if the taking of or failure to take such action violates any law, rule, or regulation implementing, or directly concerning, the merit system principles contained in section 2301 of this title. This subsection shall not be construed to authorize the withholding of information from the Congress or the taking of any personnel action against an employee who discloses information to the Congress.

CHAPTER TWO

Getting Ready

The first—and potentially most difficult—step for anyone facing a potential or actual personnel action is determining just where you stand. That means gathering information that might be needed to solve a problem informally or mount a formal challenge, and then exploring possible sources of advice and help.

Sometimes, employees don't like what they discover after going through this process and gauging how and where they stand. If honest with themselves, they're often forced to admit that they were in the wrong—at least legally speaking—and that the agency may well be justified in the steps it is taking. Other employees, though, find to their surprise and pleasure that they actually are better off than they thought they were, since they've discovered rights they didn't know they had and cases similar to their own in which complainants prevailed.

Another important consideration is determining just how and where an appeal should be filed, particularly when there are multiple and sometimes duplicative routes available to employees. Each appeal or complaint procedure tends to have its own set of procedural rules, as well as its own precedents and principles that usually end up having a significant bearing on the outcome of an employee's situation.

As part of their assessment process, employees also should consider the availability of alternative dispute resolution channels and options for settlement (see specific chapters). Such procedures can be invaluable in terms of achieving a workable solution to a workplace problem and can help keep disputes from escalating, literally, into a "federal case."

Gathering Information

What's Needed?

Federal employees preparing for a possible appeal of a personnel action usually need to gather numerous documents. Typically, these include copies of their own personnel files, such as records of dates of hire, promotions, awards, prior discipline if any, transfers, merit pay increases, and similar actions or events. The employee also may benefit from viewing other documents that were not personal in nature but may have affected the personnel action.

Most of these documents are held by the employing agency—the very agency that made the decision with which the employee disagrees. While the employee appeal channels guarantee workers access rights to certain documents, employees often find it difficult to review or gain access to some records that they believe they need. Two laws that can help in such situations are the Privacy Act and the Freedom of Information Act.

To assess where they stand, employees also may wish to research prior decisions by the administrative and judicial bodies that may be charged with handling such matters. These decisions are available through several legal reference sources that should be available to most employees (for example, at agency libraries or regional offices of an administrative agency, etc.).

Gathering information takes time, however. Employees facing tight deadlines—such as a requirement to file a formal appeal within a certain time—first should make sure they meet all such legal filing deadlines or obligations.

Researching Precedent

The decisions of the federal courts and the administrative bodies that most commonly decide federal employment disputes are indexed, making searches possible by subject matter, names, dates and so on. Some collections of decisions are published by the government, while others are put out by private companies.

The table at the end of the chapter shows where these resources might be found. However, actual availability of the different resources varies from place to place; there is no guarantee, for example, that a given agency office or law library will have a particular set of volumes. It's wise to call before going, to inquire not only about the availability of resources, but also about any restrictions on using the materials.

Legal Tools

Privacy Act

The Privacy Act of 1974 gives federal employees several rights with regard to records collected or maintained in what the Act calls a "system of records." Under the Privacy Act, a "system" of records means "a group of any records under the control of any agency from which information is retrieved by the name of the individual" or some other identifying characteristic assigned to an individual.

The Act allows federal employees to inspect and receive copies of their files, subject to various exemptions that an agency can claim (if it has published regulations pursuant to the exemptions).

Employees can request correction or amendment of any Privacy Act-covered information about them that they feel is in error. If the agency does not correct the record, the employee can appeal the agency's denial to a person whose name and address should be provided in the denial letter. Workers who lose such an appeal have the right to file a brief statement stating their reasons for disputing the information, which will accompany the record if it is sent somewhere else by the agency.

Agencies also are required to publish public notices of all systems of records they maintain.

The law requires agencies to obtain an employee's written permission prior to disclosing to other persons or agencies information about the individual, unless such disclosures are specifically authorized under the Act. Information can be disclosed without an individual's consent, for example, under circumstances in which the disclosure is:

• Required under the Freedom of Information Act;

• Is to an employee or officer of the agency that maintains the record who has a need for the information in order to perform official duties;

• Is pursuant to a court order, a showing of compelling circumstances affecting the health or safety of an individual, or a "routine use" as outlined in the agency's public notice of the system of records containing the information;

• Is to another agency for a specific civil or criminal law enforcement activity in response to the written request of the agency head.

The Privacy Act generally bars the release of personal information such as names and home addresses to unions. However, such information can be provided without the employee's consent if there are no other adequate alternative means of communicating with bargaining unit members.

Agencies are required by the Act to keep an accurate accounting of all disclosures of their employees' records to other agencies or persons, except when the disclosure was required by the Freedom of Information Act or when a disclosure was made within the agency on a need-to-know basis. With the exception of disclosures requested by law enforcement agencies, a list of all recipients of an employee's records must be provided to the worker upon request.

Under the Privacy Act, federal employees may sue an agency for refusing to release or amend their records. Employees also may sue if they are adversely affected by an agency's failure to comply with any of the other provisions of the Act. Employees may be able to obtain money damages in certain circumstances if they can prove, among other things, that they have been adversely affected as a re-

sult of the agency's intentional and willful disregard of the Act's requirements. Court costs and attorney fees may be awarded.

The Privacy Act provides criminal penalties for making a "knowing and willful" disclosure of records to those not entitled to receive them, willfully maintaining a record that is not in accordance with the law's requirements, or making a knowing and willful attempt to gain access to an individual's records under false pretenses.

Current employees who desire access to or amendment of their personnel records should contact their personnel office or their agency's designated Privacy Act officer if they need assistance in processing their request. Usually, the request will have to be made to the employing agency. Requests from former federal employees regarding information or documents in their Official Personnel Folders should be directed to the Work Force Information Division, Office of Personnel Management, 1900 E St., NW, Washington, D.C. 20415.

When making a Privacy Act request, employees should be sure to provide enough identifying information to allow the agency to find their records, while assuring the agency of their identity. Generally, this means that employees should provide at least their full name, date of birth, and Social Security number to facilitate this process.

Freedom of Information Act

Under the Freedom of Information Act (5 U.S.C. subsection 552), individuals may request from agencies documents that otherwise might not be disclosed or published by the U.S. government.

While some documents and information are protected from disclosure for national security, business confidentiality, personal privacy, or other reasons, millions of other reports, correspondence, and regulations may be available and released under FOIA's procedures.

Agencies have an obligation under this 1966 statute to make a reasonable effort to search for and turn over copies of records they have decided are releasable. If an individual's request is denied, the agency must state the reason, and the law establishes some formal administrative appeal rights in the case of such denials.

The law specifies only two requirements for requesting information: (1) requests must "reasonably describe" the document sought and (2) they must be made in accordance with an agency's published FOIA procedures.

Agencies have up to 20 working days to answer a FOIA request and must "promptly" provide information deemed releasable. They may charge reasonable search fees, copying fees, and, in the case of commercial-use requests, fees for the review of records.

Requesters can apply for a waiver of fees under a "public interest" standard. Agencies have up to 20 working days to decide an appeal of a denial and to inform individuals that they may bring a court action to challenge a FOIA denial.

The Justice Department publishes two books, the *Freedom of Information Case List*, which contains an alphabetical listing of FOIA judicial decisions, and the *Freedom of Information Act Guide & Privacy Overview*, which contains the "Justice Department Guide to the FOIA," as well as an overview discussion of the provisions of the Privacy Act. Federal employees who do FOIA work for their agencies may obtain single copies free by calling (202) 514-5105. Other individuals may obtain copies by writing to the Superintendent of Documents, U.S. Government Printing Office, Washington, D.C. 20402, or by calling (202) 512-1800. Ask for the *Freedom of Information Case List*.

Sources of Information

Deciding Body	Resource	Where to Look	Ordering Information
Merit Systems Protection Board	*Merit Systems Protection Reporter*— current and prior decisions	Law libraries; agency libraries; agency personnel offices; agency general counsel offices	West Publishing Co., 1-800-328-9352
	Federal Merit Systems Reporter— current and prior decisions	same	Labor Relations Press, 1-800-341-7874
	Personnet Merit Systems Protection Board Database— current and prior decisions	same	Information Handling Services, 1-800-320-4555
	MSPB website— current decisions and decisions from 1994-present	http://www.mspb.gov	Download from website or contact: Office of the Clerk (202) 653-7200
Federal Labor Relations Authority	*Decisions of the Federal Labor Relations Author-ity*—prior decisions; *Reports of Case Decisions*—current decisions	Law libraries; agency libraries; agency labor relations offices; union offices	Government Printing Office (202) 512-1800
	Federal Labor Relations Reporter— current and prior decisions	same	Labor Relations Press, 1-800-341-7874
	Personnet Federal Labor Relations Authority Data-base—current and prior decisions	same	Information Handling Services, 1-800-320-4555
	FLRA Web site— current decisions and decisions from 1994-present	http://www.flra.gov	Download from website or contact: Office of Information Resources and Research Services, 607 14th St., N.W., Washington, D.C. 20424 (202) 482-6550

Federal Job Dispute Procedures

Deciding Body	Resource	Where to Look	Ordering Information
Equal Employment Opportunity Commission	*Federal Equal Opportunity Reporter*—current and prior decisions	Law libraries; agency libraries; agency equal employment opportunity offices; agency personnel offices; agency general counsel offices	Labor Relations Press, 1-800-341-7874
	Personnet Equal Employment Opportunity Commission Database–current and prior decisions	same	Information Handling Services, 1-800-320-4555
Arbitrators	*Labor Agreement Information Retrieval Service*—indexing system of decisions	Office of Personnel Management headquarters	Office of Employee and Labor Relations, LAIRS Section, 1900 E St., N.W., Room 7H28, Washington, D.C. 20415 (202) 606-2930
	Federal Labor Relations Reporter—current and prior decisions	Law libraries; agency libraries; union offices; agency labor relations offices	Labor Relations Press, 1-800-341-7874
	Personnet Arbitrators' Decisions Database–current and prior decisions	same	Information Handling Services, 1-800-320-4555
OPM, GSA, and Comptroller General decisions on pay, benefits, leave, relocation and travel compensation	*Federal Pay and Benefits Reporter*—current and prior decisions	Agency personnel offices; agency payroll offices; agency general counsel offices	Labor Relations Press, 1-800-341-7874
	Personnet Comptroller General Civilian Personnel Decisions Database (includes OPM and GSA decisions)–current and prior decisions	same	Information Handling Services, 1-800-320-4555

Federal Job Dispute Procedures

Deciding Body	Resource	Where to Look	Ordering Information
Federal District Courts	*Federal Supplement—* prior decisions	Law libraries; agency libraries; federal court buildings	West Publishing Co., 1-800-328-9352
	Current decisions (available information varies among courts)	http:// www.law.vill.edu/ Fed-Ct/fedcourt.html	
Federal Appeals Courts	*Federal Reporter 2nd Series—*prior decisions	Law libraries; agency libraries; federal court buildings	West Publishing Co., 1-800-328-9352
	Current decisions (available information varies among courts)	http:// www.law.vill.edu/ Fed-Ct/fedcourt.html	
U.S. Supreme Court	*United States Reports—* prior decisions	Law libraries; agency libraries; federal court buildings	Government Printing Office (202) 512-1800
	Current decisions	http://www.supreme courtus.gov	

—— Where to Challenge an Agency Action ——

The following table describes where actions should first be appealed. Where more than one channel is available, an employee may choose only one. However, some provide for an apeal from one agency to another — for example, to the Merit Systems Protection Board after a request for reconsideration at the Office of Personnel Management. Also, many of these matters can be appealed into federal courts once the internal government appeals have been exhausted. See the chapters on the appeals agencies and on administrative and negotiated grievances for further jurisdiction and court appeal rights.

Agency Action	Where to Appeal
• Adverse actions for misconduct • Performance-based actions • Denials of within-grade salary increases • Reduction-in-force actions • Involuntary reassignment • Coerced resignation • Violation of restoration rights following military service or recovery from compensable injury	• Merit Systems Protection Board • Negotiated grievance procedures may be available — depends on existence of local union contract, its provisions and whether an individual is in the bargaining unit
• "Mixed" cases — involving both alleged discrimination and other actions that are appealable to the Merit Systems Protection Board	• Merit Systems Protection Board • Agency EEO complaints procedure • Negotiated grievance procedure (if applicable)
• Equal employment opportunity violation — discrimination based on race, color, religion, gender or national origin • Age Discrimination in Employment Act violation — discrimination based on age (over 40) • Equal Pay Act violation — wage discrimination based on gender • Rehabilitation Act violation _ discrimination based on disabling condition	• Agency EEO complaints procedure, the Equal Employment Opportunity Commission if dissatisfied • Negotiated grievance procedure (if applicable)
• Unfair labor practices (see Federal Labor Relations Authority chapter for list) • Negotiability appeals • Exceptions to arbitration awards	• Federal Labor Relations Authority (only agency or union may take matters to arbitration or to FLRA)

Agency Action	Where to Appeal
• Prohibited personnel practices (see Office of Special Counsel chapter for list)	• Office of Special Counsel (adjudicates before Merit Systems Protection Board) • Negotiated grievance procedure (if applicable)
• Position classification appeals • Life insurance eligibility determinations • Health insurance eligibility determinations and claims disputes • Examination ratings • Retirement eligibility and other determinations • Fair Labor Standards Act (FLSA) violations • Termination of grade or pay retention after reduction in force	• Office of Personnel Management
• Monetary claims arising out of official duties	• Internal agency channels, then Office of Personnel Management for disputes over compensation and leave claims or General Services Administration for disputes over travel and relocation allowances and transportation rates
• Retaliation for whistleblowing	• Office of Special Counsel • Merit Systems Protection Board (if OSC hasn't sought corrective action within 120 days of the employee filing a complaint there)
• Final retirement decisions of the Office of Personnel Management: eligibility for annuity, survivor annuity or early retirement (including determination of law enforcement officer or firefighter status); determination of disability; entitlement to discontinued service annuity; division of annuity of divorce	• Merit Systems Protection Board
• Minor discipline (reprimands, ordered counseling, suspensions of less than 14 days, etc.) • Challenges to performance ratings not involving claims of prohibited personnel practices • Transfer or reassignment not causing reduction of pay or grade • Disputes over work assignments or tour of duty • Denial of request for training • Similar disputes not involving issues appealable to the Merit Systems Protection Board or other appeals agencies	• Agency administrative grievance procedure • Negotiated grievance procedure (if applicable)

CHAPTER THREE

Getting Advice and Help

A personnel dispute almost always is a "personal" dispute because it's charged with personal emotions and feelings to those involved—especially so for the employee, but often also for the manager or supervisor. The individual choices of the worker who is facing discipline or another type of setback largely will determine the outcome of the dispute. But there is outside help available: some of it free, some expensive; some of it reliable, some less so.

This chapter outlines many of the "typical" sources of assistance that federal workers routinely avail themselves of when work time gets tough. Of course, in addition to the help listed, many workers seek and obtain support from the "standard" sources of aid, including friends, family, community, and religious groups.

———— Unions and Similar Groups ————

Union Representation Rights

Many federal employees don't give a second thought to federal unions or their labor relations rights until they are in trouble. Often they don't even know if they belong to a bargaining unit or if one even exists at their worksite. In a few cases, veteran employees are apt to act surprised to learn that unions exist at all in the government.

But a union often will be the first place employees turn to when trouble develops. Often, workers assume that union help is available to them just for the asking and are surprised to learn that it doesn't quite work that way. Or they find that union help is available, but not to the extent they had expected—or hoped.

The first lesson such workers are likely to learn is that not all federal employees are covered by union protections, which apply only to those positions included in union bargaining units. This amounts to about 60 percent of federal executive branch positions—both blue-collar and white-collar—and about 90 percent of jobs in the U.S. Postal Service.

Simply put, a bargaining unit is a group of employees for whom the union is entitled to act. Bargaining units, which are certified by the Federal Labor Relations Authority, may or may not be limited to one site or to a certain category of employees or to a certain agency function. It depends on how the unit was organized for the union's representation. Thus, employees can be members of a bargaining unit without knowing it, or incorrectly believe they are members of the unit because someone in the next office or even at the next desk is a member. When in doubt about bargaining unit membership status, check with the local union office or with the agency labor relations office.

Eligibility for membership in a bargaining unit depends largely on an employee's job responsibilities, not a worker's grade. Thus, most managers are not in bargaining units at a worksite, even though the unit may include other white-collar employees at the same or higher grades there who do not exercise managerial or supervisory duties.

However, employees can be members of a bargaining unit without being dues-paying union members. In fact, this is the case with the majority of bargaining unit members in executive branch agencies. On average, only about 20 percent of unit members in those agencies pay union dues, with some unions having notably higher or lower percentages. In the U.S. Postal Service, by contrast, about 90 percent of unit members are dues-paying members of the union.

Federal law prohibits unions from imposing dues, representation fees, and the like on bargaining unit members who do not belong to the union; there is no "closed shop" in either the executive branch or the postal service. Unions are required to represent the interests of all bargaining unit members equally, regardless of whether they are dues-paying union members. Thus, in theory at least, union membership (as opposed to unit membership) makes no difference in whether a union will choose to pursue a dispute on behalf of an employee.

Unions have even been known to help out non-unit members from time to time and in lesser ways, out of concern that an unjust agency action or policy might later spill over into the bargaining unit and create problems there. Also, union representatives by nature are interested in becoming involved in such matters and are generally sympathetic to an employee's point of view. Personal friendships that have built up over the years also can come into play. But a nonunit member must always remember that any union help is a favor, not an entitlement.

Unions naturally are somewhat reluctant to spend time and money representing non-dues paying employees, even those in the bargaining unit, if it comes down to a choice between representing one of those employees and someone who does pay dues. At the very least, a non-member might find the union more eager to settle a grievance at a lower level, rather than take a matter through the various steps up to arbitration.

On the other hand, some union locals are very aggressive and have a policy of pushing to the limit any perceived violation by management. They may view an action taken against a non-member that goes unchallenged as a potential precedent for future actions against dues-paying members. Thus, they may decide to pursue a case, simply out of "self-preservation" concerns.

Even in unionized workplaces, grievances can be filed by individual employees, not just by the union. Thus, should the union decline to pursue such a complaint, an employee might decide to file it himself or herself. But an individual has no right to go to arbitration if the agency's decision on the grievance is unacceptable. Only the union—or the agency—can invoke arbitration.

Additional Benefits

Besides the filing of formal complaints, unions can be of value in other ways. Perhaps the most important is their expertise and experience, which an individual otherwise might have to pay an attorney to get, if it's available at all. A talk with an experienced unionist might help a person decide whether it is worthwhile to start a formal appeals process or to try to resolve the matter in another way.

Union officials by definition are more involved with the personnel policies of a workplace than is the typical employee. They tend to be "old hands" who know not only how the agency and the site operate, but also much of its history, as well as the personalities involved. All of these factors can be important in understanding what is really happening in a dispute and identifying the best way to resolve matters.

Also, unionists typically have received formal training from their national offices and can call on those offices for help—for legal advice and information, as well as political backing. They also have the advantage of having been down the same road before—typically, many times. While a dispute may seem unique to an individual, chances are that a veteran union official has seen similar situations many times before, and quickly will be able to cut to the heart of the matter. And while union officials are apt to hold certain points of view strongly, they usually also tend to keep the goal in sight. This can be invaluable in settings such as grievance hearings where unemotional, clear-headed thinking is vital.

Employees who go to unions for help should be willing to recognize words of wisdom when they are being spoken, and to act accordingly. In personnel disputes, emotions and personal feelings are never far from the surface. In fact, they are a primary cause of many of those disputes. While union officials are naturally inclined to back the employee, they can act as an important buffer for the bruised feelings that typically are inherent on both sides. For example, in most cases they will advise that they do the talking at a grievance rather than the employee. This can prevent hot words that will only make matters worse.

Unions take pride in helping employees in the workplace; if they didn't, there would be no real reason to have them at all. However, employees must not consider a union a blank check on which they are entitled to draw—even those workers who have been longtime dues-paying members.

Unions have their limits, the foremost of which is financial resources. Many union locals—and their national offices—operate on tight budgets. Partly, this is because there is no requirement that bargaining unit employees pay dues. Those who do pay dues in effect are underwriting the services for those who don't—that's why unions call these folks "free riders."

Perspective Pointers

Another factor the employee should bear in mind when approaching a union might be summed up in one word: manners. Employees angered with a personnel situation, or possibly facing discipline or even firing, naturally are resentful. This, however, is no excuse to pound desks, throw papers, slam doors and so on—all behavior that has been seen over and over in these situations. Such behavior doesn't help the situation and very often worsens matters.

When dealing with a union office, employees should remember that while they have certain rights, they are, after all, asking for help. Demanding that help isn't more likely to make it happen—and if it does come about, it could very well amount to a very grudging form of aid.

Good behavior when approaching a union for help includes accepting several facts: that the unionist has other responsibilities; that the union doesn't have limitless time and money to devote to your cause; that not every dispute in a federal office is grounds for a formal complaint; and that there may be no way to win a certain case, no matter what level of effort is applied.

When confronted with an aggrieved employee, a unionist has to perform an investigation much like that conducted by a hearing officer. The union official will try to gather the facts, put them in sequence, review pertinent documents, speak to witnesses, determine cause and effect, and sort out the relevant from the unimportant—in other words, explore the background and make lots of judgments about your complaint. Naturally, the union's conclusion in some cases will be to drop the matter. The employee who finds this unacceptable is free to file a formal grievance or pursue other available appeals routes without the union's involvement, and may even file an unfair labor practice complaint against the union for failing to carry out its representation duty.

However, this is another situation where employees should strive to exercise good judgment. Filing such a complaint will not correct the personnel action that is at the heart of the matter. Instead, the best that could happen is that after a series of formal steps the union might be compelled to take up the case. The union officials involved naturally would feel resentful after such a process, and they would be acting on a case that they consider hopeless. This would not do much to improve the employee's ultimate chances of prevailing in the dispute.

Professional Associations

Many of the considerations that apply to seeking help from unions apply equally well to professional associations and other groups. These types of organizations generally offer the same advantages as unions—e.g., experience, resources, contacts, and a willingness to help. As with unions, of course, they are most eager to provide help to their own members, but membership status might not necessarily foreclose one of these groups as a source of help. Again, it depends partly on how the employee approaches the organization, along with the facts of the case.

But also remember that professional organizations depend greatly on good will to get things done. Unlike unions, they have no direct authority with the agency—no right to bargain, to invoke a grievance process, and so on. However, if for no other reason than their expertise, contacting professional organizations in your career field is generally a good strategy in any personnel dispute.

An appendix to this chapter includes a list of federal-sector labor organizations and professional associations that readers may contact for information or assistance.

Legal Representation

Attorney Advantages

A lawyer well versed in federal personnel law can be valuable in many ways, not the least of which is as a shortcut to answering if—or how—you should act. An hour or two spent in an attorney's office could give you a good idea of what to do: if you have grounds to file a formal appeal, what that might involve and cost, and what your options are for settling matters.

If things get formal, legal help is even more valuable.

Hiring a lawyer costs money, possibly more than many workers feel they can afford—especially when all the other costs involved in a personnel appeal are considered. In addition to the lawyer's time, which probably will be billed by the hour, there are many other potential costs: copying costs, notary fees, delivery fees, travel, research materials, and on and on (remember, of course, that you will have to absorb many of these costs, regardless of whether a lawyer is handling your case).

It's difficult to do a cost-benefit analysis on whether to engage an attorney. Estimating the cost of pursuing a formal appeal is virtually impossible. It depends on how much time your lawyer, and possibly the attorney's colleagues or subordinates, has to spend researching and presenting the case. Obviously, the more complicated and arcane the legal issues and the longer the case proceeds, the greater the cost.

Attorney Fee Awards

Under the various laws that govern federal personnel matters, legal fees can be reimbursed in some situations. Generally, the rule governing attorney's fees requires that the employee be the "prevailing party" and that such reimbursement be "in the interests of justice." Exactly how much of a victory is needed to be the prevailing party and what the "interests of justice" amount to are sometimes complicated issues in their own right, and often wind up being the subject of various legal wrangles themselves. Awards of attorney's fees are thus not automatic. It is quite possible to win a case and still come out behind financially, after all the costs have been subtracted.

Generally speaking, to be a prevailing party, employees must win all, or substantially all, of the relief they originally sought. This can be shown even if the case was settled in the employee's favor before a final judg-

ment of an administrative body or court, as long as it's clear that the settlement was the result of the appeal. Examples of situations in which an attorney's fees award is considered in the interests of justice include: where the agency engaged in a prohibited personnel practice; where the agency's action was clearly without merit or wholly unfounded or the employee was substantially innocent; where the agency acted in bad faith; where the agency committed gross procedural error; or where the agency knew or should have known it wouldn't prevail on the merits.

The "right to representation" that personnel law provides doesn't include the right to free representation. It's nowhere as free or convenient as the representation rights afforded indigent people involved in criminal cases. An appeals agency will not provide you with a lawyer no matter what your financial situation—questions of the agency's willingness to do so aside, they have no legal authority to provide such help. You must pay for your own legal representative and hope to gain reimbursement.

At a Loss for Lawyers?

Bear in mind that the right to representation does include the right to be represented by someone who is not a lawyer. This is another way to reduce costs, but it's up to you to decide whether to put your career in the hands of a co-worker (or brother-in-law) who "knows a little about the law."

You also can represent yourself. Nearly half of the workers who appeal to the Merit Systems Protection Board, the agency that hears most formal appeals, do just that. You could do everything yourself (called "pro se" representation), from filing the first complaint all the way up the appeals ladder. The question is how much stock you put in the adage that "he who represents himself has a fool for a client."

The various appeals routes have jurisdictional and procedural requirements that can be baffling to the inexperienced. And the agencies and courts expect you to follow those rules—filing the right papers at the right time and in the right place, citing pertinent precedent to back up legal points, presenting evidence that meets certain legal standards, stating claims on which they have authority to grant relief, and so on.

The rules of each of these bodies are available to anyone wishing to pursue a complaint, but they often are not models of clarity. The agencies and the federal courts will afford people representing themselves some leeway for lack of legal knowledge—but only up to a certain point. It's not at all uncommon for such cases to be dismissed outright, without the agency even considering the merits of a worker's complaint, because of some paperwork or filing shortcoming. If that happens, it's almost always too late to try to go back with a lawyer and ask for another shot.

There's also a risk of being penalized for trying to push a frivolous case that an attorney would have advised against filing. Administrative appeals agencies rarely impose sanctions for filing frivolous appeals, since such cases usually are dismissed at the early stage of the appeals process. However, courts may, and sometimes do, impose such sanctions. Often these sanctions—which usually take the form of monetary penalties or restrictions on the right to file further appeals—are imposed when an employee is making an argument that clearly isn't allowed by law, or after several challenges have been mounted to the same incident using different routes or legal theories.

Another consideration in choosing whether to have a representative is deciding how much of your time and energy you want to devote to your case. Personnel disputes tend to consume people in deep and heavy fashion. You could easily find yourself spending a large amount of your off-duty time absorbed in the case—giving depositions, producing legal briefs, dealing with scheduling and other paperwork matters, and so on. Many employees become totally tied up in such efforts, often to the detriment of their personal lives and their health. Hiring a lawyer will relieve some, but not all, of that burden.

You also should remember that on the other side, you usually will encounter an array of attorneys who are skilled and experienced in personnel law. Federal agencies have access not only to in-house legal staff, but also the resources of the Justice Department and help from contract attorneys if needed. It's a good idea to think twice, at least, before deciding that by yourself you are going to tackle such formidable opponents on their own ground—even when you are convinced that justice is on your side.

Even those who unquestionably have the financial ability to hire legal help must decide whether it is worth spending the money. This of course is an individual decision, but keep in mind that attorneys spend three years in law school and much time afterward studying the law for a very good reason: the laws are complicated and full of potential traps for those unfamiliar with their complexities and nuances. This is especially true of federal personnel law, with its numerous and overlapping routes and its complicated efforts to balance the rights of the individual and the rights of the government as an employer.

Should you decide to hire legal

help, just finding someone appropriate can be a challenge in itself. An attorney with a background in federal personnel law obviously is the best bet. Attorneys specialize in certain areas of the law because there is so much to know in any one field that it is virtually impossible to stay current and effective in all. However, it certainly is possible for an attorney to take up a case in a field outside his or her normal practice. This might be necessary at times, especially for employees living in areas with relatively small federal populations where it's less likely there will be attorneys who specialize in civil service matters.

A local bar association might be able to provide a list of attorneys in your area who practice federal employment law. Other employees at your worksite who have been through legal challenges might be able to recommend someone. Also try researching cases similar to your own; the decisions often carry the names of the attorneys who handled those cases for the employee side.

The choice of representation is a highly personal one. Beyond expertise and cost considerations, it is important that you be able to work well together, since a formal appeal will require spending a substantial amount of time together and potentially discussing sensitive and even embarrassing personal issues. Trust and rapport either will build up or it won't. If it doesn't, find out what the problem is and try to correct it immediately. Working effectively as a team will greatly improve your chances of success.

Finally, remember that ultimately you are responsible for keeping the case on track. It's a well-settled legal principle in federal employment law that employees are responsible for their representatives' actions or failures to act. It is rare that workers who lost a case receive a new hearing on the grounds that their attorney failed to represent them properly.

Elected Representatives

Congressional Call?

As an American, you have a constitutional right to petition the government to seek "redress of grievances," a right that isn't altered or eliminated simply because you work for the government itself. Many employees who lack confidence in their own agencies, the appeals agencies, and even the federal courts turn to members of Congress for help. That help sometimes comes, but problems rarely are solved as quickly as most workers hope or expect, and in some cases, such assistance can end up—unintentionally—making matters worse.

House and Senate members never have to be reminded that they hold their jobs because their constituents voted them in. All members of Congress try to serve their constituents in myriad ways, from getting federal grants and spending projects to tracking down lost Social Security checks. Each has a personal staff, typically large and numerous, assigned to take care of such matters.

Writing letters to every member of Congress, or to the ones you believe might be the most sympathetic, in the hope that you'll convince several to take up your cause is likely to be a waste of time and postage. By far your best ally will be the representative from your district and the senators from your state. The naked truth is that you are their potential voter. Following them, in terms of effectiveness, would be members of the two committees that handle federal and postal matters on Capitol Hill: the Senate Governmental Affairs Committee and the House Government Reform and Oversight Committee.

Rules of the Road

A first rule in contacting Congress is to write, don't call. A phone call won't get results any faster than a letter. Should you call a congressman's office, your chances of getting through directly to the legislator are slim. Doubtless, you will be routed to one of the staff assistants. And while staffers generally will give you a certain amount of time, they almost certainly will ask you to put the facts in writing. If you must call, explain that your purpose is simply to ask if there is a particular staff member to whom you should address your letter. If you feel you must talk with that person, simply inform him or her in broad terms why you are calling, say that you will send follow-up information in writing, and ask if there is anything you can do to be helpful.

It's possible, although highly difficult, for an individual to schedule an appointment with a member of Congress to discuss a personal issue. However, since senators and representatives sometimes schedule office hours in their district offices, especially on weekends and during congressional recesses, your chances of a meeting would be best during those periods. But even if you can meet with an elected representative, it's unrealistic to expect action on the spot. Again, you almost definitely will be asked to present your points, facts, or arguments in writing.

Keep any such letter or documentation to the point and make it as brief as possible. State what the problem is, what you have done to try to get it corrected, and what you would like to see done. Give your name and phone number for follow-up contacts. Don't threaten, don't try to pull strings that you don't hold, and don't demand action by a certain date. Remember, most congressional offices receive hundreds of such letters each day.

A letter complaining of personnel actions will be treated in the same way as any other constituent complaint. It will start with a junior staff member (probably the same person you would reach if you called), who handles routine inquiries. Since your situation probably will defy quick solution, it likely will be sent to a more senior staff member and eventually might be seen by, or at least summarized to, the representative or senator.

At that point, the course of action depends much on the personality of the member of Congress. Some legislators might see personnel matters as outside their authority and simply write back, suggesting you go through the normal appeals channels. Others, who place a high priority on constituent service, may call or write a letter to an agency official who has authority over the matter.

Federal agency officials take contacts from Congress very seriously— and especially so if the member is viewed as a leader or happens to sit on a committee that oversees the agency. Congress's ultimate power is the power of the purse, and no agency official wants to be known as the one who angered a member of Congress enough to get the purse strings tightened. Often, that's the reason a simple letter or phone call from Capitol Hill has produced quick results.

But agency officials do not work for the congressman; they take their orders from agency management. Because of this, writing to a member of

Congress can backfire. Agency officials may feel that you have tried to skirt normal channels or even embarrass or blackmail them. Even if they do take the action you're requesting, it likely will be a grudgingly delivered solution. They won't forget what happened and may look for a way to even the score in the future.

Also, because of legal and privacy considerations, agency officials may be powerless to change a decision even at the urging of a member of Congress. Again, a potential result will be the creation of a grudge against the employee, which could wind up making matters worse.

The Media

Power of the Press

It's undeniable that newspapers, TV, and other forms of media do influence government decisions and policies. Additionally, the media obviously rely heavily on government sources for information that in turn helps create and shape that influence. It's also undeniable that some of that information comes from federal employees who are motivated at least in part by disagreements with management that are intertwined with personnel disputes.

Basically, the power of the press is the power to bring or focus attention on an issue or subject. In only a few days of following the news, a person usually can find several examples of government decisions being changed because of unfavorable publicity. These decision reversals can, and sometimes do, include federal personnel matters. Moreover, by making disclosures to the media, a federal employee can gain whistleblower protections that could make the difference between keeping a job and losing it.

However, the power of the media is indirect. As numerous as the cases in which the government changed its mind after bad publicity are instances of agencies staying the course. A news story, even a very harsh one, doesn't guarantee change.

Simply presenting information to a news organization doesn't guarantee that a story will be published or broadcast. It will have to pass the test of newsworthiness. What's considered "news" varies from place to place and from individual to individual; there are no written standards for what gets published or broadcast. But personnel disputes in a government office will be low on just about every reporter's and editor's list. They are not likely to find a fight between a federal employee and agency management very newsworthy, unless some type of provable misconduct or national issue is involved.

Even then, not every publication or broadcast outlet is interested in doing such stories. They frequently require much effort, a long time, and high costs to develop. And most news operations are very wary about publishing anything derogatory about someone who is not a public figure in the legal sense of the term. Numerous libel suits that have resulted in huge dollar awards have put them on guard.

Also, the subject may be far afield from what they normally cover. In these days of increasingly specialized coverage, a problem in a federal office may seem hopelessly arcane to most reporters and many will be reluctant to tackle such a story. Moreover, story ideas are routinely rejected in newsrooms, regardless of the eagerness of the person providing the information. Thus you may take the whistleblowing risk and wind up never reading any story based on your disclosure.

Whether anonymity is desired or not, there is another career-risking consideration. The reporter will want to see personnel or other files in order to document the story—information that ordinarily might be restricted from public view, or at least that you normally do not have access to. Providing such information means risking disciplinary charges that might be even more serious than whatever you are facing initially. Making a charge of misconduct against an agency or against someone else does not shield you from punishment for misconduct of your own.

Union and Professional Groups

Federal Employee Unions

• **American Federation of Government Employees, AFL-CIO.** 80 F Street, NW, Washington, DC 20001. Bobby Harnage, Nat. Pres. Phone (202) 639-6419.

• **National Air Traffic Controllers Association, AFL-CIO.** Suite 701, 1150 17th Street, NW, Washington, DC 20036. Michael McNally, Pres. Phone (202) 223-2900. Internet: *www. natca.org*

• **National Association of Government Employees.** 159 Burgin Parkway, Quincy, MA 02169. Kenneth Lyons, Pres. Phone (617) 376-0220.

• **National Federation of Federal Employees.** 1016 16th Street, NW, Washington, DC 20036. Richard N. Brown, Pres.; Phone (202) 862-4400.

• **National Treasury Employees Union.** 901 E Street, NW, Suite 600, Washington, DC 20004. Colleen Kelley, Nat. Pres.; Frank Ferris, Nat. Exec. Vice Pres. Phone (202) 783-4444.

• **National Weather Service Employees Organization.** 601 Pennsylvania Ave. Suite 900, Washington D.C. 20004. Phone (703) 293-9651. Fax (703) 293-9653. Internet: *www.nwseo.org*

• **Professional Airways Systems Specialists.** District No. 6-PASS/NMEBA, AFL-CIO, 1150 17th St.,

Suite 702, Washington, DC 20036. Michael D. Fanfalone, Pres. Phone (202) 293-7277. Fax (202) 293-7727. Internet: *www.passnational.org*

Postal Employee Unions and Professional Groups

• **American Postal Workers Union, AFL-CIO.** 1300 L Street, NW, Washington D.C. 20005. Moe Biller, Pres.; William Burrus, Exec. Vice-pres.; Robert Tunstall, Sec. Treas.; Roy Braunstein, Legis. Dir.; Greg Bell, Dir. of Industrial Relations; Frank A. Romero, Dir. of Org.; Cliff Guffey, Clerk Director; James Lingberg, Maintenance Director; Robert Pritchard, MVS Director. Phone (202) 842-4200. Internet: *www.apwu.org*

• **National Alliance of Postal and Federal Employees.** 1628 11th Street, NW, Washington, DC 20001. James McGee, Pres.; Wilbur L. Duncan, Sec. Phone (202) 939-6325. E-mail: *napfe@patriot.net* Internet: *www. napfe.com*

• **National Assistance for Federal Employees.** Box 160191, Clearfield, UT 84016-9998. Kerwin Hill. (800) 957-4481

• **National Association of Letter Carriers, AFL-CIO.** 100 Indiana Avenue, NW, Washington, DC 20001.

Vincent R. Sombrotto, Pres.; William H. Young, Exec. Vice-pres., A.P. "Tony" Martinez, Vice-pres., William R. Yates, Sec.-Treas. Phone (202) 393-4695. Internet: *www.nalc.org*

• **National Association of Postal Supervisors.** 1727 King St., Ste. 400, Alexandria, VA 22314-2753. Vince Palladino, Pres.; Ted Keating, Exec. Vice-pres., Adolph Ruiz, Sec.-Treas. Phone (703) 836-9660. Internet: *www.naps.org*

• **National Association of Postmasters.** 8 Herbert Street, Alexandria, VA 22305-2600. Ted J. Carrico, Nat. Pres.; Edward J. Baer, Exec. Dir. Phone (703) 683-9027. Internet: *www.napus.org*

• **National Postal Mail Handlers Union, AFL-CIO.** 1101 Connecticue Ave., Suite 500, Washington, DC 20036. William Quinn, Pres.; Mark Gardner, Sec./Treas; Phone (202) 833-9095, Fax (202) 833-0008. Internet: *www.npmhu.org*

• **National League of Postmasters.** 1023 North Royal Street, Alexandria, VA 22314-1569. Joseph W. Cinadr, Pres., Richard A. Weinberg, CPA, Exec. Dir. Phone (703) 548-5922, Fax (703) 836-8937.

• **National Rural Letter Carriers Association.** 1630 Duke Street, 4th Floor, Alexandria, VA 22314-3465, Steven R. Smith, Pres., Dale A. Holton, Vice Pres., (703) 684-5545. Internet: *w w w . n e w c . c o m / n r l c a i n f o / default2.html*

Skilled Trade, Professional, Retirement, and Miscellaneous Groups

• **AFL-CIO Metal Trades Department.** 815 16th Street, NW, Washington, DC 20006. John F. Meese, Pres. Phone (202) 347-7255.

• **Air Traffic Control Association, Inc.** 2300 Clarendon Boulevard, Suite 711, Arlington, VA 22201 Gabriel A. Hartl, Pres.; Carol Newmaster, Sr. V-Pres. Phone (703) 522-5717, Fax (703) 527-7251. Internet: *www. atca.org*

• **Alliance of Government Managers.** 1331-A Pennsylvania Ave., NW, Suite 159, Washington D.C. 20004. John M. Ellis, Pres. Phone (916) 591-9210.

• **American Federation of State, County, and Municipal Employees.** 1625 L. Street, NW, Washington, DC 20036. Gerald W. McEntee, Pres.; William Lucy, Sec-Treas. Phone (202) 429-1000. Internet: *www.afscme.org*

• **American Federation of Teachers, AFL-CIO.** 555 New Jersey Avenue, NW, Washington, D. C. 20001. Sandra Feldman, Pres.; Edward J. McElroy, Nat LaCour, Exec. Vice-pres. Sec.-Treas.; Gregory Humphrey, Exec. asst. to the Pres. and the Sec.-Treas. Phone (202) 879-4400. Internet: *www.aft.org*

• **American Foreign Service Association.** 2101 E. Street, NW, Washington, DC 20037. Marshall Adair, Pres. Phone (202) 338-4045.

• **American Nurses Association.** 600 Maryland Ave., SW, #100W, Washington, DC 20024-2571. David W. Hennage, Exec. Dir.,. Phone 800-274-4ANA. Internet: *www.nursing world.org*

• **American Society for Public Administration.** Mary R. Hamilton, Ph.D., Exec. Dir., Suite 700, 1120 G Street, NW, Washington, DC 20005-3885. Phone (202) 393-7878. Internet: *www.aspanet.org*

• **Association of Civilian Technicians.** 12510-B Lake Ridge Drive, Lake Ridge, VA 22192. John T. Hunter, Pres. Phone (703) 494-4845. Internet: *www.actnat.com*

• **Association of Government Accountants.** 2200 Mount Vernon Avenue, Alexandria, VA 22301. Charles W. Culkin, Exec. Dir. Phone (703) 684-6931. Internet: *www.agacgfm. org*

- **Association of Part-Time Professionals.** 7700 Leesburg Pk, Suite 216, Falls Church, VA 22043. Phone (703) 532-8961.
- **Blacks in Government.** Gerald Reed., Nat. Pres., 1820 11th Street, NW, Washington, DC 20001. Phone (202) 667-3280. Internet: *www. bignet.org*
- **The Federal Bar Association.** Composed of present and former federal government attorneys and private practitioners with a federal practice. Jackie A. Goff, Pres., 2215 M Street, NW, Washington, DC 20037. Phone (202) 785-1614. Fax (202) 785-1568. Internet: **www.fedbar.org**
- **Federal Bureau of Investigation Agents Association.** P.O. Box 250, New Rochelle, NY 10801. Phone (914) 235-7580. John J. Sennett, Pres., John Gray, V-pres. Internet: *www. fbiaa.org*
- **Federal Education Association.** 1201 16th Street, NW, Suite 117 Washington, DC 20036. Jan Mohr, Pres. Phone (202) 822-7850. Internet: *www.feaonline.org*
- **Federal Criminal Investigators Association.** C. Robert Tate, Natl. Pres., P.O. Box 23400, Washington, DC 20026-3400 (800) 961-7753. Internet: *www.fedcia.org*
- **Federal Law Enforcement Officers Association.** P.O. Box 508, East Northport, NY 11731-0472. Richard J. Gallo, Nat. Pres. Phone (516) 368-6117. FAX (516) 368-6429. Internet: *www.fleoa.org*
- **Federal Managers Association.** 1641 Prince Street, Alexandria, VA 22314, Michael B. Styles, Nat. Pres., (703) 683-8700. Internet: *www. fedmanagers.org*
- **Federal Physicians Association.** P.O. Box 45150, Washington, DC 20026, Dennis W. Boyd, Exec. Dir. Phone (800) 403-3374. Fax 800-528-3492. *Internet: www.fedphy.org*

- **Federally Employed Women.** 1400 I Street, NW, Suite 425, Washington, DC 20005. Jeanette Miller, Pres.; Alma Riojas Esparza, Exec. Dir. Phone (202) 898-0994, Fax (202) 898-0998, Internet: *www.few.org*
- **Federation of Organizations for Professional Women.** 1825 I St., NW, Suite 400, Washington D.C. 20006. Viola M. Young-Horvath, Ph.D., Exec. Dir., Phone (202) 328-1415. Fax (301) 949-3459
- **Forum of United States Administrative Law Judges.** Edward Silverstein, Pres.; P.O. Box 14076, Washington, DC 20044-4076. Phone (202) 219-2556.
- **Government Accountability Project.** 1402 Third Avenue, Ste. 1215, Seattle, WA 98101. Phone (206) 292-2850 or in Washington, D.C. (202) 408-0034. Internet: *www.whistleblower.org*
- **Graphic Communications International Union.** 1900 L Street, NW, Washington, DC 20036. James J. Norton, Pres. Phone (202) 462-1400. Internet: *www.gciu.org*
- **International Association Of Fire Fighters.** 1750 New York Avenue, NW, Washington, DC 20006. Alfred K. Whitehead, general Pres.; Vincent J. Bollon, general Sec-Treas. Phone (202) 737-8484 Internet: *www.iaff.org*
- **International Association of Machinists and Aerospace Workers**, 9000 Machinists Place, Upper Marlboro, MD 20772-2687. R. Thomas Buffenbarger, Nat. Pres..Phone (301) 967-4700. Internet: *www. iamaw.org*
- **International Brotherhood of Boilermakers, Iron Ship Builders, Blacksmiths, Forgers and Helpers.** Charles W. Jones, Int. Pres., 753 State Ave, Kansas City, Kansas 66101, Phone (913) 371-2640. Internet: *www.boilermakers.org*
- **International Brotherhood of Electrical Workers.** 1125 15th Street,

NW, Washington, DC 20005. Phone (202) 833-7000. Internet: *www.ibew.org*

• **International Brotherhood of Teamsters.** 25 Louisiana Avenue, NW, Washington, D.C, 20001. James P. Hoffa, General Pres. Phone (202) 624-6800. Internet: *www.teamsters.org*

• **International Federation of Professional and Technical Engineers.** 8630 Fenton St., Suite 400, Silver Spring, MD 20910. Paul E. Almeida, Pres. Phone (301) 565-9016. Internet: *www.ifpte.org*

• **International Personnel Management Association.** 1617 Duke Street, Alexandria, VA. 22314. Philip M. Kundin, Pres. Phone (703) 549-7100. Internet: *www.ipma-hr.org*

• **International Union of Operating Engineers.** 1125 17th Street, NW, Washington, DC 20036. Frank Hanley, Gen. Pres. Phone (202) 429-9100. Internet: *www.iuoe.org*

• **National Association of Air Traffic Specialists.** 11303 Amherst Avenue, Suite 4, Wheaton, MD 20902. Walter W. Pike, President, Phone (301) 933-6228. *www.naats.org*

• **National Association of Federal Injured Workers.** 2701 Coed Place, Grants Pass, OR 97527 Phone (541) 472-8940 Fax (541) 472-9101 Internet: *www.jps.net/blugoose/nafiw.htm.*

• **National Association of Federal Veterinarians.** 1101 Vermont Avenue, NW, Suite 710, Washington, DC 20005. Dr. Christopher Bratcher, Pres.; Dr. Dale D. Boyle, Exec. Vice Pres. Phone (202) 289-6334. Internet: *www.erols.com/nafv*

• **National Association of Retired Federal Employees.** 606 N. Washington Street, Alexandria, VA 22314-1943 Frank G. Atwater, Pres., Phone (800) 627-3394, Internet: *www.narfe.org.*

• **National Conference of Shomrim Societies, Inc.** 45 E. 33rd Street, Suite 310, New York, NY 10016. Phone (212) 689-2015.

• **National Marine Engineers Beneficial Association (AFL-CIO).** Lawrence O'Toole, Natl. Pres., 444 North Capitol Street, NW, Suite 800, Washington, DC 20001, Phone (202) 638-5355.

• **National Society of Professional Engineers.** 1420 King Street, Alexandria, VA 22314-2794. Patrick J. Natale, P.E., Exec. Dir. Phone (703) 684-2800; FAX (703) 836-4875. Internet: *http://www.nspe.org*

• **Organization of Professional Employees of the U.S. Department of Agriculture.** P.O. Box 381, Washington, DC 20044. Phone (202) 720-4898, Fax (202) 720-2799. Internet: *www.usda.gov/opeda*

• **Overseas Federation of Teachers, AFT, AFL/CIO.** Dr. Marie Sainz-Funaro, Pres.; CMR 426-Box 541, APO AE 09613. Phone 39-0586-503418 (Italy). Ernest J. Lehmann, European Director, CMR 428 - Box 1276, APO AE 09628 Phone (39-045-8034943 (Italy). Mel Cann, Vice Pres., CMR 427 - Box 1174, APO AE, phone 39-0444-597196 (Italy). E-mail: *sainz-funaro_oft@odedodea.edu*

• **Patent Office Professional Association.** P.O. Box 2745, Arlington, VA 22202. Ronald J. Stern, Pres. Phone (703) 308-0818.

• **Police Emerald Society of the Washington D.C. Area.** 6006 Greenbelt Road, Suite 320, Greenbelt, MD 20770. Patrick F. O'Brien, Pres., Brian Manion, V. Pres. Phone (301) 858-0972, Fax (301) 858-0974. E-mail: *peswashdc@aol.com*

• **Professional Engineers in Government (A division of NSPE).** 1420 King Street, Alexandria, VA 22314. Nick Wright, Dir. Phone (703) 684-2863 Fax (703) 684-2863 Internet: *www.nspe.org* E-mail: *nwright@nspe.org*

• **Public Employees Roundtable.** P.O. Box 44801 Washington, DC 20026-4801. Phone: (202) 401-4344, Fax: (202) 401-4433 Internet: *www.theroundtable.org*

• **Public Employees for Environmental Responsibility** 2001 S Street, NW, Suite 570, Washington DC 20009 Jeff Ruch, Exec. Dir. Phone (202) 265-7337 Fax (202) 265-4192 Internet: *www.peer.org*

• **Senior Executives Association.** P.O. Box 44808, Washington, DC 20026-4808. Carol A. Bonosaro, Pres. Phone (202) 927-7000. Internet: *www.seniorexecs.com*

• **Service Employees International Union.** 1313 L. Street, NW, Washington, DC 20005. Andrew Stern, Pres. Phone (202) 898-3200. Internet: *www.seiu.org*

• **Society of Federal Labor Relations Professionals.** P.O. Box 25112, Arlington, VA 22202. Paco Martinez-Alvarez, Exec. Sec., Phone (703) 685-4130. Fax (703) 685-1144

• **Uniformed Services Benefit Association.** P.O. Box 418258, Kansas City, MO 64141. Larry G Vogt, Rear Admiral, USN (Ret.), Phone (800) 821-7912. Fax (800) 368-7030 Internet: *www.usba.com*

Part 1

Types
of
Disputes

CHAPTER FOUR

Discipline

Discipline—whether it be for misconduct or poor performance—obviously is a mine field filled with all sorts of explosives in the federal job disputes arena. Many of the criticisms about the federal employment program—that it's too complicated, for example, not to mention hidebound and cumbersome—stem from what critics view as the system's excessive layers of employee protections in disciplinary cases. Many supervisors consider the procedures so onerous and frustrating that rather than initiate formal disciplinary action, they prefer to try to ignore or accommodate their problem employees—or find a way to reassign them or "send" them elsewhere. Other managers, however, are determined to take more aggressive action, although the wise ones are careful to follow the required procedures to build a case that will hold up against a potential appeal.

On the other hand, from the employee's viewpoint, protections against discipline are not as strong or complete as they might seem at first glance. Agencies are under increasing pressure from the public and Congress to assure that taxpayers are getting good value for their dollars. While federal workers do enjoy certain due process rights that are rarely visible in private-sector jobs, it is not true that the government cannot fire or demote employees who perform poorly or who engage in misconduct. The truth is discipline happens all the time.

Conduct-Based Actions

Chapter 75 Actions

When disciplining employees for misconduct, agencies usually resort to adverse actions brought under Chapter 75 of Title 5 of the U.S. Code. Some of the most common grounds for misconduct charges are: insubordination or other disrespectful behavior toward supervisors; habitual tardiness; abuse of leave; absence without leave; physical altercations or threats; falsifying documents, such as an employment application or time, attendance, or travel records; disrupting the workplace; misuse of government property; conflicts of interest; sexual harassment and other discriminatory acts; nepo-

tism; and criminal behavior.

These types of offenses may result in an "adverse action," a range of penalties that include a removal, suspension of more than 14 days, reduction in pay or grade, or furlough of 30 days or fewer. In this type of disciplinary decision, the agency typically claims that the "efficiency of the service" demands that it take such action. Such actions ordinarily are based on a worker's conduct or performance deficiencies, although other reasons related to the efficiency of the service, such as a budget shortfall that requires a furlough, also sometimes are used

The Douglas Factors

The Douglas factors are a set of standards agencies must consider when deciding whether a penalty is appropriate in an adverse action. Generally, an agency will have to show that it considered the factors and why it chose a particular penalty. It is not required that every standard be weighed in every case, however. The factors include:

• The nature and seriousness of the offense. Actions taken intentionally, or repeatedly, or maliciously, or for personal reasons are considered the most serious.

• The employee's job level and the type of employment. The higher an employee's level of trust, the more serious misconduct can be viewed.

• Past discipline taken against the employee. Particularly important is discipline for the same or similar violations.

• The employee's previous work record. A long and previously unblemished record will be seen in the employee's favor.

• How the offense affected the employee's ability to work at a satisfactory level. Considerations include the supervisor's ability to maintain confidence in the employee, especially in positions of trust.

• Consistency of the penalty with other employees in similar situations. The other cases to which the decision is being compared must have

been in the same organization and involve positions of similar responsibility, however.

• Whether the discipline met the agency's table of penalties. If the agency has such a table, a deviation must be supported by strong evidence.

• How well known was the offense. Conduct that causes a public scandal or other embarrassment to the agency can merit a more severe penalty.

• How well the agency informed employees of rules that were violated. Breaking an obscure rule will be viewed less harshly than breaking one that is well publicized, and particularly one on which the employee was given specific notice.

• The potential for rehabilitating the employee. An employee can help here by being willing to accept responsibility for misconduct, rather than blaming others.

• Other mitigating circumstances. These can include personal problems, unusual tension in the workplace, provocation, and many other factors.

• Whether alternative penalties would prevent the same thing from happening again. This consideration especially applies to relatively minor offenses in which an apology or other less serious step can be taken.

as justification.

A resignation or retirement can qualify as an adverse action if it was obtained through fraud, coercion, or misrepresentation on the part of the agency. However, an employee's resignation or retirement normally is presumed to be a voluntary decision.

An adverse action also may be

taken for off-duty conduct as long as there is a connection between the worker's misconduct and the efficiency of the service. Off-duty conduct as grounds for discipline most commonly involves criminal acts away from work, such as illegal drug use.

Conduct-related cases often involve investigations. The employee is generally obligated to cooperate unless there is a possibility that criminal charges will result. Normally, union representatives are allowed to be present at interviews to help protect the rights of bargaining unit employees.

Other variables affecting disciplinary decisions include the employee's position and type of job. For example, supervisors and law enforcement personnel are held to a higher standard of conduct than are most other employees.

Agency disciplinary decisions in conduct cases are judged in accordance with a set of principles developed by the Merit Systems Protection Board, known as the "Douglas Factors." These principles, which MSPB announced in a 1981 decision, *Douglas v. Veterans Administration* (6 MSPB 313), outline the review criteria that the Board (and the courts) use in judging the appropriateness of an agency's disciplinary action against an employee. It helps to be generally familiar with these principles long before a situation turns into an adverse action, since ultimately the agency's decision may well be scrutinized to see how they comport with the Douglas Factors. They also serve as a guide during the earlier stages of a dispute, since the agency will have to show that a supervisor who takes an action considered these factors and that the discipline choice was reasonable in light of them.

When taking an adverse action on conduct grounds, an agency generally must comply with certain requirements in personnel laws and rules. These requirements include 30 days' advance notice of the charges (unless there is reasonable cause to believe the employee has committed a crime for which a sentence of imprisonment might be imposed). This notice must be a written explanation of the charges that is specific enough to permit a detailed reply. Employees also must be informed of their right to review the material on which the disciplinary decision is based.

An agency generally may not suspend employees or place them on annual leave during a notice period. However, an agency may shorten the notice period or indefinitely suspend workers if it has reason to believe they have committed a crime, as long as there is a connection between the alleged crime and the efficiency of the service.

Appeal Rights and Routes

After receiving a notice of a proposed action, employees have the right to a reasonable period (not less than seven days) to respond either orally or in writing. They also have rights to representation, to review pertinent material, and to receive a written decision giving specific reasons for the discipline. Typically, any reply by the worker must be heard by an official of high enough rank to make the final decision or to make a recommendation to the final decision-maker. Many agencies require that a supervisor other than the one proposing the action serve as the deciding official.

Appeals of final agency actions may be filed either with the Merit Systems Protection Board or through grievance procedures—either administrative or those negotiated under union contracts. The employee may use one route or the other, but not both. Also, the employee must meet all applicable eligibility requirements—for example, the completion of a mandatory probationary period.

MSPB and arbitrators have the authority to impose lesser penalties, if, for example, a Douglas Factor review indicates that a penalty is inappropriate for an offense or was not consistent with past disciplinary actions in similar situations.

All of the factors won't necessarily be considered in each case—for example, not all agencies have tables of discipline. However, the Douglas Factors serve as the best single indicator of which side is likely to prevail in an adverse action case.

An employee also can successfully challenge a conduct-based action by showing that it was the result of a prohibited personnel practice. If this claim is raised, the agency must show that it had legitimate reasons for making the disciplinary decision. If a prohibited practice is proved, the Office of Special Counsel may seek discipline against the responsible supervisor or manager by filing a complaint with MSPB.

Also, an agency's failure to meet procedural requirements in taking an adverse action that is determined to constitute "harmful error" to the employee can be grounds for overturning the decision.

Additionally, an employee who believes a disciplinary action was motivated by discrimination also can challenge the decision through equal employment opportunity channels.

—Performance-Based Disciplinary Actions—

Chapter 43 Actions

Performance-based actions normally are taken under Chapter 43 of Title 5 of the U.S. Code, which specifies procedures for dealing with poor performance in the workplace and carries certain guarantees such as an opportunity for the employee to improve. Less commonly, performance-based discipline may be meted out under Chapter 75 (see above), which generally is used for conduct-based disciplinary actions. An example of a Chapter 75 performance-based situation would be where the agency determines that a worker's level of performance is so poor that it constitutes misconduct.

Disciplinary actions taken against employees under Chapter 43 must be based on formal performance appraisal systems. These systems are used not only to periodically rate employees, but also as the basis for decisions on training, rewarding, reassigning, promoting, demoting, or firing employees. Performance appraisals also are used in decisions to grant employees within-grade pay increases.

An action taken under Chapter 43 requires that the agency prove its case by "substantial evidence" and that it meet certain procedural requirements, such as giving the employee a chance to improve. Chapter 75 has a higher standard of proof—"a preponderance of the evidence"—that the agency must satisfy in proving a connection between the employee's performance and the efficiency of the service.

Employees who are subject to Chapter 75 actions for performance-based reasons are not entitled to an opportunity to demonstrate acceptable performance before the action takes effect. However, the agency must show that all relevant factors were considered in selecting the penalty.

Performance Appraisals and PIPs

Individual agencies draw up their own performance rating systems depending on the nature of the work to be done. However, to be valid, these systems must have been approved by the Office of Personnel Management. Each rating system must: identify "critical elements" of a position—those for which performance below the minimum standard would require remedial action—describe how performance will be weighed against the standards, and explain how personnel decisions will be made based on an appraisal. The standards must be based as much as possible on objective criteria, although not necessarily on strictly numeric measures. And it is not necessary that standards for employees having the same job be identical.

In general, standards must be reasonable, sufficient to permit adequate measurement, and adequate to inform employees of what is needed to get a satisfactory rating. They must be described in positive terms, stating what must be done, rather than what must not be done.

Standards must use objective criteria and must be specific in setting forth how the employee is expected to do the job and identifying the performance level that the employee is expected to maintain.

However, the fact that a standard could be written more objectively does not, standing alone, render the standard invalid.

Unacceptable performance in only one critical element can be sufficient to warrant removal. Also, failure to perform some, but not all, of the components of a critical element can warrant an unacceptable rating on the element as a whole.

Before being disciplined under Chapter 43, an employee must be given a reasonable chance to demonstrate performance at an acceptable level. During this period, supervisors must offer assistance to improve the worker's performance. Commonly this is done through a performance improvement plan (PIP) established under individual agency rules.

Agencies may not use such plans to reduce or increase performance standards established at the beginning of the appraisal period, and the

agency may rely solely on performance during the plan period only if it shows that the employee's performance is unacceptable under the annual performance standards.

While an agency generally may rely on performance deficiencies occurring at any time during the year before taking a performance-based action, if an employee demonstrates acceptable performance under a performance improvement plan the agency may not base an action solely on the worker's performance predating the PIP. The agency may, however, use unacceptable performance predating the PIP to present a more complete context for the charged deficiencies.

Where performance standards are numeric measures set on an annual basis, those standards will be prorated during PIP periods, unless seasonal or other variations in the workload make such a division unfair.

An agency generally may rely on instances of unacceptable performance in the critical elements that occur after the successful completion of a PIP. However, an agency may not delay taking action more than one year after the beginning of the PIP. Beyond that date, if a worker's performance again shows deficiencies, a new PIP must be initiated before taking a Chapter 43 action. The agency bears the burden of proving that it provided the employee with a bona fide opportunity to demonstrate acceptable performance.

Where the agency relies on an employee's performance deficiencies before, after, and during a PIP period, it must present substantial evidence of genuinely unacceptable performance under the applicable performance standard.

Where a performance appraisal was used to deny within-grade increases, the determination must be based on performance throughout the entire waiting period for the within-grade raise. These waiting periods vary. In such cases, employees must be informed in writing that they are not performing acceptably and what must be done to improve. A within-grade raise can be denied without giving the employee a chance to improve.

Appeal Rights and Routes

Employees disciplined under Chapter 43 have the right to 30 days' advance notice, which must include specific examples of unacceptable performance and the critical elements of their performance appraisals that are involved. The employee may respond orally or in writing (or both), may be represented by counsel, and is entitled to a decision by an official higher than that made by the one who proposed the disciplinary action.

An employee disciplined for performance under either Chapter 43 or Chapter 75 has the right to appeal to the Merit Systems Protection Board, as long as the worker meets MSPB appeals eligibility. Violations of the agency obligations or employee rights mentioned above can be grounds for overturning the agency action. When an agency uses the Chapter 75 disciplinary system, MSPB will weigh the Douglas Factors in reviewing penalties for conduct.

While employees disciplined under Chapter 75 for performance reasons are not entitled to an opportunity to improve their performance before the action, the issue of whether such an opportunity was given is relevant in assessing the reasonableness of a penalty. That's because one of the Douglas Factors is the extent to which employees have been placed on notice that their deficient performance or conduct may be the basis for an adverse action.

In instances where a Chapter 75 action is initiated and the employee is provided with an improvement opportunity, the requirements of Chapter 43 don't apply—for example, that only unsatisfactory (rather than minimally acceptable) performance be the basis for the action or that the improvement period occur before the notice of proposed action. An agency may rebut a challenge to its failure to afford an opportunity period or notice of performance deficiencies by showing that the worker's deficiencies were willful or that affording the employee more time to improve would have resulted in unreasonable costs or risked the health and safety of others.

Negotiated grievance procedures also may be available to employees disciplined under either chapter for poor performance. Denials of within-grade raises also are appealable to MSPB and may be appealed through negotiated procedures.

Additionally, employees who believe the agency's decision was motivated by discrimination have the right to challenge the action through equal employment opportunity channels.

Practical Considerations

Questions and Concerns

A threshold question in nearly every personnel problem or situation that results in discipline is whether the problem is related to the worker's performance or conduct. Sometimes the dividing line between the two is not clear. But the two types of problems, despite a certain amount of overlap, can be handled in very different ways.

Conduct problems in general involve a failure or refusal to comply with some type of rule or requirement, and penalties imposed by management are designed to correct those problems. Performance problems, on the other hand, involve a worker's failure to perform official duties at the expected or desired level, and usually are addressed through attempts to improve the individual's work—although penalties up to and including removal may eventually be imposed.

One thing that disputes over both conduct and performance have in common is that they tend to turn personal. While to an extent this is perhaps inevitable, given the amount of time people spend together in the workplace and the pressures that arise in any working environment, it's best for everyone involved to separate feelings from facts as much as possible.

Fortunately, fairly reliable measures of the facts usually are available to be considered. For example, most agencies have performance appraisal systems in place that let employees know what they are supposed to be doing. Some of those ratings criteria describe the performance expected by management in numeric terms, while others, because of the nature of the work, include measures or rating scales that are not expressed as definitively. Even those, though, must be specific enough so that a neutral assessment will be able to determine whether or not the employee is doing what is expected. When an agency decides to formally address a perceived performance problem, it typically goes through the formal PIP process (i.e a performance improvement plan) that lays out what is expected and that warns the employee of potential consequences for failure to live up to those expectations.

Similarly, in misconduct cases, there are rules of conduct, both government-wide and agency-specific, to which both workers and managers can refer. While some of these sets of rules are expressed only in general terms and others are so densely written that they're difficult to understand, a detached look at them should tell just about anyone whether certain actions are on the right or wrong side of the line.

It's worth remembering that in surveys, about four-fifths of federal managers routinely say they have had a problem with a poorly performing employee, but only about a quarter of those managers took any action that might result in the worker's removal or demotion. Typical reasons why supervisors don't take formal actions are because they lack confidence that their decisions will be supported at higher levels and because they feel they don't have the time to defend their actions in a potential appeal. Instead of imposing discipline, they often will counsel the employee—sometimes with the help of the personnel office—or try in other ways to work around the problem, such as providing training or a performance improvement plan or even looking to restructure the position or move the employee into a more suitable job.

Managers commonly express similar reservations about taking actions on conduct grounds.

The bottom line is that there usually is ample time and opportunity to resolve either conduct or performance issues before push comes to shove. In many cases, the real issue boils down to whether the employee and the manager would rather make that effort than launch a nasty, potentially bruising fight.

Rulings Review

Conduct

• An agency's penalty determination for employee misconduct will not be changed unless it is clearly disproportionate and unreasonable. *(Hagmeyer v. Dept. of Treasury, 757 F.2d 1281, Fed. Cir. 1985)*

• An agency may consider an employee's past disciplinary record when choosing a penalty even if the conduct for which the prior discipline was imposed was unrelated in nature to the present circumstances. *(Lewis v. Dept. of the Air Force, 51 MSPR 475, 1991)*

• In an adverse action based on alleged falsification of an employment application, the Board will not consider the employee's good work record in mitigation of the penalty unless the deciding official had considered that work record. *(Beardsley v. Dept. of Defense, 55 MSPR 504, 1992)*

• Employees may not escape disciplinary action for refusing to obey an order because of their belief that the order is not legitimate. The proper course is to obey first and grieve later, absent extraordinary circumstances such as physical danger. *(Wiggins v. National Gallery of Art, 980 F.2d 1436, Fed. Cir. 1992)*

• To prove a claim of self-defense, employees must show that they used only as much force as was reasonably necessary to free themselves from an unwanted grasp. *(Fuller v. Dept. of the Navy, 60 MSPR 187, 1993)*

• To support a charge of falsification, the agency must prove by preponderant evidence that the employee provided false information with the intent to defraud the government. An agency must support its charges with evidence, not mere assumptions and opinions. *(Jacobs v.*

Department of Justice, 35 F.3d 1543, Fed. Cir. 1994)

• Proof of the employee's intent is required to sustain the charge of attempted removal of government property. *(Chauvin v. Department of the Navy, 38 F.3d 563, Fed. Cir. 1994)*

• When an agency charges an employee with theft, it must establish that the worker intended to permanently deprive the owner of the property. *(King v. Nazelrod, 43 F.3d 663, Fed. Cir. 1994)*

• Where an employee uses a government-issued credit card to rent a car and is personally liable for the charges, the car does not qualify as a government-leased vehicle, and the employee may not be suspended for misuse of a government-leased vehicle. *(Chufo v. Department of the Interior, 45 F.3d 419, Fed. Cir. 1995)*

• To sustain a charge of misuse of a government vehicle, the agency must prove that the employee had actual knowledge that the use would not be characterized as official or acted with reckless disregard for whether or not its use was official. *(Kimm v. Dept. of the Treasury, 61 F.3d 888, Fed. Cir. 1995)*

• A charge of misuse of a government credit card does not require proof of intent. *(Baracker v. Dept. of Interior, 70 MSPR 594, 1996)*

• A charge of failure to follow instructions is different than a charge of insubordination because it does not require proof of intentional and willful refusal to obey an order that the worker had to obey. *(Hamilton v. U.S. Postal Service, 71 MSPR 547, 1996)*

• A cancelled action that may not be considered as prior discipline may nonetheless be considered as evidence that a worker had been warned about such misconduct. *(Rush v. Air Force, 69 MSPR 417, 1996)*

• Where only some of the agency's charges are sustained, MSPB will itself independently select what it determines to be a reasonable penalty. The Board may consider statements by deciding officials as to the penalties they would have imposed if only some of the charges had been sustained, although it will not necessarily defer to them. *(White v. U.S. Postal Service, 71 MSPR 521, 1996)*

• A worker's lengthy service is a factor that supports lenience in a penalty and does not support an agency's choice of stronger discipline on grounds that the employee should have known better. *(Shelly v. Dept. of the Treasury, 75 MSPR 677, 1997)*

Performance

• Removal from a position that requires certain professional credentials because the worker has lost those credentials is analogous to a performance-based action under Chapter 75 and only the standards used in such an action should apply. The agency need not establish a valid performance standard before taking an action on those grounds. *(Graham v. Dept. of the Air Force, 46 MSPR 227, 1990)*

• An agency may take a performance-based action against an employee based on incidents of unacceptable performance during the year before the proposed action as long as it shows that the worker failed to demonstrate acceptable performance or to sustain it after receiving a reasonable opportunity to do so. *(Brown v. Veterans Administration, 44 MSPR 635, 1990)*

• In a Chapter 75 action for unacceptable performance, it is reasonable for an agency to base its decision on a sample of the employee's work, but the agency must establish a method for choosing the examples of alleged unacceptable performance, similar to

the obligation it would have in a Chapter 43 action. *(Bowling v. Dept. of the Army, 47 MSPR 379, 1991)*

• An invalid performance standard cannot be "rehabilitated" by calling it an absolute standard, but must instead be rewritten to become valid. Also, an agency must communicate to the employees that the standard was absolute. *(Ortiz v. Dept. of Justice, 46 MSPR 692, 1991)*

• In taking a performance-based action, the agency is entitled to rely on performance that occurred within the last year, and is not limited to performance that occurred during a performance improvement plan. *(Addison v. HHS, 945 F.2d 1184, Fed. Cir. 1991)*

• Where an employee qualifies for discontinued service retirement because of a performance-based removal that MSPB has reversed, the basis for the retirement has been wiped out and the Board can enforce its decision to reinstate the employee. *(Dobratz v. Dept. of Health and Human Services, 53 MSPR 9, 1992)*

General Discipline

• An agency's decision to place an employee in an "absent without leave" status is not an appealable adverse action when the employee voluntarily chose not to report for work. *(Perez v. MSPB, 931 F.2d 853, Fed. Cir. 1991)*

• A reassignment without a reduction in pay is not appealable to the Merit Systems Protection Board. *(McEnery v. MSPB, 963 F.2d 1512, Fed. Cir. 1992)*

• Where an agency substitutes deciding officials after the first had already decided on a penalty, and the penalty ultimately imposed is harsher, it must meet the burden of showing that the final penalty is reasonable. If it does not do so, the first official's penalty selection is the maximum reasonable penalty. *(Williams v. Army, 58 MSPR 646, 1993)*

• When MSPB mitigates a penalty, the worker is entitled to be restored as close to the status quo as the mitigated penalty allows, including restoring the employee to the former work location, unless the agency shows that overriding circumstances require reassignment to a different location. A claim of overstaffing and a desire for a clean state do not constitute such a showing. *(Holtgrewe v. Federal Deposit Insurance Corporation, 57 MSPR 307, 1993)*

• A reduction in a position's organizational level, without a change in pay or duties, and the rewriting of the employee's position description to reflect that change, are not adverse personnel actions. *(Fleming v. Interior, 68 MSPR 222, 1995)*

• Employees may be disciplined for failure to follow leave-requesting procedures, even if the leave ends up being approved. *(Wilkinson v. Air Force, 68 MSPR 4, 1995)*

• An agency's failure to issue a decision regarding an employee's proposed removal within 30 days after the expiration of the notice period does not invalidate the action, unless the employee can show harmful error. *(Diaz v. Dept. of the Air Force, 63 F.3d 1107, Fed. Cir. 1995)*

• Where an AWOL charge is based on the failure to report for a directed reassignment, the agency must prove that its reassignment decision was bona fide and based on legitimate management needs. *(Cooke v. U.S. Postal Service, 67 MSPR 401, 1995)*

• The "reasonable suspicion" requirement for drug testing of federal employees must be based on factual information known to agency officials at the time they ordered the test, and not on the basis of additional information that subsequently was disclosed or could have been discovered by

further inquiry. *(Garrison v. Dept. of Justice, 72 F.3d 1566, Fed. Cir. 1995)*

• The Family and Medical Leave Act has its own leave-requesting procedures, and an AWOL charge does not necessarily cancel an employee's rights under it. *(Ramey v. U.S. Postal Service, 70 MSPR 463, 1996)*

• An employee's unexcused absences under a flexitime program are proper grounds for disciplinary action because such absences are inherently connected to the efficiency of the service. *(Bryant v. National Science Foundation, 105 F.3d 1414, Fed. Cir. 1997)*

• When an agency takes a personnel action in accordance with a judicial order and ongoing judicial proceedings, it is not required to follow statutory adverse action procedures. *(Diamond v. United States Agency for International Development, 108 F.3d 312, Fed. Cir. 1997)*

• The U.S. Supreme Court held that federal employees must tell the truth during investigatory interviews related to an agency's administrative charges or face the prospects of additional charges of lying to the investigators. The High Court unanimously declared that employees "cannot with impunity knowingly and willfully answer with a falsehood," rejecting the argument that the prospect of separate charges related to the person's answers in such an interview would violate the employee's right to due process of law. *(Lachance v. Erickson, 118 S.Ct. 753, 1998)*

• In the course of an investigation by an agency inspector general, federal employees have the right to union representation if they are interviewed by the IG, the Supreme Court ruled. In its decision, the Court agreed with union arguments that the IG is a "representative" of agency management and thus employees who fear disciplinary action can invoke their legal right to have a union representative present. (*NASA v. Federal Labor Relations Authority, 119 S.Ct. 1979, 1999*)

• The U.S. Court of Appeals for the Federal Circuit held that if, during the adverse action process, a deciding official considers "new and material" information from an *ex parte* source (i.e., unknown to the worker) that the employee had no chance to address or rebut, then the disciplinary action must be reversed pursuant to the constitutional guarantee of due process. This new "objective" test replaced the "subjective" test that had previously been applied by MSPB. Under the new rule, the Board must assess whether the *ex parte* or unknown contact in question provided the deciding official with "new" (as opposed to merely "cumulative") information and also must determine whether the new information was "material." (*Stone v. FDIC, 179 F.3d 1368, Fed. Cir. 1999*)

• Wading once more into the murky waters of "mitigation of penalty," the U.S. Court of Appeals for the Federal Circuit decided that when MSPB determines that an agency's choice of punishment is too severe in a case where all the charges against an employee have been sustained, then the Board should substitute the "maximum reasonable penalty" as a reduced punishment. On the other hand, if the Board sustains some, but not all, of the charges against an employee, then MSPB may impose the "maximum reasonable penalty" only if the agency has not indicated that it would impose a lesser penalty in the event of fewer sustained charges. If the agency has so indicated, then the Board must provide the agency with a new opportunity to determine a lesser penalty. (*Lachance v. Devall, 178 F.3d 1246, Fed. Cir. 1999*)

• Civil service law does not ordinarily permit employees covered by negotiated grievance procedures a choice between that route and the Merit Systems Protection Board, unless the union and agency agree to exclude specific types of appeals from the grievance process, the U.S. Court of Appeals for the Federal Circuit held. Only in matters involving prohibited personnel practices and certain performance-based actions is the employee given the choice of using either the grievance mechanism or MSPB procedures. (*Dunkelbarger v. MSPB, Fed. Cir., No. 96-3200, 1997*)

• The U.S. Court of Appeals for the Federal Circuit held that an agency violated a union's rights by denying its request for the investigative file records related to a disciplinary action, plus five-year records of all regional disciplinary actions. (*INS v. FLRA, Fed. Cir., No. 97-1388, 1998*)

• The U.S. Court of Appeals for the Federal Circuit formally adopted the MSPB's standards on removing employees for non-performance after reassignments, but held that the Board misapplied its own precedent in the case at hand. According to the court, MSPB should have followed the precedent previously established in such situations: determining whether the efficiency of the service would be promoted more by removing the reassigned employee than by returning him to his former position. (*Vidal v. USPS, Fed. Cir., No. 97-3386, 1998*)

• The presenting of internal agency documents "of an advisory nature" to an agency official who was deciding on a personnel action against an employee did not improperly taint that decision, the U.S. Court of Appeals for the Federal Circuit held. It said the documents were simply nonessential evidence in support of the proposed action and did not constitute additional charges against the employee and thus did not trigger application of the worker's due process rights. (*Hendrix v. Dept. of Agriculture, Fed.*

Cir., No. 98-3071, 1998)

• A federal firefighter who refused a random drug test on the grounds that it was an invasion of his rights was not entitled to appeal the agency's decision to remove him from his position, according to the U.S. Court of Appeals for the Federal Circuit. The court held that employees responsible for the safety of others—such as firefighters—may be subject to drug testing even if there is no suspicion that they are using illegal drugs. (*Hatley v. Dept. of Navy, 164 F.3d 602, Fed. Cir., 1998*)

• A federal agency cannot apply stricter Family and Medical Leave Act standards than those called for in the law, MSPB ruled, overturning the removal of an employee who was unable to provide all the medical documentation required by the agency to justify medical leave. According to MSPB, in such situations agencies may follow their own policies only if they're less restrictive than the FMLA guidelines. (*Burge v. Air Force, 82 MSPR 75, 1999*)

• A postmaster was improperly demoted for writing a letter to the union that USPS contended had "compromised the agency's ability to defend its removal action" taken against one of the postmaster's workers, MSPB ruled. The Board agreed with the postmaster's contentions that the grade reduction violated his free speech rights and amounted to interference with the collective bargaining process. (*Wills v. USPS, 84 MSPR 90, 1999*)

CHAPTER FIVE

Discrimination

Federal and postal employees are protected by most of the same anti-discrimination laws that generally apply to private-sector workers. Among the major laws prohibiting various forms of discrimination in the government workplace are:

- Title VII of the Civil Rights Act of 1964, which makes it illegal to discriminate in employment based on race, color, religion, sex, or national origin.
- The Equal Pay Act of 1963, which prohibits agencies from discriminating on the basis of sex in compensating male and female employees for substantially equal work performed under similar working conditions.
- The Rehabilitation Act of 1973, which makes it illegal to engage in disability discrimination against federal employees and job applicants. Federal agencies are required to make reasonable accommodations to the known physical and mental limitations of qualified employees or applicants with disabilities. The law also requires agencies to undertake affirmative action with respect to hiring, placing, and promoting qualified individuals with disabilities.
- The Age Discrimination in Employment Act of 1967, which protects people 40 years of age and older from age-based discrimination in hiring, discharge, pay, promotions, and other terms and conditions of employment.

Enforcement responsibility for these laws generally rests with the Equal Employment Opportunity Commission, a five-member federal agency that is primarily responsible for ensuring EEO compliance in both private and public-sector workplaces in the U.S. However, in the federal sector, employees who are victims of illegal discrimination may have other complaint and appeals routes available, which in some cases may substitute for EEOC procedures.

This chapter first summarizes the basic types of workplace discrimination prohibited under various federal laws, and then reviews the complaint-processing channels established by the Equal Employment Opportunity Commission—the primary enforcer of federal workers' EEO rights—to resolve federal-sector discrimination disputes.

Prohibited Bias

Race/Color Discrimination

Title VII makes it unlawful to discriminate against employees or job applicants because of their race or color with respect to a hiring, termination, promotion, compensation, or training decision, or any other term, condition, or privilege of employment. Title VII also prohibits basing any employment decision on stereotypes or assumptions about a racial group's abilities, traits, or job performance. The law bars not only intentional discrimination, but also facially-neutral job policies that are not job-related and tend to disproportionately exclude minorities.

Title VII's ban on race discrimination is quite broad. For example, under the law equal employment opportunity cannot be denied because of: an individual's marriage to or association with a person of a different race; membership in or association with ethnic organizations or groups; or attendance or participation in schools or places of worship generally associated with certain minority groups. Moreover, discrimination on the basis of an immutable characteristic associated with race—such as an individual's skin color, hair texture, or other physical features—violates Title VII, even though not all members of the race share the same characteristic.

Title VII also prohibits discrimination on the basis of a condition that predominantly affects one race, unless the employment procedure or practice is job related and consistent with business necessity.

Harassment on the basis of race and/or color also violates Title VII. Ethnic slurs, racial jokes, offensive or derogatory comments, or other verbal or physical conduct based on an individual's race or color constitutes unlawful harassment if the conduct creates an intimidating, hostile, or offensive working environment, or interferes with the individual's work performance.

Requesting pre-employment information that discloses or tends to disclose an applicant's race suggests that race will be unlawfully used as a basis for hiring. However, agencies may legitimately gather information about their employees' or applicants' race for affirmative action purposes or to track applicant flow.

National Origin Discrimination

Title VII also makes it unlawful to discriminate against any employee or applicant because of the individual's national origin. No one can be denied equal employment opportunity because of birthplace, ancestry, culture, or linguistic characteristics common to a specific ethnic group.

Similarly, these prohibitions extend to discrimination on the basis of an individual's: marriage or association with persons of a national origin group; membership or association with specific ethnic promotion groups; attendance or participation in schools, churches, temples, or mosques generally associated with a national origin group; or possession of a surname associated with a national origin group.

A rule requiring employees to speak only English at all times on the job may violate Title VII, unless the employer can show that it is necessary for conducting business. An agency must show a legitimate non-discriminatory reason for denying an employment opportunity because of an individual's accent or manner of speaking. Requiring employees or applicants to be fluent in English may violate Title VII if the rule is adopted to exclude individuals of a particular national origin and is not related to job performance.

Harassment on the basis of national origin is a violation of Title VII. An ethnic slur or engaging in other ethnic-based verbal or physical conduct toward individuals constitutes harassment if such actions create an intimidating, hostile, or offensive working environment, unreasonably interfere with another's work performance, or negatively affect an individual's employment opportunities.

Religious Discrimination

Tile VII also prohibits discriminating against individuals because of their religion in hiring, firing, or other terms and conditions of employment. Agencies are required to reasonably accommodate the religious practices of an employee or prospective employee, unless doing so would create an undue hardship or significantly interfere with operations. Flexible scheduling, voluntary substitutions or swaps, job reassignments, and lateral transfers are all examples of ways to accommodate an employee's religious beliefs.

Once again, the ban on religious discrimination covers a wide range of actions. For example, agencies cannot: schedule examinations or other selection activities that conflict with a current or prospective employee's religious needs; inquire about an applicant's future availability at certain times; maintain a restrictive dress code; or refuse to allow an employee's observance of a Sabbath or religious holiday, unless the agency can prove that permitting the practice or exception would cause an undue hardship.

An agency can support its claim of undue hardship resulting from a proposed religious accommodation by showing that granting the request or permitting the practice would require it to incur more than ordinary administrative costs. Similarly, undue hardship also may be shown if changing a bona fide seniority system to accommodate one employee's religious practices denies another employee the job or shift preference guaranteed by the seniority system.

Title VII's ban on religious discrimination also may be violated by required participation in "New Age" training programs that are designed to improve employee motivation or productivity through meditation, yoga, biofeedback, or other practices. Agencies must accommodate any employee who notifies management that

---

Sexual Orientation Discrimination

No federal job bias statute prohibits an employer (either public or private) from discriminating on the basis of an employee's sexual orientation. However, if a federal agency is shown to have taken an adverse action against an employee based on that individual's sexual orientation, the Merit Systems Protection Board may reverse the adverse action because it was taken for a non-merit-based reason. Also, many federal agencies have formally adopted policies prohibiting sexual orientation discrimination; this does not, however, create a claim for relief either through EEOC's processes or court actions. Workers and agencies also should keep in mind that in May 1998, President Clinton issued Executive Order 13087, stressing that all executive branch agencies were prohibited from discriminating against federal workers on the basis of sexual orientation.

participation in these types of programs is inconsistent with the worker's religious beliefs, whether or not the agency believes there is a religious basis for the employee's objection.

Sex-Based Discrimination

Under Title VII, an employer may not discriminate between men and women with regard to their pay, benefits, job opportunities, or other terms and conditions of employment.

It is illegal to classify a job as "male" or "female" or to maintain separate lines of progression or seniority lists based on sex, except in the rare instances when a person's gender is a bona fide occupational qualification for a particular job. Co-workers' or customers' preferences generally are not considered a bona fide requirement.

Sexual harassment is a form of sex discrimination that violates the Act. Unwelcome sexual advances, requests for sexual favors, and other verbal or physical conduct of a sexual nature constitutes sexual harassment when submission to or rejection of this conduct explicitly or implicitly affects an individual's employment, unreasonably interferes with an individual's work performance, or creates an intimidating, hostile, or offensive work environment (see the Sexual Harassment chapter).

Discrimination on the basis of pregnancy, childbirth, or related medical conditions also constitutes unlawful sex discrimination under Title VII. Women affected by pregnancy or related conditions must be treated in the same manner as other applicants or employees with similar abilities or limitations. An agency cannot refuse to hire a woman because of her pregnancy-related condition as long as she is able to perform the major functions of her job, nor may it refuse to hire because of its prejudices against pregnant workers or the prejudices of co-workers, clients, or customers. An agency may not single out pregnancy-related conditions for special procedures to determine an employee's ability to work.

If an employee is temporarily unable to perform her job due to pregnancy, the agency must treat her the same as any other temporarily disabled employee—for example, by providing modified tasks, alternative assignments, disability leave, or leave without pay. Pregnant employees must be permitted to work as long as they are able to perform their jobs. If an employee has been absent from work as a result of a pregnancy-related condition and recovers, management may not require her to remain on leave until the baby's birth.

Reasonable Accommodation Requests

The laws prohibiting disability discrimination contemplate a "dialogue" between an employee and management regarding the types of accommodation that may be appropriate for the disabled worker in a given situation. For many reasons, it is important for employees to identify acceptable accommodations throughout this "dialogue" process. Generally, disabled workers are well-advised to provide management with accommodation options in writing, accompanied by written medical support where applicable. Employees (and managers) may call the Job Accommodation Network at 1-800-526-7234 to obtain assistance in identifying possible accommodation ideas.

Salary Discrimination

Although the Equal Pay Act originally did not apply to the federal sector, Congress approved amendments in 1974 to the Fair Labor Standards Act that extended EPA's coverage to government workers. The Equal Pay Act prohibits paying men and women different wages for equal work, which essentially means work that requires equal skills, effort, and responsibility and is performed under equal working conditions. However, this "equal work" principle requires only that the jobs be substantially equal, not identical.

The EPA's protections apply only to situations where pay disparities exist between comparably situated workers of different sexes. Certain job classification, seniority, and merit systems are exempt from coverage, as are disparate pay systems for which a legitimate business necessity exists—e.g., those in which pay differences are based on factors other than sex, such as production levels.

Sex-based disparities in pay may violate either the Equal Pay Act or Title VII's sex discrimination provisions, or both.

Disability Discrimination

Under Section 501 of the 1973 Rehabilitation Act, it is illegal for federal agencies to discriminate against employees or applicants based on an individual's disability. The Rehabilitation Act also requires agencies not only to make reasonable accommodations to the known physical or mental limitations of qualified employees or applicants, but also to develop and carry out affirmative action plans for hiring, placing, and promoting persons with disabilities. (The Rehabilitation Act requirements imposed on federal agencies were the model for the many similar disability protections applied to private-sector employers and state and local governments under the 1990 Americans With Disabilities Act).

The Rehabilitation Act's protections generally extend to persons who: have a physical or mental impairment that substantially limits one or more of their major life activities, have a record of such an impairment, or are regarded as having such an impairment. "Major life activities" are such functions as caring for one's self, performing manual tasks, walking, seeing, hearing, speaking, breathing, learning, and working. The term "physical or mental impairment" covers a broad range of conditions, including anatomical losses, cosmetic disfigurements, mental, emotional, or psychological disorders or illnesses, and specific learning disabilities.

The Act's rights and protections do not extend to individuals who currently are using illegal drugs. This exception, however, does not remove the Act's protections from individuals who have successfully completed a supervised drug rehabilitation program or have otherwise been rehabilitated successfully and are no longer using illegal drugs or who are participating in a supervised rehabilitation program and are no longer using illegal drugs.

An agency must make reasonable accommodation to the known physical or mental limitations of qualified applicants or employees, unless it can demonstrate that the accommodation would impose an undue hardship on its program operations. Examples of reasonable accommodations include making facilities more accessible, job restructuring, part-time or modified work schedules, acquisition or modification of equipment or devices, adjustment or modification of examinations, and the provision of readers and interpreters.

A number of factors can come into play in determining whether a proposed accommodation would create an undue hardship on an agency. Typically, these factors include the overall size of the agency's program with respect to the number of employees involved or affected, number and type of facilities and size of budget, the type of agency operation, and the nature and cost of the proposed accommodation.

Agencies generally may not use any employment test or other selection criterion that tends to screen out qualified individuals with disabilities. They also generally are barred from conducting preemployment medical examinations and may not ask applicants whether they have a disability or inquire into its extent or nature.

An agency may, however, make preemployment inquiries into an applicant's ability to perform the job's essential functions or meet any applicable medical qualification requirements. Agencies may condition a job offer on the results of a medical exam if all entering employees are subject to such exams.

If nonprobationary disabled employees become unable to perform the essential functions of their position—even with a reasonable accommodation—their agency must offer to reassign such workers to a funded vacant position in the same commuting area and at the same grade or level, unless the agency can show that the reassignment would impose an undue hardship on its program.

If no position is available at the same grade or level, an agency must offer reassignment to a vacant position at the highest available grade or level below the employee's current grade or level. If the agency has already posted a vacancy announcement for a position, the agency is not obliged to offer to reassign the individual to that position, but it must consider the individual on an equal basis with those who applied for the position.

Age Discrimination

The Age Discrimination in Employment Act (ADEA) protects individuals who are 40 years of age or older from age-based employment discrimination. The ADEA's protections, which apply to both employees and job applicants, generally make it unlawful to discriminate against individuals because of their age with respect to any term, condition, or privilege of employment. These include, but are not limited to, hiring, firing, promotion, layoff, compensation, benefits, job assignments, and training. The Act also makes it unlawful to retaliate

---

Dual Option Complaint Process for Postal Employees

Postal employees, unlike most other federal workers, have an additional option when it comes to pursuing an EEO complaint. Along with seeking redress through the agency's EEO administrative process, postal workers who are covered by a collective bargaining agreement also may file an EEO grievance under their contractual grievance/arbitration procedure. (In such situations, processing of the administrative charges may be deferred pending resolution of the grievance proceedings.) This dual option is limited to the postal workforce. Even if covered by a union contract, nonpostal federal employees do not have this additional option for pursuing discrimination complaints. Instead, they must choose between the administrative EEO-complaint process and an available contractual grievance procedure.

against an individual for opposing employment practices that discriminate based on age or for filing an age discrimination charge, testifying, or participating in any ADEA investigation or proceeding.

The ADEA does not specifically prohibit an agency from asking an applicant's age or date of birth. However, because such inquiries may deter older workers from applying for employment or may otherwise indicate possible intent to discriminate based on age, EEO enforcement officials will closely scrutinize any such requests for age information to make sure that the inquiry was made for a lawful purpose, rather than for a purpose prohibited by the ADEA.

General Ban on Retaliation

A person who files a complaint or charge, participates in an investigation or charge, or opposes an employment practice made illegal by any of the federal anti-discrimination laws is protected from retaliation. A claim of retaliation may be filed through the same procedures used to file any EEO complaint. However, if the underlying complaint is still pending, the employee may ask that the two be consolidated.

EEO Complaint Channels

Multi-Step Process

The EEO complaint process for federal employees is a multi-step procedure, with different time limits established for each stage of the process. The general complaint-processing rules for federal-sector EEO cases are spelled out in regulations issued by the Equal Employment Opportunity Commission. Employees or applicants who feel they have been discriminated against by a federal agency first must contact an equal employment opportunity counselor at the agency where the alleged discrimination took place within 45 days of the discriminatory action. Ordinarily, counseling must be completed within 30 days. If counseling does not resolve the problem, aggrieved individuals may then file a complaint with the agency.

After receiving an individual's EEO complaint, the agency must decide to accept or dismiss it. If it does not dismiss the complaint, the agency must, within 180 days, conduct an investigation. (If the parties agree to an extension, an agency may be allowed an additional 90 days to complete its investigation.)

After receiving the results of the agency's investigation, complainants have two basic choices. If the complaint is one that does not contain issues that are appealable to the Merit Systems Protection Board, employees have 30 days from the conclusion of the agency's investigation to request either:

• A hearing conducted by an Equal Employment Opportunity Commission (EEOC) administrative judge. If the employee proceeds down the EEOC route, the administrative judge must process the worker's request for a hearing, make findings of fact and conclusions of law, and issue a decision within 180 days.

• An immediate final decision from the employing agency. If the employee seeks a final agency decision, the agency must promptly comply with the worker's request (i.e., generally within 60 days). After receiving the agency's final decision, the employee may appeal a dismissed complaint (or portion of the complaint) to EEOC within 30 days of receiving notice of the agency's decision. Alternatively, the employee also may choose to file a lawsuit in a federal district court within 90 days. While either party may request reconsideration by the Commission, only complainants are entitled to seek judicial review.

Upon receiving an appeal of a final agency decision, the EEOC may determine that the dismissal was improper, reverse the dismissal, and remand the matter back to the agency for completion of the investigation. There are no time limits established for EEOC reviews of appealed agency decisions.

If the complaint involves a matter that is appealable to the Merit Systems Protection Board (e.g., a "mixed case," such as the termination of a career employee who charges the agency with discriminatory motives), the worker may appeal the agency's final decision to the MSPB within 20 days of receipt or pursue a remedy from a U.S. district court within 30 days. Thereafter, the complainant may petition the EEOC for review of the MSPB decision concerning the claim of discrimination.

Federal employees, as well as former employees or applicants, who believe that they and other similarly situated persons have been discriminated against may file a class complaint if counseling is unsuccessful. The procedures for filing a class-action complaint are found in 29 CFR 1614.204.

Federal employees or job applicants who believe they have been discriminated against under the Age Discrimination in Employment Act may follow these standard complaint procedures or forego them and file suit directly in federal district court, after they've given EEOC 30 days notice of their intent to sue. Complaints under the Equal Pay Act may be brought through the standard procedures, reported directly to the appropriate EEOC district office, or filed directly in federal district court. Class actions also are allowed in these cases, although procedures differ somewhat from those brought under the Civil Rights Act.

New EEOC Complaint-Processing Rules

EEOC issued final rules, effective November 9, 1999, which are designed to simplify and streamline the federal-sector complaint-handling process. Several provisions in these final rules modify or alter the way EEOC handles an individual's EEO complaint. The main rule changes made by EEOC include:

• In cases decided by EEOC's administrative judges, the AJs now issue final (rather than recommended) decisions, thereby eliminating the previous right of agencies to reject or modify an unfavorable administrative judge's decision. However, along with employees, agencies now are allowed to appeal an AJ's decision to EEOC.

• Federal agencies are required to establish or make available alternative dispute resolution (ADR) procedures in the early stages of the EEO complaint process.

• Rather than allowing agencies to dismiss complaints if employees decline a "certified offer of full relief," the rules allow agencies to make "offers of resolution," which must be provided in writing at least 30 days before any hearing. If an employee rejects such an offer and ends up with a ruling that is not more favorable, the worker would lose any entitlement to attorney's fees or other costs incurred after the date of the offer's rejection.

• Agencies are allowed to dismiss "spin-off" complaints based on a worker's dissatisfaction with the processing of a previous EEO claim, as well as those complaints that represent an obvious abuse of the EEO process.

Practical Considerations

Difficulties and Deadlines

Discrimination cases can be among the most difficult for employees to win for a variety of reasons, including the complexities of the various EEO laws and regulations and the lengthy, time-consuming processes that employees must follow.

Employees covered by bargaining agreements should check the provisions of those contracts for coverage of discrimination complaints under grievance procedures. If such complaints are allowed, employees generally must choose either the EEOC (or MSPB) procedure outlined above or file their charges with the contractually authorized grievance procedure. As noted above, with the exception of postal employees, most federal workers cannot pursue both remedial paths.

Many EEO complaints end up being dismissed because workers ignore or miss filing deadlines. The time requirements for pursuing EEO charges are complex and relatively tight. Complainants should keep in mind that it is imperative for them to contact an EEO counselor in a timely fashion (usually, within 45 days of the incident) and adhere to all other filing deadlines. By contrast, agencies routinely miss or seek extension beyond their "mandatory" deadlines for EEO charge-processing, usually without serious consequences. In particular, the 180-day period for completing an investigation is commonly exceeded by some agencies (generally due to case backlogs).

"Prima Facie" Showing

On the legal end, to prove discrimination cases, EEOC and the courts generally will require employees to produce credible evidence that supports their discrimination charges with substantial or reasonable probability, not just a possibility. The first thing that the enforcement agencies and courts normally require workers to do is demonstrate that their charges are sufficient to make a "prima facie" case of discrimination. Basically, this means that complainants must prove that they are part of a protected group, that an unfavorable employment action was taken, and that discrimination was a likely determining factor in the agency's decision.

Once a complainant meets this initial requirement, the burden shifts to the agency to show that it had a legitimate motive for the challenged decision. The agency need only introduce evidence that would allow a reasonable person to conclude that it had nondiscriminatory reasons for its action. If the agency can do this, the burden then shifts back to the employee to prove that the agency's asserted reason was false (or "pretextual"), and that instead discrimination was the real reason for the action.

Hurdles for Employees

Several hurdles that employees must clear are obvious just from this truncated overview. First, a complaining employee must show membership in a protected group. While in some cases, such as alleged age discrimination, this is straightforward, disputes can arise over an individual's right to protection under other anti-discrimination statutes. This is especially true in cases involving allegations of disability discrimination, where the accepted definition of who is protected is constantly evolving.

Next, showing that discrimination was the determining factor in an adverse personnel action or decision often is a difficult thing to prove. Unfavorable employment actions can be taken for many reasons, and an agency may well be able to argue that its decision was based not just on one, but on many other, non-discriminatory motivations. Moreover, an agency usually is able to produce at least some written evidence supporting its claim of nondiscriminatory motivations, such as incidents of misconduct or poor performance. Obviously, evidence of bias on the part of agency officials rarely is documented anywhere. Even if it does exist, such evidence of discriminatory motives may be contained in records that the employee is unaware of or cannot obtain due to privacy considerations.

The other major hurdle for employees is the structure of the EEO process that most discrimination complaints are funneled through. Depending on the type of allegation involved, the actions the agency took, and the union status of the employee, an EEO complaint might be handled through an agency's administrative process, a contractual grievance procedure, an EEOC or MSPB proceeding, in the federal courts, or through some combination of the above processes.

The most common route, the EEOC channel, starts with an investigation of the employee's allegations by the employing agency itself—a requirement that critics of the process have singled out as a major conflict of interest. The complaint process then can move on through numerous hearing and appeals levels, all of which can, and often do, take a long time.

On average, employing agencies now take about a year to close a case, and if EEOC gets involved, cases spend an average of a year there, too. Some cases have been known to drag on for many, many years, bouncing up and down and in and out of the various channels. The truly bad news is that the process has actually gotten slower in recent years.

Part of the reason is that more complaints are being filed, creating backlogs at both the agency and EEOC levels. To some extent, the recent upswing in EEO complaints may be due to passage of the Civil Rights Act of 1991, which allows complainants, including federal and postal employees, to receive compensatory damages of up to $300,000 and a jury trial in federal district court in cases brought under the Civil Rights Act or the Rehabilitation Act. (Punitive damages, however, are not available against governmental entities.)

Others blame the increase in complaints squarely on continuing discriminatory practices in the government and a growing realization by employees of their legal rights and protections. For example, passage of the 1990 Americans With Disabilities Act, which gave most private-sector and state and local government employees disability discrimination protections (similar to those provided federal workers by the Rehabilitation Act), has raised the national level of consciousness about the rights of the disabled.

Additionally, there's a perception among many management officials that the government's discrimination complaint process is subject to abuse by employees because many workers want to enlist a third party's assistance in resolving a workplace dispute, or simply want to harass supervisors or delay legitimate actions against them. On the other hand, many employees perceive that discrimination is an all-too-common problem in the federal workplace and feel that the complaint system is set up to discourage individuals from bringing legitimate charges.

Then too, differences in viewpoints often lie at the heart of many discrimination cases. The types of words or actions that are considered acceptable or unacceptable in the workplace often vary according to the age, gender, and ethnic or cultural backgrounds of employees and supervisors—the very factors that anti-discrimination laws say are not to be taken into account. Agencies commonly respond to such issues by providing training and other types of counseling to help the two sides understand and work with their differences, but in a workplace that is increasingly diverse, this is an uphill battle. Whatever one's viewpoint, it is important to note that despite the legal and procedural difficulties encountered in the EEO complaint process, employees regularly do win decisions involving all forms of prohibited discrimination.

Rulings Review

• The Equal Employment Opportunity Commission has the authority to award compensatory damages in deciding discrimination complaints postal and federal employees bring before the commission, the U.S. Supreme Court ruled, rejecting an argument that such awards can be made only when federal-sector bias charges wind up in federal court. The High Court's ruling upheld the policy EEOC has been following since 1991, when Title VII of the 1964 Civil Rights Act was amended to allow compensatory damage awards of up to $300,000 in discrimination cases. (West v. Gibson, 119 S.Ct. 1906, 1999)

• Upholding a white male worker's claim of "reverse discrimination," the U.S. Court of Appeals for the Third Circuit dismissed the Postal Service's argument that the manager was not discriminated against since he ended up accepting another position before the one he had originally applied for had been filled. According to the appeals court, in reverse discrimination complaints, a job applicant should simply be required to present "sufficient evidence to support the reasonable probability of discrimination"

—essentially the same standard required for members of minorities. (Iadimarco v. Runyon, CA 3, 1999, 190 F. 3d 151)

• Federal unions are not immune from suit under the Americans with Disabilities Act, according to the U.S. Court of Appeals for the Fourth Circuit. Even though the APWU successfully defended itself against discrimination claims filed by a removed postal worker, the appeals court rejected the union's argument that it was not a "labor union" subject to the ADA's disability discrimination prohibitions and therefore could not be sued or held liable under the Act. (Jones v. APWU, CA 4, 1999, 192 F. 3d 417)

• The issue of handicap discrimination can be addressed for the first time in connection with a petition for enforcement of an MSPB order. (Davis v. Dept. of the Navy, 50 MSPR 592, 1991)

• To meet its burden once an employee makes a prima facie case of intentional discrimination, an agency must introduce evidence that, if viewed as true, would permit a conclusion that it had nondiscriminatory reasons for its actions, even if it failed to prove its charges against the worker. If the agency meets this burden, the employee then must prove not only that the asserted reason was false, but that discrimination was the real reason for the action. (Carter v. Small Business Administration, 61 MSPR 156, 1994)

• Where an employee proves by direct rather than circumstantial evidence that membership in a protected category was a substantial factor contributing to the appealed action, the burden of proof shifts to the agency to show that it had a legitimate motive that was sufficient, standing alone, to induce it to make the same decision. (Johnson v. Defense Logistics Agency, 61 MSPR 601, 1994)

• A supervisor's statements that women are incapable of performing work in the warehouse and that he would never hire a woman were insufficient to support a charge that he violated the agency's EEO policies, without evidence that he actually made a discriminatory personnel decision. (Holland v. Department of the Air Force, Fed. Cir. 1994, 31 F.3d 1118)

CHAPTER SIX

Sexual Harassment

Sexual harassment, unfortunately, is an ugly—and illegal—part of too many federal workers' jobs. In a recent survey, almost half of female federal employees and a fifth of male employees said they had experienced sexual harassment in the previous two years. The most common types of reported behaviors were sexual remarks, jokes, looks and gestures, although more overt types of harassment, such as pressure for dates or sexual favors and even stalking and assaults, also were reported.

Whatever form it takes, sexual harassment violates the sex discrimination prohibitions set forth in Title VII of the 1964 Civil Rights Act. Sex discrimination in general is any practice or procedure that denies employment opportunities because of one's sex. As a "specialized" form of sex discrimination, illegal sexual harassment consists of unwelcome sexual advances, requests for sexual favors, or other verbal or physical conduct of a sexual nature that employees are exposed to as either a condition of employment or the basis for an employment decision or action.

Basic Rules and Procedures

Types and Categories

Generally, Title VII, the main federal antidiscrimination law, recognizes two types of sexual harassment: "quid pro quo" and "hostile environment" harassment. As suggested by its name, a "quid pro quo" harassment situation involves an exchange, which typically consists of the grant of a job benefit or the threat of an adverse job action that is linked to someone's (generally, a supervisor's or manager's) request for sexual favors. "Hostile environment" harassment, on the other hand, typically involves the creation of a work situation in which an employee is subject to severe, persistent sexually-oriented behavior or attention. While "quid pro quo" cases are considered the classic type of harassment, they tend to be less common than "hostile

environment" situations.

Federal regulations (29 C.F.R. 1604.11(a)) define sexual harassment as an employee's exposure to unwelcome sexual advances, requests for sexual favors, and other verbal or physical conduct of a sexual nature if one of the following is involved:

• An employee's submission to such conduct is made either explicitly or implicitly a condition or term of the individual's employment;

• A worker's submission to or rejection of such conduct is used as the basis for employment decisions affecting that individual; or

• The objectionable behavior or conduct has the purpose or effect of unreasonably interfering with an individual's work performance or creating an intimidating, hostile, or offensive working environment.

Behavior or conduct that falls into the first two categories is considered "quid pro quo" harassment, while activities in the third category constitute "hostile environment" harassment. Usually, quid pro quo harassment is easy to recognize, since by definition it involves real or threatened harm to the employee's career and/or financial well-being by someone in a position to impose such harm.

Hostile Environment Factors

While the distinguishing characteristics of hostile environment harassment are still being identified by the courts, commonly recognized types of improper actions include: discussing sexual activities, unnecessary touching, comments on an individual's physical attributes, displaying sexually suggestive pictures, or using demeaning or inappropriate language or unseemly gestures.

The degree or amount of such conduct that is needed to create a hostile environment also is not fully defined. Generally, only one incident of objectionable behavior, unless it is truly egregious, does not constitute hostile environment harassment. Similarly, a hostile environment normally is not created by the mere use of words that an employee considers offensive. Generally, for such conduct to be judged illegal, it must influence or permeate the workplace to such an extent that an employee reasonably perceives the environment to be hostile or abusive. Whether the worker's belief is "reasonable" is based on the point of view of the alleged victim.

Among the factors that courts commonly consider in scrutinizing hostile environment claims are whether the objectionable conduct was physical and not just verbal, how often it was repeated, whether it was patently offensive, and whether the harasser was a supervisor or a co-worker.

Some other key principles:

• Sexual harassment is not limited to harassment of subordinates by supervisors; it can be found even if the improper conduct was between fellow employees. Moreover, the behavior of non-government employees operating in the federal workplace, such as contractors or their workers, also can constitute prohibited harassment.

• Harassment can be found even if the alleged harasser and victim are of the same sex. Also, the victim does not have to be the person harassed, but could be anyone adversely affected by the objectionable, unwelcome conduct.

• A hostile environment may be shown by evidence that the conduct interfered with an employee's work, created an abusive working environment, or caused serious psychological damage.

• The alleged victim must perceive the environment to be abusive in order for the conduct to be considered illegal. However, victims are not required to specifically mention in their charges that they felt that the complained-of conduct or behavior was harassing.

• The offensive conduct must be of a sexual, or at least gender-based, nature. Poor management practices or a personality conflict that does not involve such overtones is not sexual harassment.

• A victim's voluntary participation is not necessarily an indication that the conduct is welcome. The unwelcome nature of such conduct may be conveyed verbally or non-verbally, and there does not have to be resistance by the victim.

Complaints and Charges

Employees who feel that they have been the victims of sexual harassment have several possible avenues for filing complaints: Equal Employment Opportunity Commission procedures, a formal grievance (under either the administrative or collectively bargained procedures), or through MSPB procedures (if the situation involved an appealable adverse action).

In deciding whether alleged conduct constitutes sexual harassment, investigators or enforcement officials generally examine the circumstances—such as the nature of any sexual advances or the context in which the alleged incidents occurred—as well as the totality of the circumstances (i.e., not looking at each separate incident in isolation). Thus, a comment that might be excused if it was not typical of the alleged harasser's behavior could weigh more heavily against that person if it fits into a larger pattern of behavior.

In the past, when an employee won a harassment claim, the agency typically would make whatever restitution was ordered—reinstatement, attorney's fees, or payment of damages—while the harasser often went unpunished. In recent years, that has changed significantly, and a finding of sexual harassment now commonly leads to an agency's filing of charges against the harasser.

Charges against harassers generally take one of two forms. In one, management may charge the employee with violating the agency's policies against sexual harassment. In this type of action, the agency describes the harasser's alleged misconduct and explains how that conduct adversely affected the agency's mission, the efficiency of the workplace, or the employment relationship. Such charges are reviewed under the same standards that apply to any discipline for alleged violations of agency rules

In the other type, the agency may charge the employee with violating Title VII of the Civil Rights Act, meaning the agency has to prove not only that the objectionable conduct occurred under that law's legal standards, but also that the conduct involved quid pro quo harassment or created a hostile environment. In order to prove a hostile environment charge, the agency generally must show that the conduct was: offensive and unwelcome, based on the sex of the employee or employees to whom it was offensive, and sufficiently severe or pervasive to create an environment that a reasonable person would consider hostile or abusive.

Less commonly, the agency may file charges of inappropriate conduct in the workplace, of which alleged sexual harassment may have been only a part. For example, an agency might charge one of its supervisors with engaging in harassing conduct—such as phone calls or visits to the other person's home—that was not sexual in nature.

In any case, any appeal of disciplinary action meted out to an employee charged with sexual harassment typically goes into a grievance process or to the Merit Systems Protection Board as an appeal of an adverse personnel action.

Timely Complaint Considerations

In order to preserve the right to pursue legal claims involving sexual harassment, individuals must make sure they comply with applicable deadlines. Specifically, to preserve EEO complaints, employees must contact an EEO counselor within 45 days of the harassing conduct. Where a pattern of harassing conduct is involved, however, it may be possible to pursue an EEO complaint regarding "old" conduct, if at least one manifestation of the objectionable behavior or actions occurred within at least 45 days of the victim's first contact with an EEO counselor. What's important, however, is for employees to realize that they should not delay in contacting an EEO counselor, even if they fear retaliation.

Practical Considerations

Perceptions and Reactions

Beyond the textbook and legal definitions, there still exists some uncertainty about what sexual harassment actually is and what can and should be done about it. As noted earlier, surveys have confirmed that sexual harassment is a significant problem in the federal workplace. However, the same studies also found wide ranges of opinion regarding whether particular types of actions constitute harassment. For example, a recent survey found that more than half of the male respondents and nearly half of the women agreed that some people are too quick to take offense at normal remarks and attractions in the workplace, and nearly half of the men acknowledged that they don't feel comfortable giving compliments because they fear their comments will be misinterpreted.

Cultural, age, and personal differences further complicate how people interpret workplace comments and conduct. Some employees may be unaware that their actions are perceived by others as sexual harassment. On the other hand, some employees may not realize that the actions of others are in fact sexual harassment and that they do not have to tolerate those actions.

Similarly, individuals' reactions to incidents of perceived sexual harassment vary greatly. Many workers simply ignore such incidents, viewing the objectionable conduct as not serious enough to warrant a formal complaint or thinking that nothing would be done anyway or that making a complaint would hurt their own career prospects. Others address harassing actions far more directly. At a minimum, they ask the person to stop, and many follow up by reporting such incidents to a management official or EEO counselor or filing a grievance, equal employment opportunity complaint, or Merit Systems Protection Board appeal.

Issues for Complainants

Despite a lengthy string of court and administrative decisions that have helped define sexual harassment, such a complaint can be hard to prove. This is especially true when it comes to proving the existence of hostile environment harassment, which typically doesn't involve a victim's loss of tangible job benefits or protections. Usually, the harm suffered by victims of hostile environment harassment is less obvious, which can make it a lot tougher to prove.

Formal complaints, especially through equal employment opportunity channels, also can take a long time to resolve. It's worth noting that many of the survey respondents cited above said that simply asking the harasser to stop was more effective in making things better than formally reporting the conduct.

Another factor that comes into play is that many victims of sexual harassment experience feelings of shame or embarrassment, leading them to shy away from filing formal or informal complaints. While anonymous complaints may provide some help (at least in terms of stopping the objectionable conduct), keep in mid that anonymity is not a viable option for anyone seeking personal relief (e.g., emotional distress or other damages).

In addition to knowing the general law and rules on sexual harassment, it is important for employees to familiarize themselves with their individual agency's policies and procedures. Most, if not all, agencies have issued policies explicitly prohibiting sexual harassment. Frequently, these rules go beyond the requirements and prohibitions laid down in Title VII. In some cases, this is because the agency is trying to define what it does or doesn't consider harassing behavior, while in other instances, agency management has decided to take an even stronger stance against such conduct than the law requires.

Thus, conduct that isn't explicitly barred by the law might be prohibited by the employing agency. In some cases, employees who know and point out that fact may be able to bring a halt to objectionable behavior or otherwise make a difference.

Those wishing to pursue a formal sexual harassment grievance or complaint should remember that such cases often turn on disputes over what individuals said or did—or what was implied or understood by what was said or done—in a private interaction between two people. That means that the outcome of a harassment complaint may rest heavily on the hearing official's determination as to which of the two parties is more credible.

That's a main reason why it can be helpful to make contemporary notes of the situation. Write down what happened and in what context, and take note of any other employees who may have direct or indirect knowledge of what was said or done. Also put together any information you can gather about other such incidents involving the same individual. Being able to establish that the conduct was part of an ongoing pattern can considerably strengthen an individual's complaint.

When deciding how to respond to a situation, it also helps to bear in mind that only *unwelcome* conduct constitutes sexual harassment. Activities that consist of individuals' joking, flirting, or dating—or that are even more involved—do not amount to harassment as long as they are consensual. Over time, one party might come to view the attention as unwelcome and believe that sexual harassment is occurring. However, it might be difficult to prove that such conduct is unwelcome if there is an established record of consensual activity, especially if such activities continue beyond the point that the alleged victim claims that they became unwelcome.

Rulings Review

• Sexual harassment is definitively included in the forms of prohibited sex discrimination under Title VII of the 1964 Civil Rights Act. (Meritor Savings Bank v. Vinson, U.S. Supreme Court, 1986, 477 U.S. 57)

• Employees can recover from employers for a supervisor's sexual harassment that does not result in adverse job consequences, even without showing that the employer was negligent or otherwise at fault for the illegal conduct. However, in such cases, an employer can establish an "affirmative defense" if it can show that: (1) it took "reasonable care" to prevent and promptly correct any harassing behavior, and (2) the complainant "unreasonably failed to take advantage" of the employer-provided preventive or corrective measures. (Burlington Industries v. Ellerth, U.S. Supreme Court, 1998, 118 S.Ct. 2257)

• A single incident of harassment may be enough to sustain a charge of quid pro quo sexual harassment. (Downes v. FAA, Fed. Cir., 1985, 775 F.2d 288)

• An EEOC complaint is not a prerequisite to agency discipline for alleged sexual harassment. An agency is not required to tolerate alleged misconduct until it reaches the level at which victims are certain to prevail in a Title VII action against the agency. (Carosella v. U.S. Postal Service, Fed. Cir. 1987, 816 F2d 638)

• A harasser's offensive conduct need not involve sexual activity or language to constitute sexual harassment. If the conduct is based on the victim's gender, it is appropriate to consider it in determining whether a hostile or abusive environment has been created. (King v. Hillen, Fed. Cir. 1994, 21 F.3d 1572)

• Sexual harassment can be found even if no personnel action was taken, because complainants do not have to show a loss of tangible job benefits in order for a charge of sexual harassment to be sustained. (Special Counsel v. Russell, 1987, 32 MSPR 115)

• The conduct at issue must be viewed from the perspective of the person who allegedly is being harassed. (King v. Frazier, Fed. Cir., 1996, 77 F3d, 1361)

CHAPTER SEVEN

Whistleblowing

Whistleblowing disputes can turn into one of the ugliest, most acrimonious types of disagreements between employees and their agencies. That's because whistleblowing disputes typically involve not only clashes over personnel matters, but also, in many cases, very high stakes for both the agency and the employee. They also involve a complex set of procedures and, often require a long passage of time between the start of the dispute and the point at which it's finally resolved.

While agency management often sees whistleblowing as a betrayal of trust—organizational, personal, or both—employee disclosures of agency waste or abuse have the explicit sanction and support of federal law. The 1978 Civil Service Reform Act created the foundation for whistleblower protections, and the 1989 Whistleblower Protection Act and its 1994 amendments expanded these legal protections against job reprisals for employees who "blow the whistle" on illegal or inappropriate management actions.

———— Basic Rules and Procedures ————

Protected Disclosures

The Whistleblower Protection Act prohibits agencies from threatening, proposing, or taking (or failing to take) a personnel action because of an employee's disclosure of information about management misconduct. The Act stipulates that the worker must reasonably believe that the disclosed information shows that agency management engaged in conduct that involved: a violation of a law, rule, or regulation, gross mismanagement, a gross waste of funds, an abuse of authority, or activities that created a substantial and specific danger to public health or safety.

The most common types of employee "disclosures" that trigger whistleblower rights include information disclosures to agency inspectors general, the Office of Special Counsel, Congress, or the media. Whistleblowing disclosures also can be made through internal agency routes as well, such as the grievance, unfair labor practice, or equal employment opportunity processes. However, where all of an employee's disclosures are made in such internal procedures, they are not protected under the whistleblowing laws.

It is important to remember that the law does not protect all forms of employee disclosure. For example, charges that employees were poorly trained or that a supervisor did not make good use of managerial discretion would not be deemed to constitute whistleblowing. Nor is a disclosure protected if it involves a matter that the employee had the personal authority to resolve, or if release of the information was specifically prohibited by law—a provision that sometimes comes into play with employees who have access to classified information.

To gain whistleblower protection, the employee does not need to prove that a violation occurred, but only that a reasonable person in that position would believe that one occurred. The worker's "reasonable belief" of a violation or other misconduct must be shown by substantial evidence.

Also, to be entitled to the law's protections, employees must show that have been subject to a definite personnel action, which generally consists of either an action or refusal to act on the agency's part. For example, a supervisor's non-binding recommendation that management take adverse personnel action against a whistleblower would not be deemed a personnel action triggering the Act's protections. Similarly, management's rejection of an employee's suggestion for improving agency operations would not be grounds for a whistleblowing complaint.

Two Complaint Channels

There are two routes to challenge alleged retaliation for whistleblowing, both of them leading to the Merit Systems Protection Board (MSPB):

• *Otherwise appealable action*— In this kind of case, an employee is subject to a personnel action that is ordinarily appealable to the Board and charges that the action was taken because of the individual's whistleblowing activities. The types of personnel actions that normally can be appealed to MSPB include adverse actions, performance-based removals or reductions in grade, denials of within-grade salary increases, reduction-in-force actions, or denials of restoration or reemployment rights. In

situations involving an "otherwise appealable action," the worker may seek the assistance of the Office of Special Counsel (OSC) or may appeal directly to MSPB.

• *Individual right of action*—This second remedial path for a whistleblowing employee is known as the "individual right of action" (IRA), a category created by the 1989 Whistleblower Protection Act. These types of cases involve a personnel action that is not normally appealable to MSPB, but that the Office of Special Counsel has jurisdiction over due to its authority over prohibited personnel practices. Examples of personnel actions that can trigger IRA rights include adverse decisions regarding appointments, promotions, details, transfers, and reassignments, as well as decisions concerning pay, benefits, awards, and educational or training opportunities. In IRA cases, individuals first must file a complaint with the OSC. That office in turn may file requests with the Board for stays, corrective actions, or disciplinary actions. Employees may file their own IRA appeal with MSPB if: (1) OSC issues a written decision saying that it will not take any action on a worker's complaint, or (2) 120 days have elapsed from the filing of the complaint and OSC has not said whether it will seek corrective action.

An individual's eligibility to file the two types of appeals varies somewhat. The categories of employees eligible to file an IRA complaint are the same as those who have the right to file prohibited personnel practice complaints with the OSC. This includes competitive service employees and most excepted service employees in an executive agency and the Government Printing Office, except for workers employed by a government corporation, the General Accounting Office, or the FBI and intelligence agencies.

The eligibility criteria for filing an "otherwise appealable action" complaint vary based on the type of personnel action being appealed. In general, competitive service and preference-eligible employees have MSPB appeal rights with respect to most actions, while most excepted service employees may appeal only adverse actions and performance-based actions.

If you are unsure about your eligibility to file a complaint, MSPB advises that you file anyway in order to preserve any rights you may have. Only in exceptional circumstances will the Board accept cases filed after the expiration of a deadline.

Appeal Rules and Stages

Both IRA and "otherwise appealable action" appeals must be filed in writing with the MSPB regional office serving the area where the employee's duty station was located when the action occurred. After filing, the following rules generally apply:

• **Time Limits**—The time limits for filing an "otherwise appealable action" are the same as for all other direct appeals to MSPB. That means that employees must file their appeals within 30 calendar days of the effective date of the action, or in the case of actions that do not have a definite, effective date, within 35 days of the agency's issuance of the decision. An IRA appeal must be filed with MSPB within 65 calendar days after the date of a written notice from OSC that it will not seek a corrective action. However, if 120 calendar days have passed since the complaint was filed at OSC and the whistleblowing employee has not been notified by OSC that it plans to seek corrective action, the worker may file an IRA appeal "anytime thereafter." In IRA cases where the

individual's complaint already has gone to the Special Counsel, MSPB may not take into account the Special Counsel's decision not to file a complaint.

• **Burden of Proof**—Whistleblowers generally must prove that they engaged in a protected disclosure and that the disclosure was a contributing factor to a personnel action that the agency has threatened, proposed, taken, or not taken. The appeal must contain the standard information required in all MSPB cases, plus a description of the whistleblowing disclosure, a chronology of facts concerning the personnel action, including the name and position of the person or persons taking the action, and a description of which laws, rules, or regulations allegedly were broken. In cases involving the threat of an agency action, employees must provide specific information as to why they felt threatened.

If the employee meets the "contributing factor" burden, then the agency must show that it had a legitimate management reason for the decision—in other words, that it would have taken the same action without the protected disclosure.

• **Stay Requests**—In both types of whistleblower appeal actions, an employee may ask MSPB to issue a stay of the adverse or objectionable personnel action. Generally this may be requested no earlier than the time the employee becomes eligible to file the appeal and no later than the end of the discovery period before the MSPB administrative judge. Stay requests must be filed in writing with the MSPB regional office handling the appeal and must include information such as a chronology of the facts, as well as evidence that the personnel action was or will be based on the worker's whistleblowing activities. The request also must indicate why there is a substantial likelihood that the employee will win the appeal.

• *Appealing Decisions*—Parties who are dissatisfied with decisions of an MSPB administrative judge may appeal to the three-member Board in Washington. If no party files a petition for review, the AJ's initial decision becomes final 35 days after it is issued.

If a petition for review is filed, the decision issued by the Board becomes the final decision. Final MSPB decisions may be appealed to the U.S. Court of Appeals for the Federal Circuit. The time limit for appeals court review is 30 days after receipt of the Board's final decision.

Practical Considerations

Disclosure Deliberations

Despite the formal legal protections provided employees under the Act, whistleblowing is not something to be done on the spur of the moment or to be taken lightly. Despite the law's protections, many whistleblowers' careers have been ruined, and an all-too-common refrain among whistleblowers is that "had I known then what I know now, I probably never would have done it." On the other hand, despite the aggravation and frustration they endured, a number of other whistleblowers remain proud of their disclosures of impropriety, and insist that the changes they helped bring about were worth the effort.

Keep in mind, however, that the Act's general support for disclosures that expose uncomfortable truths does not mean that every type of disclosure is entitled to protection. The law's definitions of what types of disclosures are protected are not as broad as many employees seem to believe. It's also important to remember that the Act does not protect a whistleblower from legitimate personnel actions that the agency would have taken anyway.

Employees have many motives for whistleblowing. Some disclosures are motivated by a genuine desire to see a wasteful, abusive, or dangerous situation corrected, particularly where an individual thinks chances are slim of getting the problem corrected by working through regular channels. In other cases, though, a whistleblower's motives are more complicated. Many whistleblowing situations, for example, involve employees who are dissatisfied with their agencies, or their agencies with them. Tensions escalate and so do the tactics each side uses.

After the Fact

The outcome and aftermath of whistleblowing also vary widely. In many well-publicized cases, disclosures by federal employees have focused attention on long-standing problems that had gone unaddressed, ended the wasteful spending of taxpayers' money, or corrected hazards that created health or safety risks. In recent years, for example, whistleblowers have been credited with helping to eliminate major cost overruns in Defense Department programs, deficiencies in meat and poultry inspection procedures, and lax enforcement of environmental protection laws.

In many other cases, however, there has not been a clear cause-and-effect relationship between an employee's disclosure and an achieved solution or outcome. In most cases, whistleblowing rarely brings quick action against the problem identified in the disclosure. Frequently, investigation of the worker's complaint—whether by Congress, an inspector general, the media, or some other party—can drag on indefinitely and end inconclusively. Also, many potential whistleblowers have been surprised to discover that an issue of high importance to them may be viewed by outsiders as of only minor, or even no, interest. This is especially true in situations—which are very common in whistleblowing cases—where internal personal and policy disputes between agency employees are intertwined with instances of the alleged fraud, waste, or abuse.

Another frequent outcome is that little changes after a disclosure except that the employee is now labeled by some in the agency as a troublemaker. In fact, many experienced whistleblowers say that the only guaranteed results are retaliatory actions—some overt, some subtle—against the employee.

Some whistleblowers try to protect themselves by making their disclosures anonymously. However, it's extremely difficult to remain anonymous, once an investigation into the charges starts. And in something of an irony, to be protected by the whistleblower law, employees must show that the agency knew that they were the ones who blew the whistle in order to prove their disclosure was a contributing factor in an adverse personnel decision.

Whistleblowing cases also are among the most emotionally charged—not to mention mentally and financially draining—of employment disputes. Even with a representative handling the legal side, the employee often finds that becoming a whistleblower turns into a full-time job on its own.

Before you blow the whistle, you might want to ask yourself if the wrongdoing you're exposing—and the good you can achieve by disclosing it—are significant enough to offset the likely risk of reprisal. You also should consider whether you're in a good position to prove your allegations, or at least to show why you reasonably believe them to be true.

Whistleblower Hotlines

Most federal departments and agencies have established whistleblower hotlines (see list below) to serve federal employees who have complaints or information about fraud, waste, or mismanagement. The calls will be to the offices of the inspectors general who were appointed to the various departments and agencies to help wipe out waste and corruption in government. The identity of those furnishing information is kept confidential.

Special Counsel Hotline

The Office of the Special Counsel investigates charges or reprisals against federal employees for lawful disclosure of information relating to fraud, illegalities, corruption, or mismanagement in government. The number is 202-653-7188, toll-free 800-872-9855.

Rulings Review

• Where only some of the agency's alleged grounds for its personnel actions are sustained by MSPB, the agency must prove by a preponderance of evidence that it would have taken the same action against the employee on the basis of only the sustained charges. (Berube v. General

Services Administration, Fed. Cir. 1998, 820 F.2d 396)

• MSPB can dismiss for lack of jurisdiction an IRA appeal in a case where the petitioner did not first present a basis for corrective action to OSC. (Knollenberg v. Merit Systems Protection Board, Fed. Cir. 1992, 953 F.2d 623)

• Employees are not required to demonstrate that the agency had a retaliatory motive based on their status as a whistleblower. Rather, an employee's burden of proving the disclosures were a contributing factor to the agency action is satisfied if the content of the employee's disclosures is related to the action. (Marano v. Department of Justice, Fed. Cir. 1993, 2 F.3d 113)

• An agency's rejection of an employee's suggestion for improving agency operations is not a personnel action reviewable in an IRA, although the denial of an award can serve as the basis for an IRA. (Weber v. Department of the Army, Fed. Cir. 1993, 9 F.3d 97)

• A protected disclosure cannot be a contributing factor to a personnel action that was proposed before the disclosure was made. Also, a disclosure to the person who is the subject of the disclosure is generally not protected whistleblowing. (Horton v. Department of the Navy, Fed. Cir. 1995, 66 F.3d 279)

• Where the facts supporting discipline are intertwined with those disclosed by the whistleblower, the agency must show only that it would have taken the same action absent the disclosure, not that it would have eventually discovered the contents of the disclosures from independent sources. (Watson v. Dept. of Justice, Fed. Cir. 1995, 64 F.3d 1524)

• The Whistleblower Protection Act is meant to protect employees who report genuine infractions of the law, not to encourage employees to report arguably minor and inadvertent incidents that might occur in an individual's conscientious carrying out of assigned duties. (Frederick v. Department of Justice, Fed. Cir. 1996, 73 F.3d 349)

• An agency action is not retaliatory even if the worker's whistleblowing may have been a contributing factor in the decision, if the agency can prove by clear and convincing evidence that it would have taken the same step regardless of the whistleblowing. (Caddell v. Merit Systems Protection Board, Fed. Cir. 1996, 96 F.3d 1367)

• When employees seek corrective action from the Office of Special Counsel, they must cite each matter raised as a personnel action in order to appeal those matters to MSPB in a subsequent IRA case. (Mintzmyer v. Department of Interior, Fed. Cir. 1996, 84 F.3d 419)

• The disclosure of matters that are only potential violations may be protected where the facts indicate that the employee had a reasonable belief of wrongdoing. (Ward v. Department of the Army, 1995, 67 MSPR 482)

• Any weight that an agency gives to the employee's disclosure, alone or in combination with other factors, can satisfy the employee's burden of proving that the disclosure was a contributing factor in the adverse personnel action. (Powers v. Department of the Navy, 1995, 69 MSPR 150)

• An employee's motive in making a disclosure is not relevant to a determination of whether the worker had a reasonable belief that it evidenced a violation as specified in the whistleblower law. (Bump v. Department of Interior, 1996, 69 MSPR 354)

• In an IRA appeal, employees must have raised to OSC the same issue they raise to the Board, and must have characterized it in the same manner. The fact that OSC conducted an investigation of the employee's claims shows that the office was informed of the precise basis for the whistleblowing charge. (Lloyd v. EPA, 1996, 71 MSPR 671)

• The fact that an employee's case was complex and took OSC longer than 120 days to investigate does not excuse the employee from missing the deadline for filing an IRA appeal after OSC decided to end its investigation. (King v. Department of Health and Human Services, 1996, 71 MSPR 22)

• The U.S. Court of Appeals for the Federal Circuit provided new guidance regarding the proper test for analyzing whether a purported whistleblower had a "reasonable belief" as to a disclosure of gross mismanagement. The proper test, according to the appeals court, is this: "Could a disinterested observer with knowledge of the essential facts known to and readily ascertainable by the employee reasonably conclude that the actions of the government evidence gross mismanagement?" The appeals court specifically took issue with the MSPB's test in such cases, which had focused on whether other employees shared the whistleblower's view as to the alleged mismanagement. (Lachance v. White, 174 F.3d 1378, Fed. Cir., 1999)

• Confirming information that another employee disclosed to the inspector general's office does not amount to an act of disclosure on its own and does not fall under whistleblower protections, said the U.S. Court of Appeals for the Federal Circuit. The court noted that although the employee later said he believed he was making the type of disclosures protected by the law, his initial complaint to the Office of Special Counsel did not characterize the actions in that way and thus the whistleblower law didn't apply. (Eisinger v. MSPB, 194 F.3d 1339, Fed. Cir.,1999)

• A federal employee claiming retaliation for whistleblowing must show that the disclosures he made were a contributing factor in the agency's decision, the U.S. Court of Appeals for the Federal Circuit said, stressing that the worker's most recent disclosures occurred several years before the agency action. (Holtgrewe v. FDIC, Fed. Cir., No. 98-3068, 1998)

• Noting that the purpose of the whistleblower protection law is to shield employees "who risk their own personal job security for the benefit of the public," the U.S. Court of Appeals for the Federal Circuit decided that an employee didn't gain whistleblower protections when he complained to his supervisors regarding the reversal of several decisions he made. According to the court, "It is entirely ordinary for an employee to fairly and reasonably disagree with a supervisor who overturns the employee's decision." (Willis v. Dept. of Agriculture, Fed. Cir., No. 97-3250, 1998)

• The filing of an "individual right of appeal" complaint of retaliation for whistleblowing is not itself the type of disclosure that merits protection under the whistleblower law unless the employee shows "substantive details" that the complaint involved a protected disclosure, the U.S. Court of Appeals for the Federal Circuit said. (Lessard v. Dept. of the Navy, Fed. Cir., No. 98-3172, 1998)

• Stressing that the Whistleblower Protection Act was passed to protect employees who report misconduct, not to make their lives more difficult, the Merit Systems Protection Board rejected an administrative judge's ruling that the WPA doesn't apply unless the whistleblower's disclosure "contains the degree of detail necessary to launch a formal investigation. (Keefer v. USDA, 82 MSPR 687, 1999)

Hotline Contact Information

Most federal departments and agencies have established whistle-blower hotlines to serve federal employees who have complaints or information about fraud, waste, or mismanagement. The calls will be to the offices of the inspectors general who were appointed to the various departments and agencies to help wipe out waste and corruption in government. The identity of those furnishing information is kept confidential.

Agency for International Development
Everett L. Mosley,
Acting Inspector General
(202) 712-1150
1300 Pennsylvania Ave, N.W.
Washington, D.C. 20523
Hotline Number:
(202) 712-1023; (800) 230-6539

Department of Agriculture
The Honorable Roger C. Viadero,
Inspector General
(202) 720-8001
12th and Independence Avenue,
S.W.; Room 117-W
Washington, D.C. 20250
Hotline Number:
(800) 424-9121; (202) 690-1622;
Hearing Impaired (202) 690-1202

Amtrak
Fred W. Weiderhold, Jr,
Inspector General
(202) 906-4600
400 North Capitol Street, N.W.
Washington, D.C. 20002-4285
Hotline Number: 1-800-468-5469

Appalachian Regional Commission
Hubert Sparks, Inspector General
(202) 884-7675
1666 Connecticut Avenue, N.W.;
Suite 215
Washington, D.C. 20235
Hotline Number:
(800) 532-4611; (202) 884-7667

Central Intelligence Agency
The Honorable L. Britt Snider,
Inspector General
(703) 874-2555
Room 2X30 New Headquarters
Washington, D.C. 20505
Hotline Number: None

Department of Commerce
The Honorable Johnnie E. Frazier,
Inspector General
(202) 482-4661
14th and Constitution Avenue, N.W.
Washington, D.C. 20230
Hotline Number:
(800) 482-5197; (202) 482-2495;
Hearing Impaired (800) 854-8407

Commodity Futures Trading Commission
A. Roy Lavik, Inspector General
(202) 418-5110
Three Lafayette Centre;
1155 21st Street, N.W.
Washington, D.C. 20581
Hotline Number: (202) 418-5510

Consumer Product Safety Commission
Mary B. Wyles, Inspector General
(301) 504-0573
4330 East West Highway;
Bethesda, MD 20814-4408
Hotline Number: (301) 504-0573

**Corporation for
National and Community Service**
The Honorable Luise S. Jordan,
Inspector General
(202) 606-5000
1201 New York Avenue, N.W.;
Suite 8100, Washington, D.C. 20525
Hotline Number: (800) 452-8210

Corporation for Public Broadcasting
Kenneth Konz, Inspector General
(202) 879-9660
901 E Street, N.W.
Washington, D.C. 20004
Hotline Number: (800) 599-2170;
(202) 783-5408

Department of Defense
Donald Mancuso,
Acting Inspector General
(703) 604-8300
400 Army Navy Drive
Arlington, VA 22202-2884
Hotline Number: (800) 424-9098;
(703) 604-8546; Fax #: (703) 604-
8597 email—*hotline@dodig.osd.mil*;
website— *http://www.dodig.osd.mil*

Department of Education
The Honorable Lorraine Pratte Lewis,
Inspector General
(202) 205-5439
600 Independence Avenue, S.W.
Washington, D.C. 20202-1510
Hotline Number: (800) 647-8733;
(202) 205-5770

Department of Energy
The Honorable Gregory H. Friedman,
Inspector General
(202) 586-4393
1000 Independence Avenue, S.W.
Washington, D.C. 20585
Hotline Number:
(800) 541-1625; (202) 586-4073

Environmental Protection Agency
The Honorable Nikki L. Tinsley,
Inspector General
(202) 260-3137
401 M Street, S. W.; (2410)
Washington, D.C. 20460
Hotline Number: (888) 546-8740

**Equal Employment
Opportunity Commission**
Aletha L. Brown, Inspector General
(202) 663-4379
1801 L Street, N.W.; Suite 3001
Washington, D.C. 20507
Hotline Number: 800-849-4230

Farm Credit Administration
Eldon W. Stoehr, Inspector General
(703) 883-4030
1501 Farm Credit Drive
McLean, VA 22102
Hotline Number:
(800) 437-7322; (703) 883-4316

**Federal Communications
Commission**
H. Walker Feaster, III,
Inspector General
(202) 418-0470
445 12th St, SW; Room 2-C762
Washington, D.C. 20554
Hotline Number: (202) 418-0473

**Federal Deposit Insurance
Corporation**
The Honorable Gaston L. Gianni, Jr.,
Inspector General
(202) 416-2026
801 17th St. N.W., Room 1096
Washington, D.C. 20434
Hotline Number: (800) 964-3342

Federal Election Commission
Lynne A. McFarland,
Inspector General
(202) 694-1015
999 E Street, N.W.; Room 940
Washington, D.C. 20463
Hotline Number: (202) 694-1015

**Federal Emergency
Management Agency**
The Honorable George J. Opfer,
Inspector General
(202) 646-3910
500 C Street, S.W.; Room 505
Washington, D.C. 20472
Hotline Number: (800) 323-8603

Federal Housing Finance Board
Edward Kelley, Inspector General
(202) 408-2544
1777 F Street, N.W.
Washington, D.C. 20006
Hotline Number: (202) 408-2900
or (800) 276-8329

Federal Labor Relations Authority
Francine C. Eichler, Inspector General
(202) 482-6570
607 14th Street, N.W.
Washington, D.C. 20424
Hotline Number: (800) 331-3572

Federal Maritime Commission
Tony P. Kominoth, Inspector General
(202) 523-5863
800 North Capitol Street, N.W.;
Room 1072
Washington, D.C. 20573
Hotline Number: (202) 523-5865

Federal Reserve Board
Barry R. Snyder, Inspector General
(202) 973-5003
20th and Constitution Avenue, N.W.
Stop 300, Washington, D.C. 20551
Hotline Number: (800) 827-3340;
(202) 452-6400

Federal Trade Commission
Frederick J. Zirkel, Inspector General
(202) 326-2800
600 Pennsylvania Avenue, N.W.
Washington, D.C. 20580
Hotline Number: (202) 326-2581

General Services Administration
The Honorable William R. Barton,
Inspector General
(202) 501-0450
18th and F Streets, N.W.
Room 5340, Washington, D.C. 20405
Hotline Number:
(800) 424-5201; (202) 501-1780

Government Printing Office
Robert G. Andary, Inspector General
(202) 512-0039
North Capitol and H Streets, N.W.;
Stop:IG
Washington, D.C. 20401
Hotline Number: (800) 742-7574

**Department of
Health and Human Services**
The Honorable June Gibbs Brown,
Inspector General
(202) 619-3148
330 Independence Avenue, S.W.
Washington, D.C. 20201
Hotline Number: (800) HHS-TIPS;
email: htips@os.dhhs.gov

**Department of
Housing and Urban Development**
The Honorable Susan Gaffney,
Inspector General
(202) 708-0430
451 7th Street S.W.
Washington, D.C. 20410
Hotline Number: (202) 708-2451 TTY
Department of the Interior
The Honorable Earl E. Devaney,
Inspector General
(202) 208-5745
1849 C Street, N.W.; Mail Stop 5341
Washington, D.C. 20240
Hotline Number: (800) 424-5081

International Trade Commission
Dev Jagadesan,
Acting Inspector General
(202) 205-2210
500 E Street S.W.; Room 515
Washington, D.C. 20436

Department of Justice
Robert L. Ashbaugh,
Acting Inspector General
(202) 514-3435
950 Pennsylvania Avenue, N.W.;
Suite 4706
Washington, D.C. 20530
Hotline Number: (800) 869-4499

Department of Labor
The Honorable Charles C. Masten,
Inspector General
(202) 693-5100
200 Constitution Avenue, N.W.;
Room S1303
Washington, D.C. 20210
Hotline Number: (800) 347-3756;
 (202) 219-5227

Legal Services Corporation
Edouard Quatrevaux,
Inspector General
(202) 336-8830
750 First Street, N.E.; 11th Floor
Washington, D.C. 20002-4250
Hotline Number: (800) 678-8868;
(202) 336-8936

**National Aeronautics and
Space Administration**
The Honorable Roberta L. Gross,
Inspector General
(202) 358-1220
300 E Street, S.W.;
Code W, Room 8V69
Washington, D.C. 20546
Hotline Number: (800) 424-9183

National Archives
Ralph E. McNamara,
Acting Inspector General
(301) 713-7300
8601 Adelphi Road
College Park, MD 20740-6001
Hotline Number: (800) 786-2551;
(301) 713-7305

National Credit Union Administration
H. Frank Thomas, Inspector General
(703) 518-6350
1775 Duke Street; Alexandria
VA 22314-3428
Hotline Number: (703) 518-6357;
(800) 778-4806

National Endowment for the Arts
Edward Johns, Inspector General
(202) 682-5402
1100 Pennsylvania Avenue, N.W.
Washington, D.C. 20506
Hotline Number: (202) 682-5402

**National Endowment for the
Humanities**
Sheldon L. Bernstein,
Inspector General
(202) 606-8350
1100 Pennsylvania Avenue, N.W.
Room 419, Washington, D.C. 20506
Hotline Number: (202) 606-8423;
Internet Address: *oig@neh.fed.us*

National Labor Relations Board
Jane E. Altenhofen, Inspector General
(202) 273-1960
1099 14th Street, N.W.
Room 9820, Washington, D.C. 20570
Hotline Number: (800) 736-2983

National Science Foundation
Philip L. Sunshine,
Acting Inspector General
(703) 306-2100
4201 Wilson Boulevard; Room 1135
Arlington, VA 22230
Hotline Number: (703) 306-2004;
Internet Address: *OIG@NSF.GOV*

Nuclear Regulatory Commission
The Honorable Hubert T. Bell,
Inspector General
(301) 415-5930
Mail Stop T5 D28
Washington, D.C. 20555
Hotline Number: (800) 233-3497

Panama Canal Commission
Victor Diamond, Inspector General
(800)622-2625, ext. 3142
Unit 2300; APO AA 3401-2300
Hotline Number: (800) 622-2625
ext. 272-7801

Peace Corps
Charles D. Smith, Inspector General
(202) 692-2900
1111 20th Street, N.W.
Washington, DC 20526
Hotline Number: (800) 233-5874

Pension Benefit Guaranty Corporation
Wayne Robert Poll, Inspector General
(202) 326-4030
1200 K Street, N.W.
Washington, D.C. 20005

Office of Personnel Management
The Honorable Patrick E. McFarland,
Inspector General
(202) 606-1200
1900 E Street, N.W.; Room 6400
Washington, D.C. 20415-0001
Hotline Number: Fraud, Waste and
Abuse (202) 606-2423; Health Care
Fraud Hotline (202)418-3300

U.S. Postal Service
Karla W. Corcoran, Inspector General
(703)248-2300
1735 North Lynn Street
Arlington, VA 22209-2005
Hotline Number:(888)877-7644

Railroad Retirement Board
The Honorable Martin J. Dickman,
Inspector General
(312) 751-4690
844 North Rush Street; Room 450
Chicago, Illinois 60611
Hotline Number: (800) 772-4258;
Hotline Homepage

Securities and Exchange Commission
Walter Stachnik, Inspector General
(202) 942-4461
405 5th Street, N.W. (1107)
Washington, D.C. 20549
Hotline Number: (202) 942-4460

Small Business Administration
The Honorable Phyllis K. Fong,
Inspector General
(202) 205-6586
409 3rd Street, S.W.; 7th Floor
Washington, D.C. 20416
Hotline Number: (800) 767-0385;
(202) 205-7151

Smithsonian Institution
Thomas D. Blair, Inspector General
(202) 287-3326
955 L'Enfant Plaza; Mail Stop 905;
Room 7600
Washington, D.C. 20560
Hotline Number: (202) 287-3676

Department of State
The Honorable Jacquelyn Williams-
Bridgers, Inspector General
(202) 647-9450
2201 C Street, N.W.; Room 6817
Washington, D.C. 20520-6817
Hotline Number: (202) 647-3320
Collect Calls Accepted

Social Security Administration
James G. Huse, Jr,
Acting Inspector General
(410) 966-8385
6401 Security Boulevard; Suite 300
Baltimore, MD 21235
Hotline Number: (800) 269-0271

Tennessee Valley Authority
Robert L. Thompson,
Acting Inspector General
(423) 632-4120
400 West Summit Hill Drive
Knoxville, TN 37902-1499
Hotline Number: (800) 323-3835

Department of Transportation
The Honorable Kenneth M. Mead,
Inspector General
(202) 366-1959
400 Seventh Street, S.W.; Room 9210,
Washington, D.C. 20590
Hotline Number: (800) 424-9071;
(202) 366-1461

Department of the Treasury
The Honorable Jeffrey Rush, Jr.,
Inspector General
(202) 622-1090
1500 Pennsylvania Avenue, N.W.;
Washington, D.C. 20220
Hotline Number: (800) 359-3898

**Treasury Inspector General
for Tax Administration**
The Honorable David C. Williams,
Inspector General,
(202) 622-6500
1111 Constitution Ave. NW,
Room IR-3031
Washington, DC 20224

Hotline Number: (800) 366-4484

Department of Veterans Affairs
The Honorable Richard J. Griffin,
Inspector General
(202) 565-8620
810 Vermont Avenue, N.W.
Washington, D.C. 20420
Hotline Number: (800) 488-8244;
email: *VAOIG.HOTLINE@FORUM.
VA.GOV*

Special Counsel Hotline

The Office of the Special Counsel
investigates charges or reprisals against
federal employees for lawful disclosure of information relating to fraud,
illegalities, corruption, or mismanagement in government. (See separate
section on Special Counsel.) The number is 202-653-9125, toll-free 800-
572-2249.

CHAPTER EIGHT

Injury Compensation and Disability

Work-related illnesses and injuries are among the most catastrophic career-related setbacks an individual can suffer. Unfortunately, they also result in some of the most contentious and complicated personnel disputes that an employee can experience in the federal workplace.

The contentiousness is rooted in the basic mistrust many employees feel toward their agencies, which often leads to disputes over payment of injury benefits. Claimants frequently feel they are improperly being denied injury-related benefits they have "earned." Many agencies, under pressure to hold down costs and keep the work moving, feel that they have too often been the victim of employee or provider fraud. According to some observers, while undoubtedly there has been a certain amount of abuse on both sides, abuses of the workers' compensation system occur far less frequently than advocates of either point of view might believe.

The complications arise, at least in part, because workers' rights to injury compensation and the closely related issue of disability retirement are governed by two separate laws and are administered by two different agencies—the Office of Personnel Management and the U.S. Department of Labor.

In addition to the relationship between workers' comp benefits and disability retirement, there are several other issues arising in injury and disability situations that often spark disputes between workers and their agency. These include employee eligibility for continued benefit payments under FECA, the agency's obligation to "reasonably accommodate" employees who are disabled, and job restoration rights for workers who have recovered.

———— Basic Rules and Procedures ————

Administrative Responsibilities

Workers' compensation benefits paid under the Federal Employees Compensation Act are administered by DOL's Office of Workers' Compensation Programs. Rather than the employing agency, it is OWCP's responsibility to authorize the payment of wage loss, as well as medical, benefits if an employee's injury results in disability. If the disability is total, compensation is paid at two-thirds of monthly pay, while workers who are married or have dependents are entitled to benefits paid at three-fourths of their wage rate.

OPM, on the other hand, is the federal agency in charge of approving disability retirement claims. An injured worker's entitlement to benefits under one program does not automatically establish entitlement to benefits under the other. Often, injured employees apply for both disability retirement and injury compensation. If both are approved, workers then must decide between receiving one or the other, since they generally can't draw FECA benefits and a retirement annuity at the same time. (Many workers, at least initially, opt for workers' compensation benefits because such payments are not subject to income tax liability.)

FECA Overview

The Federal Employees' Compensation Act (FECA), which is administered by the Office of Workers' Compensation Programs, provides compensation benefits to civilian employees of the United States for disability due either to personal injuries sustained in the performance of duty or to employment-related disease. FECA also pays benefits to a worker's dependents if the injury or disease causes the employee's death.

Benefits will not be paid if the injury or death is caused by the willful misconduct of the employee or by the employee's intentional or deliberate act to bring about injury or death, or if the worker's intoxication caused the injury or death.

Employees who sustain a job-related injury must be allowed to seek treatment from a physician of their choice without agency interference. The agency can require the employee to undergo a medical examination by its own doctors for the purpose of determining the worker's employability. An agency-required examination has no effect on the payment of compensation benefits by OWCP.

Employees who are unable to perform the full duties of their position may be placed on leave without pay or separated at any time. Such a termination is considered a non-disciplinary action and has no effect on the employee's restoration rights upon recovery.

An employee who sustains a disabling, job-related traumatic injury may request sick or annual leave or to be placed in a "continuation of pay" status for the period of disability (not to exceed 45 calendar days). If the disability continues beyond 45 days or the worker is not entitled to continuation of pay, the employee may use sick or annual leave or enter a leave-without-pay status and claim compensation from OWCP.

When disability results from an occupational disease, the employing agency is not authorized to continue the employee's pay. The employee may use sick or annual leave or enter a LWOP status and file a FECA compensation claim.

Compensation is generally paid at the rate of 2/3 of the salary if the employee has no dependents and 3/4 of salary if workers have one or more dependents.

OWCP also may authorize a "schedule award" for a permanent impairment to certain members or functions of the body (e.g., loss of use of an eye or arm, or loss of function or removal of a kidney due to injury). The schedule-award amounts payable are specified by FECA. An additional award may be paid under FECA for serious disfigurement of the head, face, or neck.

OWCP may arrange for vocational rehabilitation or training for the injured worker, and may pay an allowance if the employee's condition requires a constant attendant.

Additionally, survivor benefits are payable in the event of death due to the employment-related injury. All FECA compensation payments on account of a disability or death are inflation-adjusted.

Where an employee's injury or death in the performance of duty occurs under circumstances that involve the legal liability of a party other than the United States, a portion of the cost of compensation and other benefits paid by OWCP may have to be refunded from any settlement subsequently obtained by the injured worker. OWCP will assist FECA beneficiaries in obtaining such settlements, and the law guarantees that the employee may retain a certain proportion of the settlement (after any attorney's fees and costs are deducted).

FECA compensation can be ended if OWCP determines that the employee can return to the former job without limitations, or the worker's agency makes a suitable job offer that a partially recovered worker unreasonably refuses. However, it is OWCP—not the employing agency—that determines whether the job being offered is suitable and if a worker's refusal is reasonable. Similarly, OWCP can suspend a worker's FECA compensation for a failure to respond to requests for information on employment and earnings.

FECA beneficiaries who refuse to cooperate in vocational rehabilitation programs or to make good faith efforts to obtain reemployment also face the possible reduction or termination of their compensation benefits.

General Appeal Rights

An employee or survivor who disagrees with a final determination of OWCP may, within 30 days of the decision, request an oral hearing from the Branch of Hearings and Review. Oral and/or written evidence in support of the claim may be presented. The request for a hearing should be addressed to the Office of Workers' Compensation Programs, Branch of Hearings and Review, P.O. Box 37117, Washington, D.C. 20013-7117.

In lieu of an oral hearing, you may request a review of the written record by an OWCP representative. During this process, you may submit additional written evidence in support of your claim. The request should be sent to the address above. You are not entitled to have both an oral hearing and a review of the written record on the same issue.

You may request a reconsideration of a decision by submitting a written request within one year to the district office that issued the decision. No special form is required, but the request must clearly state the grounds on which you are basing your reconsideration request. The request must be accompanied by evidence not previously submitted, such as medical reports, affidavits, or statements.

If there is no new evidence available after the OWCP decision, you may request a review by the Employees' Compensation Appeals Board within 90 days from the date of the decision. The address is Employees' Compensation Appeals Board, U.S. Department of Labor, 200 Constitution Ave., N.W., Room N-2609, Washington, D.C. 20210. The board rules solely on the evidence of record at the time the decision was issued.

Decisions of the ECAB are final and may not be appealed to federal or state courts.

Accommodation Requirements

Agencies are required to consider whether the job and/or the work environment can be adjusted to enable a disabled person to perform the duties of the position. Such accommodations may include modifying the worksite, adjusting the work schedule, restructuring the job, or providing special assistance such as readers or other types of help.

A disabled person has a right to a light-duty job if a position can be restructured to remove nonessential functions the employee cannot perform. However, an assignment to light duty does not establish any entitlement to it on a permanent basis. Also, there is no requirement that an agency accommodate an employee with a light-duty assignment where the tasks do not comprise a complete and separate position.

Agencies also are obligated to review all vacant positions at the same pay or grade and tenure within the commuting area for which the person is qualified to determine if placement is possible.

The requirement to accommodate through reassignment arises when workers establish their status as a "qualified employee with a disability." An agency that receives a reassignment request to accommodate an employee's disability is entitled to a reasonable time to assess the evidence and the worker's need for accommodation. Additionally, an agency need not put all other personnel actions on hold while it is doing so, even those involving a position the employee is seeking.

An employee generally is entitled to a disability accommodation on an agency-wide basis, not just within the employing component. However, since different components may have separate missions, budgets, and appointing authorities, reassignments across component lines may be viewed as creating an "undue hardship" on the agency. In such cases, to gain entitlement to a reassignment to another component, an employee would have to show that the agency

would not suffer a hardship or that the agency's hardship claim actually is a pretext for discrimination. Also, keep in mind that the agency's obligation to accommodate an employee's condition by reassignment is limited geographically to the commuting area where the employee is currently assigned.

In some cases, collective bargaining units might require that certain workers be placed in vacancies that a disabled person might otherwise get— for example, positions for which other employees have "bidding rights." These types of contractual arrangements may suffice to support an agency's claim of undue hardship.

General factors considered when deciding whether an accommodation would impose an undue hardship on the agency include the overall size of the agency and type of operation involved, including the composition and structure of the workforce and the nature and cost of the accommodation.

Accommodation Appeals

Employee claims that an agency failed to make a reasonable accommodation are appealable to the Merit Systems Protection Board or, where applicable, through the negotiated grievance process.

In general, employees must prove that they are disabled, that there was a causal relationship between their disability and a personnel decision, and that they could continue working with a reasonable accommodation. The agency then would have to prove it had a legitimate reason for the action and that the accommodation being sought would have imposed an undue hardship or that the employee couldn't perform the essential functions of the position even with the accommodation.

The Civil Rights Act of 1991 allows complainants to receive monetary awards based on either intentional discrimination or failure to accommodate a disability. An employee who prevails before the Board on a finding of discrimination may recover compensatory damages from an agency under that law. However, there is no right to punitive damage awards against a government agency. Requests for compensatory damages must be made with the appeal on the merits of the case and cannot be raised for the first time in a petition for enforcement, except where the agency's failure to comply itself constitutes a separate incident of discrimination.

Restoration Rights

FECA guarantees employees certain job rights upon recovery. Upon their return to work, employees will be treated as though they had never left for purposes of rights and benefits based on length of service.

An agency must tell an employee who is being separated or placed on leave without pay how the worker's benefits will be affected and what the employee's restoration rights are. To be eligible for restoration, the employee must have been receiving benefits from OWCP (or have been eligible for OWCP benefits).

Not only must the agency make an effort to place a recovered employee, but employees also have a responsibility to return to work as soon as they are able. A partially disabled employee who refuses to work after suitable work is offered is not entitled to compensation under FECA. An individual who is ordered to return to work is required to comply with instructions that are within agency authority, unless obedience would place the person in a clearly dangerous circumstance—for example, being exposed once again to conditions that endanger personal health.

The obligation to reemploy rests with the injured worker's former agency; other agencies have no obligation to reemploy a recovered worker.

Full recovery is determined by an OWCP decision to cut off FECA compensation payments on the basis that the employee is medically able to resume regular employment.

Employees have an obligation to cooperate with the agency, to keep the agency informed of their medical status, and to seek restoration as soon as their medical condition permits.

The restoration rights of employees who sustain compensable injuries fall into four categories:

• *Fully recovered within one year*—Workers have mandatory restoration rights to the position they left, or to an equivalent position in the former commuting area. If a suitable vacancy does not exist, the restoration right is agency-wide. Recovered employees must apply for restoration immediately and must be restored immediately and unconditionally by their former agency.

• *Fully recovered after one year*—Workers are entitled to priority consideration for their former position or an equivalent one, provided they apply for restoration within 30 days of the date compensation ceases. Priority consideration means the agency enters the individual on its reemployment priority list. If the agency cannot place such workers in their former commuting area, they are entitled to priority consideration for an equivalent position elsewhere in the agency.

• *Physically disqualified (medically unable to return to former occupation, but able to do other work)*—Such workers are entitled, within one year of the date compensation begins, to agency-wide placement in a position that most closely approximates the seniority, status, and pay to which they otherwise would be entitled, depending on the circumstances of the case. After one year, such workers are entitled to the same restoration rights as individuals who partially recover.

• *Partially recovered (not fully recovered but able to work in some capacity)*—These workers are entitled to employment consideration in the former commuting area. The agency must make every effort to place such employees, but they do not have an absolute right to restoration. If such workers subsequently recover, they are then entitled to the restoration rights of a fully recovered employee, based on the timing of their recovery. Partially recovered workers have an obligation to seek employment within their capabilities. If a partially recovered employee refuses to accept a suitable job offer, OWCP may terminate compensation.

The OWCP decides whether a position offered by an agency is suitable for a partially disabled employee according to the individual's medical restrictions, education, and vocational background. OWCP will evaluate such offers in light of the nature of the employee's injury, the degree of the employee's impairment, the employee's age and qualifications for other work, and other factors. When an agency removes an employee who has a compensable injury solely for refusal to return to work and OWCP has not made a suitability determination, the employee is entitled to priority consideration for restoration.

Other factors affecting restoration rights are the timeliness of the application for restoration, the employee's performance and conduct prior to the injury, and the availability of positions.

If an employee was separated because of a compensable injury, the agency cannot refuse to restore the individual because of alleged poor performance prior to the injury. Similarly, an injury may not be used as a basis to circumvent performance-based or adverse action procedures that otherwise would apply. An allegation of an on-the-job injury by an employee does not stop an agency from taking action against the employee for performance or conduct. An employee who is removed for cause (performance or conduct) has no restoration rights.

Employees who are restored following a compensable injury generally are entitled to be treated as though they never left. This means that the entire period the employee was receiving compensation or continuation of pay is creditable for purposes of rights and benefits based upon length of service, including within-grade increases, career tenure, time-in-grade restrictions, leave rate accrual, and completion of the probationary period. However, an employee does not earn sick or annual leave while off the rolls or in a non-pay status.

An employee on FECA compensation also is generally entitled to be considered for promotion as though still present. This means that an employee who occupies a career ladder position, or whose position is reclassified at a higher grade, is entitled to be considered for promotion under the provisions of the agency's merit promotion plan. However, employees on compensation generally are not entitled to a promotion unless it is clear that they would have been promoted if the injury had not occurred.

An injured employee enjoys no special protection in a reduction in force (RIF) and can be separated like any other worker. An injured employee separated by RIF has no restoration rights.

Restoration Appeal Rights

Executive branch employees who are entitled to restoration or priority consideration because of a compensable injury may appeal to the Merit Systems Protection Board as follows:

• An employee who fully recovers within one year or who is physically disqualified may appeal an agency's failure to restore (or an improper restoration).

• An employee who takes longer than one year to fully recover may appeal the agency's failure: to place the worker on its reemployment priority list; to reemploy the individual from the priority list (by showing that restoration was denied because of the employment of another person who otherwise could not properly have been appointed); or to place the employee in an equivalent position with credit for all rights and benefits.

• A partially recovered employee may appeal by showing that the agency's failure to reemploy was arbitrary and capricious.

• If reemployed, the employee may appeal the agency's failure to credit time spent on FECA compensation for all benefits based upon length of service.

———— Practical Considerations ————

Preparations and Protections

Possibly the last thing on the mind of an employee who has just suffered a work-related injury or illness is preparing to present a case that meets FECA's legal standards and principles, but unfortunately, such preparation can be critically important. Gathering the proper documentation and complying with filing deadlines are vital to an individual's obtaining benefits, as well as prevailing in any later challenge that might arise out of a dispute.

It's important to know the lay of the land at the outset, in order to prepare for various possibilities.

OWCP makes the determination of an employee's disability status on a case-by-case basis, focusing on whether the particular impairment substantially limits the individual's ability to work or otherwise constitutes a significant barrier to employment. Relevant considerations are the number and type of jobs from which the person is disqualified, the geographic area to which the worker has reasonable access, and the person's job expectations and training.

The fact that a work-related injury or impairment forecloses an employee from performing the duties of a particular position does not automatically establish that the impairment constitutes a disabling condition. The disabling condition generally must foreclose the type of employment involved, not just the demands of a particular job.

By comparison, the test for determining entitlement to a disability retirement annuity is whether an employee can perform "useful and efficient service" for the agency—i.e., whether the worker can demonstrate acceptable performance of the critical elements of the job and maintain satisfactory attendance and conduct.

Following are some steps employees should take to protect themselves:

• In case of injury, obtain first aid or medical treatment, even if the injury or accident seems to be only "minor." This might head off more serious medical problems that can be avoided with treatment, and also serves to establish a record of what happened, along with when, where and in what circumstances, in case any of these factors later come into dispute.

• Report every injury or illness to your supervisor. Submit written notice of your injury on Form CA-1 if you sustained a traumatic injury, or Form CA-2 if the injury was an occupational disease or illness. Once again, this helps establish a record of the sequence of events.

• For traumatic injuries, ask the agency to provide authorization for medical treatment (Form CA-16) before you go to the doctor. Take that form when you go to the doctor, along with Form OWCP-1500, which the doctor must use to submit bills to OWCP. Submit all medical bills promptly to OWCP.

• Gather the documents you may need to establish a claim. To ensure entitlement to FECA benefits, you must provide evidence showing, for example, that you filed for benefits in a timely manner, that the injury occurred as reported and in the performance of duty, and that your condition or disability is related to your federal employment.

• File a wage-loss compensation claim (Form CA-7) if you cannot return to work because of your injury and you are losing (or expect to lose) pay for more than three days. All wage-loss claims must be supported by medical evidence of injury-related disability for the period of the claim.

• Cooperate with agency actions or directives—such as offers of light-duty assignments or orders for medical exams—unless you can make a case that your health and safety would be endangered. You could lose benefits or be subject to personnel actions for refusing. If you disagree with agency orders, follow the "obey now, grieve later" principle. Disagreements will be sorted out later and you can't count on a decision that you were justified in refusing an order, no matter how strongly you may feel about it.

• Find out what the relevant deadlines are and make sure you meet them. That's far easier than trying to make a case later that time limits should be waived to cover your situation.

• Document everything. Keep records of all official communications between yourself and your employing agency and of all medically related paperwork. Take notes of conversations and write up those notes as things happen. Although you might not expect to become permanently or even temporarily disabled, you'll greatly improve your chances of gaining FECA coverage should matters come to that.

Disability Retirement

CSRS Disability Benefits

Disability retirement benefits are payable to you if you are unable to perform useful and efficient service in your position because of disease or injury. However, you cannot be considered disabled if you decline your agency's offer of a position that accommodates your disability and that is at the same grade or pay level and is within your commuting area. To qualify, the disabling condition must be expected to last at least one year, and you must have completed five years of federal civilian service and have been covered under CSRS when disabled.

The amount of annuity payable depends on the amount of federal service you have, as well as your salary level. There also is a guaranteed minimum benefit. If you qualify for both disability retirement and FECA compensation benefits, generally you will be allowed to choose the higher FECA benefit over disability retirement. If your agency separates you, you should apply for disability retirement to protect your and your survivor's future annuity rights. Disability retirement benefits are suspended while you are receiving FECA benefits, but can be activated should the compensation benefit stop or drop below the amount of the annuity benefit. The exception is if you are entitled to a scheduled award, which may be paid at the same time disability benefits are paid.

If you also are covered by Social Security as a CSRS Offset employee, your disability benefit would be offset by the part of your Social Security benefit that is based on your CSRS Offset service. You must apply for Social Security disability benefits if you are a CSRS Offset employee.

Retirement benefits are payable under certain circumstances where FECA benefits may not be payable. For instance, retirement benefits may be payable to a former spouse if a court order awarded them, but FECA benefits are not payable to a former spouse. In addition, if a widow or widower remarries before age 55 and that marriage ends, the retirement benefit may be reinstated (provided the survivor has not received a refund of your retirement contributions). In contrast, FECA benefits may not be reinstated. Also, if you become disabled because of a job-related illness or injury, but die of unrelated causes, your survivors would not be eligible for FECA benefits, but may be eligible for CSRS survivor benefits.

FERS Disability Benefits

The eligibility requirements for FERS disability benefits are similar to those under CSRS except that you

need only 18 months, rather than 5 years, of federal civilian service. FERS disabled employees also may qualify for Social Security disability benefits if they are unable to work in any substantial gainful activity and their disability is expected to last at least one year or result in death.

FERS disability benefits are offset if you also are eligible for Social Security disability benefits. Therefore, you must apply for Social Security benefits at the same time you file an application for FERS disability benefits. The rules concerning concurrent payment of FECA benefits and disability retirement benefits are the same as the rules for CSRS employees.

Other General Rules

If you also are receiving workers' compensation, your disability benefit may be reduced. The total of all disability benefits (Social Security, workers' compensation, and benefits under CSRS or FERS) may not exceed 80 percent of your earnings before the disability began.

OPM has the authority to reevaluate disability annuitants up to age 60 to determine whether they have recovered. Disability annuitants are not precluded from working while collecting an annuity, but they must annually report income from wages and self-employment to OPM. If their earnings amount to more than 80 percent of the current rate of pay of their former position, they will be deemed restored to earning capacity.

Disability retirees who are deemed recovered or restored to earning capacity are eligible for temporary continuation of their benefits and may be eligible for priority job placement with the government. If the disabling condition recurs later, the individual can request reinstatement to the disability rolls.

Unlike FECA benefits, disability retirement can be paid whether or not the illness or injury was incurred on the job. Also unlike FECA, there is no provision in disability retirement for "scheduled" awards to compensate for the loss of certain body parts or functions. However, in such situations employees may be entitled to accidental dismemberment payments under their Federal Employees Group Life Insurance coverage.

Disability Appeal Rights

Disability retirement applications under CSRS or FERS are filed with the employing agency, which assembles necessary documentation concerning the employee's medical condition, its relationship to work abilities, attempts or requests to reassign or accommodate the employee, and similar information. In some cases, the agency initiates the proceedings. The Office of Personnel Management examines the application and documents and decides whether a disability retirement is warranted.

Generally, disability retirement applicants have the burden of proving that they meet all of the requirements for disability retirement, and are responsible for ensuring that all documents are submitted within time limits. If employees have been removed for a "physical inability to perform," there is a presumption that they meet the requirements for disability retirement.

If OPM denies an application, the employee can ask for reconsideration by submitting a written and signed request. The request must be received by OPM within 30 days of issuance of the initial decision. The applicant may submit additional medical or other information at the reconsideration stage. OPM then reevaluates the decision, taking any additional information into account.

A final denial of an application by OPM can be appealed to the Merit Systems Protection Board within 35 days of the reconsideration decision. An MSPB hearing officer will review the case and issue a written decision based on the preponderance of the evidence. The applicant can then appeal to the three-member Board and from there to the U.S. Court of Appeals for the Federal Circuit.

Rulings Review

• In the absence of a finding of disability discrimination, an agency is under no general obligation to reassign an employee unless an agency regulation requires it. (*Konieczko v. U.S. Postal Service*, 47 MSPR 509, 1991)

• An earlier light duty assignment does not establish an employee's entitlement to continued light duty once it is established that the disabling condition is permanent. (*Joyner v. Dept. of the Navy*, 47 MSPR 592, 1991)

• The relevant question in disability retirement appeals is not whether the agency has refused to accommodate an employee, but whether it is unable to reasonably accommodate the employee. (*Dec v. OPM*, 47 MSPR 72, 1991)

• A former employee who has partially recovered from a work-related injury and has been restored to the agency rolls may not appeal the details or the circumstances of the restoration to MSPB. The Board has jurisdiction only over denials of restoration. (*Booker v. MSPB*, 982 F.2d 517, Fed. Cir. 1992)

• The employee's position at the time a disability retirement application is forwarded to OPM is the one for which the worker must prove a disability. Voluntary acceptance of a demotion would constitute the withdrawal of an application, and reassignment to another position would constitute evidence that the employee was not disabled for a position at the same pay and grade.(*Malan v. Dept. of the Air Force*, 55 MSPR 283, 1992)

• Different medical restrictions over a several year period for various illnesses and injuries cannot be cumulated with a later injury that lasts for a few months to make the latter disability a permanent condition. (*Crew v. Navy*, 58 MSPR 597, 1993)

• An employee with a disability is entitled to accommodation by reassignment only to components of the agency served by the same appointing authority. (*Hurst v. Dept. of the Navy*, 61 MSPR 277, 1994)

• The inability to perform a specific job is not sufficient for an employee to be deemed disabled under the Rehabilitation Act of 1973; rather, the issue must focus on whether the worker is foreclosed generally from the type of employment involved. (*Groshans v. Dept. of the Navy*, 67 MSPR 629, 1995)

• An applicant for disability retirement who can perform limited duties as an accommodation must show that the limited-duty status will not continue and that there is no vacant position to which the worker can be reassigned. (*Gomez v. OPM*, 69 MSPR 115, 1995)

• A qualified disabled employee who accepts a demotion because the agency would not provide an accommodation to which he is entitled has shown that his acceptance was coerced. (*O'Connell v. U.S. Postal Service*, 69 MSPR 438, 1996)

CHAPTER NINE

Monetary Claims

In the past, the settlement of most monetary or financial claims arising between employees and agencies in the executive branch was traditionally handled by the General Accounting Office. However, effective in 1996, GAO's former duties were transferred to and divided between the Office of Personnel Management and the General Services Administration.

Disputes over travel and relocation allowances (as well as transportation rates) now fall under the authority of GSA's Board of Contract Appeals. Disputes over compensation and leave claims, as well as deceased employees' compensation and proceeds of canceled checks for veterans' benefits payable to deceased beneficiaries, are handled by OPM.

OPM also is authorized to resolve overtime claims under the Fair Labor Standards Act, except for claims arising under the equal pay provisions of that law, which are administered by the Equal Employment Opportunity Commission.

GAO is not entirely out of the pay-dispute business, however. GAO's Office of the Comptroller General still has the authority to issue advance decisions, which agencies sometimes seek before processing an employee's pay or reimbursement claim.

GSA Jurisdiction

Travel and Relocation Claims

GSA reviews claims made against the government by civilian employees who are seeking reimbursement of expenses incurred while on official temporary duty travel, as well as claims for reimbursement of expenses incurred in connection with relocation to a new duty station.

Any claim for entitlement to travel or relocation expenses must first be filed with the employee's own department or agency, which initially adjudicates the claim. Workers who disagree with an agency's determination may request review of their claim by GSA's Board of Contract Appeals. Employees have the burden of estab-

lishing both the agency's liability for, and their right to, the disputed payment.

The Board of Contract Appeals will issue a final decision on the claim based on the information submitted by the employee and the agency.

A claim must be in writing and must be signed by the employee or by the employee's attorney or authorized representative. No particular form is required. However, the request should describe the basis for the claim and state the amount sought. It also should include: the worker's name, address, telephone number, and facsimile machine number, if available; the name, address, telephone number, and facsimile machine number, if available, of the agency employee who denied the claim; a copy of the denial of the claim; and any other information that the employee believes the Board should consider.

If an agency has denied a claim for travel or relocation expenses, it may, at the employee's request, forward the claim to the Board. The agency must include the same type of information required of individual claimants.

A claim should be sent to the Board at: Office of the Clerk of the Board, Room 7022, General Services Administration Building, 1800 F Street, NW, Washington, D.C. 20405, phone (202) 501-0116.

The employee must send copies of all material provided to the Board to the individual designated by the agency to handle the claim. If an agency forwards a claim to the Board, it must, at the same time, provide the employee with a copy of all material sent to the Board. All submissions to the Board must indicate that a copy has been provided to the employee or the agency.

When a claim has been filed by an employee, within 30 calendar days after it has been docketed by the Board, the agency must submit to the Board: a simple, concise, and direct statement of its response to the claim; citations to applicable statutes, regulations, and cases; and any additional information the agency considers necessary to the Board's review of the claim. A copy of these submissions also must be sent to the employee.

Employees may file a reply to the agency response within 30 calendar days after they receive it (or within 60 calendar days after receiving the response, if the employee is located outside the 50 states and the District of Columbia).

The employee or the agency may request additional time to make any filing.

A Contract Appeals Board judge may hold a conference with the employee and the individual designated as the agency contact and may provide the participants a memorandum reflecting the results of the conference. A Board judge also may require the submission of additional information at any time. The judge will issue a written decision based on the record, which includes submissions by the employee and the agency, and information provided during any conferences.

The employee and the agency will be furnished copies of the judge's decision by the Office of the Clerk of the Board. Either side may request reconsideration by the Board within 30 calendar days after the date the decision was issued (or within 60 calendar days after the date the decision was issued, if the employee or the agency office making the request is located outside the 50 states and the District of Columbia).

The request for reconsideration should state the reasons why the Board should consider the request. Neither mere disagreement with a decision nor the reargument of points already made will be considered sufficient grounds for granting Board reconsideration.

The agency must pay the worker any amounts the Board determines are due the employee.

OPM Jurisdiction

Compensation and Leave Claims

OPM has authority to resolve employees' compensation or reimbursement claims involving wage or leave disputes. Employees generally are required to submit such claims in writing to OPM, stating the basis for the claim as well as the amount sought. The statement also should include contact information on the claimant, the agency employee who denied the claim (if known), a copy of the denial of the claim, and any other information the claimant believes OPM should consider. In addition, a claim filed by an employee's representative must be supported by a power of attorney or other documentary evidence of the representative's right to act for that person.

At its discretion, the agency may forward a pay-dispute claim to OPM on the employee's behalf. In such cases, however, the employee is responsible for ensuring that OPM receives all the information required.

OPM may request the agency to provide an administrative report, which typically includes the agency's factual findings, its conclusions of law, its recommended decision, and copies of rules, memos, or other guidance agency officials used in making their decision. The report also should note whether or not the employee is a member of a collective bargaining unit, and if so, whether the claim is covered by a negotiated grievance procedure that might specifically exclude the claim from OPM review.

The burden of proof is on the employee to establish a claim's timeliness—most claims are subject to a six-year statute of limitations—along with the government's liability for the disputed payment and the employee's right to payment. OPM will base the terms of any claim settlement only on the written record. Keep in mind that OPM also will accept facts asserted by the agency in the absence of "clear and convincing evidence to the contrary."

All claims should be submitted to the Claims Adjudication Unit, Room 7535, Office of the General Counsel, Office of Personnel Management, 1900 E Street, N.W., Washington, D.C. 20415, phone (202) 606-2233.

OPM will send a copy of its decision to the employee, advising the worker whether it has decided to allow the claim in whole or in part. If OPM requested an agency report or if the agency forwarded the claim on behalf of the claimant, OPM also will send the agency a copy of its decision.

There is no further channel of review within OPM. However, in some situations, employees have the right to carry their claim on to federal court.

OPM does not have jurisdiction over claims under the exclusive authority of administrative agencies or claims concerning matters subject to negotiated grievance procedures or certain claims arising under the Fair Labor Standards Act (e.g., postal workers' FLSA disputes and congressional employees' claims).

Fair Labor Standards Act Claims

OPM's pay-dispute procedures generally extend to federal workers' claims involving FLSA exemption-status determin- ations (i.e., exempt or nonexempt status under FLSA) and FLSA minimum wage or overtime pay disputes for work allegedly covered under the Act. Employees have the right at any time to file a complaint challenging the correctness of an agency's determination of their FLSA exemption status (which usually is triggered by a dispute over a worker's entitlement to overtime pay). Employees also may file an FLSA claim concerning their entitlement to minimum wage or overtime pay for work hours that arguably should be covered under the Act. It is important to remember, however, that time limits apply to such FLSA pay claims.

All new FLSA pay claims are subject to a two-year statute of limitations (three years for willful violations). An employee or a worker's designated representative may preserve the claim period by submitting a written claim either to the employing agency during the claim period or to OPM. The date the agency or OPM receives the claim is the date that determines the period of any back pay entitlement. The employee is responsible for proving when the claim was received by the agency or OPM.

If at any time during the claim period, an employee was a member of a bargaining unit covered by a negotiated agreement that did not specifically exclude matters under the Act from the scope of the contractual grievance procedure, the worker must use that grievance procedure as the exclusive administrative remedy for all claims under the Act. There is no right to further administrative review by the agency or by OPM.

Workers who are not covered by such a contract may file a claim with the employing agency or with OPM, but not both simultaneously. Nothing in OPM's rules limits the right of an employee to bring an action in an appropriate federal court. However, filing a claim with an agency or with OPM does not satisfy the statute of limitations governing FLSA claims filed in court. OPM will not decide an FLSA claim that is in litigation.

An employee may designate, in writing, a representative to assist in preparing or presenting a claim. However, such representatives may not participate in OPM interviews unless specifically requested to do so by OPM. An agency may disallow an employee representative who also is a federal employee in certain circumstances.

Filing Requirements

OPM encourages, but does not require, employees to obtain a decision on their pay-dispute claim from the agency before filing a claim with OPM. An employee who receives an unfavorable decision on a claim from the agency may still file the claim with OPM. However, an employee may not file the claim with the agency after receiving an unfavorable decision from OPM.

An FLSA claim filed with an employing agency should be made according to appropriate agency procedures. At the request of the employee, the agency may forward the claim to OPM on the worker's behalf. The employee is responsible for ensuring that OPM receives all the information requested.

An FLSA claim filed with OPM must be in writing and signed by the employee or the employee's representative. It also must include: the identity of the employee and any designated representative; the employing agency during the claim period; the position (job title, series, and grade) occupied by the worker; the employee's (and designated representative's) current mailing address, commercial telephone number, and facsimile machine number, if available; a description of the nature of the claim and the issues or incidents giving rise to the claim, including the time period covered; a description of actions taken by the employee to resolve the claim within the agency and the results of any such actions; a copy of any decision or written response by the agency; evidence that supports the claim; and the remedy sought by the employee.

Employees also must provide: a statement that they were (or were not) a member of a collective bargaining unit at any time during the claim period, and if they belonged to a bargaining unit, a statement that they were (or were not) covered by a negotiated grievance procedure at any time during the claim period. If covered by a grievance procedure, claimants must indicate whether that procedure specifically excluded such claims from the scope of the grievance procedure. Employees also must indicate whether or not they have filed an action in an appropriate federal court, and provide any other information that they believe OPM should consider.

For all FLSA claims, the employee or representative must provide any additional information requested by OPM within 15 workdays after the date of the request, unless the worker (or the designated representative) requests additional time and OPM grants a longer time in which to provide the requested information.

While the disclosure of information by an employee is voluntary, OPM may be unable to render a decision on a claim unless the worker provides the information requested. In cases where workers fail to disclose necessary information, the claim will be cancelled without further action being taken by OPM. If the employee wishes the pay dispute to be treated confidentially, the claim must specifically request that the identity of the employee not be revealed to the agency.

In claims involving an FLSA exemption status determination, the burden of proof rests with the agency that asserts the FLSA exemption. The agency must provide the employee with a written acknowledgment of the date the claim was received. Upon an employee's request, and subject to any Privacy Act requirements, an agency must provide the employee with information relevant to the claim.

The agency must provide any information requested by OPM within 15 workdays after the date of the request, unless the agency requests additional time and OPM grants a longer period of time in which to provide the requested information.

Post Decision Procedures

OPM will send a copy of its FLSA claim decision to the employee or the employee's representative and the agency. An FLSA claim decision made by OPM is final and is not subject to further administrative review. However, workers have the right to pursue their claims by filing an action in the U.S. Court of Federal Claims, 717 Madison Place, N.W., Room 103, Washington, D.C. 20005, phone (202) 219-9561, subject to timeliness and jurisdictional restrictions.

At its discretion, OPM may agree to reconsider its decision based on a showing that material information was not considered or there was a significant error of law, regulation, or fact in the original decision. A decision by OPM under the Act is binding on all administrative, certifying, payroll, disbursing, and accounting officials of agencies for which OPM administers the Act.

Upon receipt of a decision, the employing agency during the claim period must take all necessary steps to comply with the decision, including adherence with compliance instructions provided with the decision. All compliance actions must be completed within the time specified in the decision, unless an extension of time is requested by the agency and granted by OPM.

The agency should identify all similarly situated current and, to the extent possible, former employees, ensure that they are treated in a manner consistent with the decision, and inform them in writing of their right to file an FLSA claim with the agency or OPM.

OPM FLSA Claim Locations

Workers must file their FLSA claims with the OPM office that serves the area where the basis of the claim originated. Following are OPM office addresses and the service areas they cover:

OPM Atlanta Oversight Division
75 Spring Street SW., Suite 972,
Atlanta, GA 30303-3109
(Alabama, Florida, Georgia, Mississippi, North Carolina, South Carolina, Tennessee, Virginia, excluding the Virginia locations listed under the Washington, DC Oversight Division)

OPM Chicago Oversight Division
230 S. Dearborn Street,
DPN 30-6,
Chicago, IL 60604-1687
(Ilinois, Indiana, Iowa, Kansas, Kentucky, Michigan, Minnesota, Missouri, Nebraska, North Dakota, Ohio, South Dakota, West Virginia, Wisconsin)

OPM Dallas Oversight Division
1100 Commerce Street,
Room 4C22,
Dallas, TX 75242-9968
(Arizona, Arkansas, Colorado, Louisiana, Montana, New Mexico, Oklahoma, Texas, Utah, Wyoming)

OPM Philadelphia Oversight Division
600 Arch Street, Room 3400,
Philadelphia, PA 19106-1596
(Connecticut, Delaware, Maine, Maryland—excluding the Maryland locations listed under the Washington, DC Oversight Division—Massachusetts, New Hampshire, New Jersey, New York, Pennsylvania, Rhode Island, Vermont, Puerto Rico, Virgin Islands)

OPM San Francisco Oversight Division
120 Howard Street, Room 760,
San Francisco, CA 94105-0001
(Alaska, California, Hawaii, Idaho, Nevada, Oregon, Washington, Pacific Ocean Area)

OPM Washington, D.C., Oversight Division
1900 E Street NW., Room 7675,
Washington, D.C. 20415-0001
(District of Columbia, Maryland counties of Charles, Montgomery, and Prince George; Virginia counties of Arlington, Fairfax, King George, Loudoun, Prince William, and Stafford, along with the cities of Alexandria, Fairfax, Falls Church, Manassas, and Manassas Park; and any overseas areas not listed in the service area of another oversight division)

CHAPTER TEN

Security Clearances

Thousands of federal employees need to hold security clearances to be qualified for their jobs. Many others may need limited access to confidential information on a temporary basis for a short-term assignment or project. Federal agencies generally have very broad powers over a worker's entitlement to a security clearance. Moreover, an agency's powers are almost as broad when it takes personnel actions based on a management decision that a particular individual or employee doesn't qualify for a security clearance.

This has been a tough lesson for many employees who have had their clearances revoked, as well as for individuals whose applications for positions requiring classified access are rejected because a clearance was denied. Basically, the courts have held that no one has a right to either a security clearance or employment in a position requiring one, which leaves most people with only limited means, at best, of challenging an adverse security clearance decision.

However, these long-standing security-clearance practices have resulted in complaints through the years that agencies were acting as investigator, prosecutor, and judge with respect to possible infringements of basic employee job rights. Finally, employee rights were broadened somewhat by an August 2, 1995, Executive Order (E. O. 12968). For the first time, the E.O. laid out a government-wide policy for granting or denying individuals access to classified information, replacing the general patchwork of procedures that individual agencies had developed on their own. The order also created a basic set of employee protections and appeals procedures to handle disputes over denials or revocations of security clearances. However, the procedures established by the E.O. still fall well short of employee protections in most other types of personnel disputes. Despite the protections afforded by the E.O., this is one type of personnel dispute where agencies hold virtually all the cards.

Basic Rules and Procedures

Supreme Court Guidelines

In addition to the procedures established under the E.O., the rights of employees in security clearance disputes are governed by a 1988 U.S. Supreme Court decision (*Department of the Navy v. Egan*, 484 U.S. 518). Under both the Supreme Court ruling and the E.O., employee rights with respect to adverse clearance decisions are far more limited than their rights in other types of disputes.

In the *Egan* case, the Court held that individuals have neither a property right nor a liberty interest in access to classified material, and therefore the loss of such access does not implicate any due process rights. The Court also decided that the Merit Systems Protection Board has no authority to review the merits of an agency's decision to revoke a security clearance, but instead can review only whether the procedural steps satisfying due process have been followed. Subsequently, the executive order spelled out what those procedural steps should consist of, but specified that the final decision on whether an employee can have a clearance—and thus, in many cases, will remain employed—remains in the hands of the employing agency.

Revocation Steps

Federal employees are granted security clearances only after undergoing background investigations that become increasingly rigorous as higher levels of access are involved. Government workers also are subject to periodic reinvestigations after clearances have been granted. When an investigation brings to light information or actions that make the granting or continuance of a clearance questionable, an agency may move to deny or revoke the worker's access rights to classified material.

For those already holding a clearance, an agency's first step typically is a suspension of the individual's clearance until the unfavorable information is resolved. This effectively can result in a worker's suspension, if the job can't be performed without such access. Employees also may be formally suspended while the agency investigates whether a clearance should be withdrawn. An agency may put employees on enforced leave or suspend them indefinitely, even if management lacks reasonable cause to believe that the employee is guilty of a crime. Moreover, employees whose clearances are restored after such a suspension may not receive back pay for the time they were suspended.

Clearances generally are formally denied or revoked only after full investigations and a possible review by the agency's central security office. However, at times, an agency also may determine that a position no longer needs access to classified information and move to revoke a clearance on those grounds. When a clearance is revoked, an agency might proceed to remove or transfer an employee for failing to meet an essential requirement of the position—in other words, holding that the individual is no longer qualified to hold that position. Agencies have a great deal of discretion in deciding that the loss of a security clearance makes an individual unqualified for a position. (In some ways, this situation is analogous to the job security of "dual status" technicians who, in order to hold their civilian federal jobs, must maintain their military reserve status; when those employees lose their military status—for whatever reason—they also lose their civilian positions.)

Procedural Rights

The 1995 executive order outlined certain procedural rights for employees whose clearances are denied or revoked. These include rights to a detailed written explanation of the agency's basis for the decision and copies of any related documents that would be releasable under the Freedom of Information Act. Employees also must be notified of their right to be represented (at their own cost) and to request other documents and the investigative file, although the release of such materials could be restricted for national security reasons.

Employees must be given an opportunity to reply in writing and to request a review of the agency's determination. In addition, they are entitled to:

• Written notice of the results of the review that provides the identity of the reviewer;

• The right to appeal in writing to a panel appointed by the agency head;

• An opportunity to appear personally to present relevant information at some point in the process before an adjudicator or other authority, other than the investigating entity, as determined by the agency head.

Appeals Routes

Beyond the few appeal possibilities outlined in the executive order, the ultimate decision about an employee's need for or right to a security clearance is left solely to the agency's discretion. Security clearance decisions, for example, are outside the realm of union-negotiated grievance procedures. Moreover, the Supreme Court's *Egan* ruling said that MSPB has no authority to review such decisions, since that would mean involving the Board in security-related matters that are within an agency's sole discretion. This means that in clearance disputes, employees have only limited grounds for challenging an agency's suspension or removal decision, which, under other circumstances, might be fully appealable.

In reviewing a personnel action based on the revocation of a security clearance, the Board has no power to review the substance of the underlying security clearance determination. Instead, MSPB's review authority is confined to considering only whether the agency provided the employee with the procedural protections required by statute, regulation, and the Constitution.

For example, in ruling on the Board's authority to review security-related cases, courts have held that:

• MSPB could not order a clearance reinstated after an agency's alleged breach of a settlement agreement which the employee claimed had resulted in a security investigation and the lifting of his clearance; and

• MSPB cannot consider an employee's allegations of discrimination and reprisal in a security clearance revocation. Nor can the Board consider the merits of a disparate treatment allegation.

In its *Egan* ruling, the Supreme Court did say that MSPB may determine whether an employee's transfer to a nonsensitive position is feasible as an alternative to a removal action, if such transfer rights are available from some other source. However, the Court did not create any broad obligation for an agency to look for such a position, nor did it find that employees have any substantive rights to such a move. Thus, in the absence of an agency regulation providing that employees whose clearances are denied or revoked are entitled to consideration for reassignments, MSPB has no authority to review either the feasibility of a worker's reassignment to a nonsensitive position or the extent of the agency's efforts to do so.

Essentially, what this means is that agencies can be held to a transfer policy only if there is an agency regulation spelling out such transfer rights to an available nonsensitive position for employees who are denied clearances. In such situations, MSPB can review whether the agency's efforts showed that it tried to comply with its own policy rules. However, the Board's review authority extends only to the scope of the agency's rules. Thus, if the rules are narrowly drawn—and they usually are—MSPB has a very limited review role. For example, an agency might need only to show that it did consider an employee for reassignment under its rules, but that no positions for which the individual was qualified were available.

Practical Considerations

Limited Rights At Best

Realistically, there are very few paths open to employees who want to challenge the revocation or denial of a security clearance. Some employees have tried to argue that they were denied due process because they were not allowed to confront witnesses or decision-makers in the security clearance revocation process. However, the courts generally have held that such arguments are really attacks on the sufficiency of the evidence and are beyond the Board's scope of review.

In other instances, employees have challenged the agency's decision that the position required the incumbent to hold a security clearance. Once again, however, courts have ruled that MSPB cannot review an agency's judgment that a particular position requires a clearance.

Nor do employees have the right to full disclosure of information about the agency's grounds for terminating or denying their access to classified information. Employees sometimes suspect that the denial or lifting of a clearance was an improper personnel action—for example, a means of retaliation for the worker's whistleblowing—but they have few ways to document such beliefs, even if they could somehow invoke MSPB jurisdiction over their cases.

Agencies can cite a wide range of reasons for revoking or denying a security clearance. For example, an agency might simply say it has concerns regarding an employee's judgment and ability. In one case, a clearance was revoked due to an employee's refusal to take prescribed medication to control a mental disorder.

While employees may be given an opportunity to respond to derogatory information outlined in a notice letter, they might not have access to supporting information warranting a revocation, if the agency refuses to release it for national security reasons. In such cases, employees have only a limited opportunity, at best, to examine the agency's basis for its decision and to challenge any inaccuracies they believe may have influenced the action.

Overall, security clearance disputes leave little room for employees to either challenge or negotiate about the related adverse employment consequences of the agency's action. Employees basically are left in the position of making sure they are familiar with the procedures the agency must follow and then holding the agency accountable for using them.

Rulings Review

• An employee has no property or liberty interest in continued access to classified information, and the termination of that access does not have any due process implications. (Jones v. Navy, 978 F.2d 1223, Fed. Cir. 1992)

• When employees are removed based on the loss of their security clearance and do not raise a definitive constitutional claim, the Board may review only whether such individuals received procedural due process. (Brockmann v. Department of the Air Force, 27 F.3d 54, Fed. Cir. 1994)

• Employees who are removed based on the revocation of their security clearances are entitled to a review of whether the agency complied with its own procedural regulations, but may not pursue their due process claims directed toward the merits of the revocation decision. (Drumheller v. Department of the Army, 49 F.3d 1566, Fed. Cir. 1995)

• When an agency indefinitely suspends an employee because the employee's access to security information or areas has been revoked, management must ensure that either in the suspension notice or earlier access denial, the employee was notified of the reasons for the access revocation and was allowed to respond to it. (Kriner v. Dept. of the Navy, 61 MSPR 526, 1994)

CHAPTER ELEVEN

Reductions-in-Force

Of the government's innumerable acronyms, probably none is more disliked by its employees than "RIF," shorthand for reduction-in-force. RIFs became a major concern as certain agencies were cut back in the early 1980s, but the more widespread cuts of recent years have made RIF a part of the daily vocabulary at some agencies.

Even with the significant job cuts of recent times, relatively few employees have been "RIF'd" in the sense that they were involuntarily separated. But the number of people actually laid off is far smaller than the number affected by RIFs, which generally also trigger relocations, hiring freezes, downgradings and other career disruptions, to say nothing of the personal stress that employees experience when they face potential job loss from a process that few fully understand.

But there's another school of thought that welcomes RIFs because they bring with them potential benefits that otherwise might not be available to employees—the possibility for early-out or discontinued service retirement, severance pay, continuation of certain benefits after leaving government service, and, where authorized, buyout separation incentive payments. The Defense Department even has a program in which employees who would not otherwise lose their jobs in a RIF can volunteer to be separated. Usually the desire to save someone else's job is a secondary motivation to receiving the special benefits that being RIF'd can bring.

Regardless of an employee's attitude, a RIF is like a major storm hitting the office. First there are clouds gathering on the horizon in the form of budget cutbacks and program changes. Then the clouds move a bit closer and pessimists warn that major trouble is coming while optimists hope it will pass over. When the storm hits, employees scramble for shelter, in the form of getting into the positions that will be left or seeking assistance to be placed on the outside.

Basic Rules and Procedures

RIF Rules Control

RIF policies are set primarily by Office of Personnel Management regulations, not law. Individual agency regulations also may play a role—for example, the Defense Department traditionally has been able to offer certain benefits not generally available elsewhere, including buyouts. In addition, national and local collective bargaining agreements also may impose certain specific rules. Such rules and agreements may cover subjects ranging from notice procedures to policies on retention and job placement. But in general the OPM rules govern what happens in a reduction in force.

An agency has the right to decide whether a RIF is necessary, when it will take place, and what positions are abolished. Acceptable reasons for a RIF action include: reorganization; lack of work; shortage of funds; insufficient personnel ceiling; the exercise of certain reemployment or restoration rights; or a furlough for more than 30 consecutive days, or more than 22 discontinuous workdays. An agency is required to use RIF procedures when an employee is faced with separation or downgrading for a specific reason. In lieu of RIF procedures, an agency may reassign an employee to a vacant position at the same grade or pay, regardless of where the position is located.

The government generally must give 60 days of notice of an impending RIF. The notice must state the actions to be taken, their effective date, your competitive area and level, where you may review regulations and records, any applicable exceptions to retention standing rules, and your appeal rights.

The competitive area sets the limits within which employees compete for retention, and is defined on the basis of organization and geography. OPM's standard for a minimum competitive area is an organization in a local commuting area that is separate from other organizations because of differences in operation, work function, staff, and personnel management authority.

Retention Factors

Within each competitive area, the agency groups interchangeable positions into competitive levels based upon similarity of grade, series, qualifications, duties and working conditions. The agency then establishes separate retention registers for each competitive level. Employees are listed in the order of their retention standing, based on four retention factors:

• *Tenure* — Competitive service employees are ranked on a retention register in three groups according to their types of appointment:

Group I—Career employees who are not serving on probation.

Group II—Career employees who are serving a probationary period, and career-conditional employees.

Group III—Employees serving under term and similar non-status appointments.

• *Veterans' Preference* — Each of these groups is divided into three subgroups reflecting their entitlement to veterans' preference for retention purposes:

Subgroup AD—Veterans with a compensable service-connected disability of 30 percent or more.

Subgroup A—Veterans not included in Subgroup AD.

Subgroup B—Nonveterans.

• *Length of Service* — Employees are ranked by service dates within each subgroup (i.e., the employee with the most service is listed at the top of the subgroup, the employee with the least service at the bottom of the subgroup). The service includes creditable civilian and military service, and additional service credit is granted for certain performance ratings.

• *Performance* — Employees receive extra RIF service credit for performance based upon the average of their last three annual performance ratings received during the four-year period prior to the date the agency issues specific RIF notices, or the date the agency freezes ratings before issuing RIF notices. The amount of extra credit is:

—20 additional years for an "outstanding" rating;

—16 additional years for an "exceeds fully successful" rating;

—12 additional years for a "fully successful" rating.

No additional service credit is given for performance ratings below "fully successful."

RIF Procedures

Employees are released from the retention register in the inverse order of their retention standing (i.e., the employee with the lowest standing is the first individual reached for a RIF action). All employees in Group III are released before employees in Group II, and all employees in Group II are released before employees in Group I.Then within subgroups, all employees in Subgroup B are released before employees in Subgroup A, and all employees in Subgroup A are released before employees in Subgroup AD.

Any employees reached for release out of this regular order (such as under a temporary or a continuing exception in order to retain an employee with special skills) must be notified of the reasons for the exception.

Competitive service employees in Groups I or II with current performance ratings of at least "minimally successful" who are reached for release from the competitive level are entitled to an offer of assignment if they have "bump" or "retreat" rights to an available position in the same competitive area, and they would otherwise be separated by the reduction in force. The existence of an available position does not oblige an agency to offer an employee a particular position; however, it does establish the employee's right to be offered a position at the same grade of the available position

An employee with an excepted service appointment has no assignment rights under OPM's regulations. However, an agency may elect to establish its own system of RIF assignment rights for its excepted employees.

An agency is not required to offer vacant positions in a RIF, but may choose to fill all, some, or none of them. When an agency chooses to fill a vacancy with an employee affected by a RIF action, it must follow subgroup retention standing. An agency may choose to waive qualifications, except for educational requirements, in offering an employee a RIF assignment to a vacant position. An employee's right to a RIF assignment is met if the agency offers the employee a vacant position at the grade to which he or she has bump or retreat rights.

An employee who is downgraded because of a RIF is entitled to retain the same grade for two years, provided that the employee held the position for at least one year prior to the RIF, and the employee has not declined an offer of an equivalent position. After grade retention ends, the employee is eligible for indefinite pay retention. Also, an employee who is not eligible for grade retention may instead be eligible for pay retention.

Other benefits normally accruing in RIFs—each with its own set of eligibility rules—include job placement help, severance pay, unemployment insurance, early or deferred retirement, lump-sum payments of unused annual leave, and continued health and life insurance coverage.

Appeal Rights and Routes

An employee who has been separated, downgraded, or furloughed for more than 30 days by a RIF has the right to appeal to the Merit Systems

Protection Board (MSPB) if he or she believes the agency did not properly follow the RIF regulations. The appeal must be filed during the 30-day period beginning the day after the effective date of the RIF action.

The MSPB's review of an agency's action is limited to the written record, unless the MSPB determines that the facts are in dispute.

Generally, when MSPB finds that RIF rights have been violated, the Board returns employees to the status quo, including restoring the employee to the former position, potentially with back pay. However, there may be situations where that is no longer possible, due to relocated work, closed offices, and other changes occurring in the interim. In those situations, the employees are to be made as nearly whole as possible.

An employee in a bargaining unit covered by a negotiated grievance procedure that does not exclude RIF must use the negotiated grievance procedure and may not appeal the RIF action to MSPB, unless the employee alleges the action was based upon discrimination. The time limits for filing a grievance are set forth in the collective bargaining agreement.

If employees feel they have been discriminated against during a RIF, they should contact the agency EEO counselor for information on available options.

If the agency opposes your RIF appeal, it has the burden of proving that it followed the RIF procedures correctly in your case.

Practical Considerations

Steps and Options

While agency management has the discretion—in consultation with unions, where appropriate—to decide whether, where, and to what extent a RIF will be applied, there are many steps employees can take to make sure they come through the process as well as possible.

The need for early action can't be overstated. Some of the steps take some time; employees shouldn't wait until they have an actual RIF notice in their hands to take them. By that point, time will be short and many others will be trying to do the same things, clogging the process.

First, review your official papers. Examine your personnel file to make sure that all your periods of federal service are documented. This is critical because computations concerning retention rights, severance pay, voluntary early retirement, and buyouts will be computed based on this information.

Then review your position description to make sure it reflects your actual duties. Your rights and benefits as an employee in a RIF flow from the position description of record.

Also make sure that all your performance ratings from the last four years are in the records. Employees receive RIF service credit for performance based on the average of the last three ratings of record during the four-year period prior to the date the agency issues RIF notices. Obtain any missing performance appraisals from the prior four years in order to receive the full credit you are due in a RIF.

If you served in the armed forces, check your official personnel folder to ensure it contains a copy of your latest discharge papers. These papers (Form DD-214) are used to determine your entitlement to veterans' preference in a RIF.

Once you have the paperwork in order, begin to consider your personal options. It may well be that you're actually ready to leave the government but hadn't realized it until now, and an involuntary separation, with its accompanying benefits, might not be such a bad thing. Or possibly you're eligible to retire but hadn't yet seriously thought about retirement. Now may be the time to take your annuity, especially if it comes with a buyout attached.

Consider your future under the various scenarios: if you manage to ride out the RIF and stay with the agency; if you are involuntarily separated; if you voluntarily separate or retire. Each has its own good points and bad points, and different benefits apply in each situation.

If you are eligible for retirement—either under standard age and eligibility rules or under the early-out authority commonly granted during RIFs—obtain an estimate of your annuity and meet with a retirement counselor to get an explanation of your benefits. Do this even if you haven't been actively considering retirement.

If you're not eligible for retirement, explore the career assistance and job placement help that your agency has available. Finding another job might be easier (or harder) than you now think.

Regardless of your status, take time to fully review your benefit options, such as your ability to continue coverage under federally sponsored life and health insurance programs under the various scenarios. Also make sure you understand your options under the retirement Thrift Savings Plan.

Most of all, discuss the situation fully with your spouse and family. Being a step back, they may see things that are invisible to you from up close. Listen to what your colleagues at work have to say, but take their observations with a grain of salt. Each individual is different, and what makes sense for a co-worker, even one in roughly the same life situation, might not be best for you.

Also consider meeting with a financial advisor to review your money situation and help you make plans under the various scenarios. An advisor can help you figure out what tax advantages may be open to you, make projections on future income, review current and future debts, and help determine what standard of living you can expect.

Rulings Review

• Employees do not have placement rights when work is shifted to another agency if there are significant differences that prevent the new position from being a replacement for the old one. (Hayes v. Dept. of Health and Human Services, 829 F.2d 1092, Fed. Cir. 1987)

• A reduction in force is a personnel action under whistleblower protections if it is taken for reasons personal to the employee. An agency's failure to waive qualification requirements for a position in which an employee seeks to be placed during a RIF, resulting in the employee's separation, is also a personnel action. (Carter v. Dept. of the Army, 59 MSPR 531, 1993)

• RIFs are appealable despite receipt of retained grade and pay. The acceptance of a job offered at a lower grade after the employee is told that he would not be retained in his position, and with accompanying warnings about the effects of declining the position, is not voluntary and remains appealable. (Brown v. U.S. Postal Service, 58 MSPR 345, 1993)

• Where an agency collective bargaining agreement gives employees affected by a reduction in force a right to consideration for vacant positions, the Board must enforce those rights in the same manner it enforces agency regulations. (Deweese v. Tennessee Valley Authority, 35 F.3d 538, Fed. Cir. 1994)

• Where temporary positions are established after a RIF, the release of incumbent employees does not violate the bar against retaining temporary employees over permanent ones. Such actions may show that the agency did not lack work at the time of the RIF, but the agency still would be upheld if it showed the employees would not have been retained in any event. (Metger v. Navy, 68 MSPR 225,1995)

• An agency has no obligation to give a retiring employee notice of RIF appeal rights if he retired before the agency took an appealable RIF action against him. (Krizman v. Merit Systems Protection Board, 77 F.3d 434, Fed. Cir. 1996)

• An employee's acceptance of an offer of a demotion during the agency's restructuring is voluntary and beyond the MSPB's jurisdiction if the employee accepts before being notified of, or subjected to, a reduction-in-force action. (Torain v. U.S. Postal Service, 83 F.3d 1420, Fed. Cir. 1996)

• Employees who requested and accepted reassignments to positions in their local commuting area after the agency informed them that their facility would be closed were not subjected to appealable RIF actions where they were never told they would not be retained in positions at the same grade and pay. (Roche v. U.S. Postal Service, 80 F.3d 468, Fed. Cir. 1996)

• An agency is within its discretion when it sets a specific and uniform cutoff date by which employees are required to update their qualifications. The fact that the agency created a new position after that date does not entitle an employee to a chance to update his qualifications where he did not do so during the specified period. (Gregg v. Navy, 71 MSPR 127, 1996)

• An agency does not act prematurely when it separates an employee despite a continuing resolution then funding an agency; the agency does not have to wait until it runs out of funds before carrying out a RIF to stave off a deficit situation. (Cook v. Dept. of the Interior, 74 MSPR 454, 1997)

• As long as the agency had legitimate reasons to abolish positions, the RIF is proper even if performance or conduct issues involving an affected employee were a factor in the decision to carry out the RIF. (Buckler v. Federal Retirement Thrift Investment Board, 73 MSPR 476, 1997)

• Agencies may waive RIF regulations when authorized to do so under demonstration project authority. (Kohfield & Porter v. Dept. of the Navy, 75 MSPR 1, 1997)

• Although a reorganization and a reduction-in-force happened in roughly the same time frame, they were not related and an employee who lost his job in the RIF wasn't improperly denied the right to accompany a position that moved to an office in a different state during the reorganization, ruled the U.S. Court of Appeals for the Federal Circuit. (Byrnes v. Dept. of the Interior, Fed. Cir., No. 97-3097, 1997)

•The "relatively small size" of an agency branch did not disqualify it from being considered a major subdivision of the agency and a self-contained competitive area during a reduction-in-force, the U.S. Court of Appeals for the Federal Circuit decided. The court said that although government-wide rules provide only "limited guidance" as to how a competitive area is to be defined, they focus on whether the office in question "enjoys substantial independence in operation, function, and personnel." (Whitsell v. OPM, Fed. Cir., No. 97-3054, 1998)

• A reduction-in-force notice that identified ways to request additional information and identified materials that explained appeal rights constituted sufficient notice to the employee, the U.S. Court of Appeals for the Federal Circuit ruled. The court pointed out that although no one remembered whether the appeals rights attachments had been sent with the employee's notice, the notice itself specifically identified those attachments by title and also explained ways to request additional information (Flores v. Dept. of the Air Force, Fed. Cir., No. 97-3392, 1998)

• The size of an agency subunit does not determine whether or not it can be a separate competitive area during a reduction in force, nor does the authority of that subunit's head official to make appointments, the U.S. Court of Appeals for the Federal Circuit held. The court rejected an employee's argument that a competitive area was drawn too narrowly, thereby reducing the worker's job placement possibilities. (Markland v. OPM, Fed. Cir., No. 97-3249, 1998)

• An employee who accepted a lower-graded position in the face of a RIF acted voluntarily and thus does not have the right to appeal that action, the U.S. Court of Appeals for the Federal Circuit held. Since he had the chance to remain in his higher grade in the RIF, the court observed, the worker had no grounds for complaining that he had not been told he couldn't be retained at the lower grade. (Ovens v. Dept. of the Army, Fed. Cir., No. 97-3429, 1998)

• An agency need not show that it had a funds shortage at the time it issued reduction-in-force notices, only that it had a reasonable expectation of such a shortage, the U.S. Court of Appeals for the Federal Circuit held in rejecting a separated employee's argument that the agency was required to show its expenditures exceeded its income. (Wreen v. Dept. of the Army, Fed. Cir., No. 98-3078, 1998)

• Agencies have "wide discretion" in dealing with funding shortfalls, which extends to a decision not to follow reduction in force procedures but establish a placement program that resulted in an employee's removal on charges of failure to comply with a directed reassignment, said the U.S. Court of Appeals for the Federal Circuit. Finding that the decision was within the agency's discretion, the court added that an employee's recourse in such a situation is to accept the reassignment and then appeal the action. (Mears v. Dept. of Agriculture, Fed. Cir., No. 98-3137, 1998)

• A Senior Executive Service member was properly demoted to a GS-15 position during a reduction in force, the U.S. Court of Appeals for the Federal Circuit decided, rejecting the employee's argument that his agency used an improper bureau-wide, rather than department-wide, procedure for making RIF decisions. The court pointed out that "there is no language in the statute that requires that an agency conducting a RIF of SES employees adopt department-wide competitive areas." (Schmidt v. Interior, Fed. Cir., No. 97-3379, 1998

• An agency failed to justify its use of one-person competitive levels and thus improperly eliminated the job of a Census Bureau attorney during a reduction-in-force, the U.S. Court of Appeals for the Federal Circuit decided. While acknowledging that a one-person competitive level may be appropriate in certain situations, the court added "rarely will a position entail work that only the incumbent can perform without causing undue disruption to train a replacement." (Heelen v. Department of Commerce, Fed. Cir., No. 97-3413, 1998)

CHAPTER TWELVE

Veterans Protections

For more than a century, military veterans have benefited from special employment rights with the federal government as partial recompense for the sacrifices of military duty.

Veterans' preference in its present form comes from the Veterans' Preference Act of 1944, which has been amended numerous times in the succeeding years. In general, veterans who are disabled or who served on active duty in the armed forces during certain specified time periods or in military campaigns are entitled to preference over others in hiring and also to retention during reductions in force.

In addition to receiving preference in competitive appointments, veterans may be considered for special noncompetitive appointments for which only they are eligible.

The various provisions in some cases have differing definitions of who is covered, so it's important to make sure in advance that you are eligible for each of the specific rights and benefits.

Hiring

Coverage and Eligibility

Veterans' preference in hiring applies to permanent and temporary positions in the competitive and excepted services of the executive branch. Preference does not apply to positions in the Senior Executive Service or to the legislative or judicial branches unless the positions are in the competitive service.

This preference applies to hiring based on civil service examinations conducted by the Office of Personnel Management and by agencies for most excepted service jobs, including Veterans' Readjustment Appointments (VRA). It also applies when agencies make temporary, term, and overseas limited appointments. Veterans' preference does not apply to personnel actions such as a promotion, reassignment, change to lower grade, transfer, or reinstatement.

Veterans' preference does not require an agency to use any particular appointment process. Agencies have broad authority to hire from any appropriate source of eligible veterans, including special appointing authorities.

To receive preference, a veteran must have been separated from active duty with an honorable or general discharge from the Army, Navy, Air Force, Marine Corps or Coast Guard. Certain other conditions apply, however. For example, military retirees at the rank of major, lieutenant commander, or higher are not eligible for preference in appointment unless they are disabled veterans, and active duty for training or inactive duty by National Guard or Reserve soldiers does not qualify as "active duty" for preference.

Categories and Points

The following preference categories and points apply:

• *Five-Point Preference*—Five points are added to the passing examination score or rating of a veteran who served: during a war; during the period April 28, 1952 through July 1, 1955; for more than 180 consecutive days, other than for training, any part of which occurred after January 31, 1955, and before October 15, 1976; during the Gulf War from August 2, 1990, through January 2, 1992; or in a campaign or expedition for which a campaign medal was authorized. Certain restrictions apply to campaign medal holders who originally enlisted after September 7, 1980 or who began active duty on or after October 14, 1982.

• *10-Point Compensable Disability Preference*—Ten points are added to the passing examination score or rating of a veteran who served at any time and who has a compensable service-connected disability rating of at least 10 percent, but less than 30 percent.

• *10-Point 30 Percent Compensable Disability Preference*—Ten points are added to the passing examination score or rating of a veteran who served at any time and who has a compensable service-connected disability rating of 30 percent or more.

• *10-Point Disability Preference*—Ten points are added to the passing examination score or rating of a veteran who served at any time and has a present service-connected disability or is receiving compensation, disability retirement benefits, or a pension from the military or the Department of Veterans Affairs but does not qualify under the above provisions; or to a veteran who received a Purple Heart.

• *Derived Preference*—Ten points are added to the passing examination score or rating of certain spouses, widows, widowers, or mothers of veterans. Both a mother and a spouse (including widow or widower) may be entitled to preference on the basis of the same veteran's service if they both meet the requirements. However, neither may receive preference if the veteran is living and is qualified for federal employment. Ten points are added to the passing examination score or rating of a mother of a living disabled veteran under certain conditions.

Agencies are responsible for adjudicating all preference claims except claims for preference based on common-law marriage, which should be sent to the Office of Personnel Management, Office of the General Counsel, Washington, DC 20415.

How Preference Works

Names of eligible applicants are placed on lists, or registers of eligible veterans, in the order of their ratings. For scientific and professional positions in grade GS-9 or higher, names of all qualified applicants are listed on a register in order of ratings, augmented by veterans preference, if any. For all other positions, the names of 10-point preference eligible veterans who have a compensable, service-connected disability of 10 percent or more are listed at the top of the register in the order of their ratings ahead of the names of all other eligible veterans.

The names of other 10-point preference eligible veterans, five-point preference eligible veterans, and other applicants are listed in order of their numerical ratings. A preference eligible is listed ahead of a nonpreference eligible having the same final rating. After the preference lists are compiled, the following general rules apply:

• *Filling a Position from a Competitive Examination*—To fill a vacancy by selection from a competitive examination, the selecting official requests a list of eligible veterans from the examining office. The examining office must announce the competitive examination to the public and report it to OPM, which notifies the state employment service. The examining office determines which applicants are qualified, rates and ranks them based on their qualifications, and issues a certificate of eligible veterans.

Selection generally must be made from the highest three eligible veterans on the certificate who are available for the job—the "rule of three." However, an agency may not pass over a preference eligible to select a nonpreference eligible with the same or lower score.

• *Crediting Experience of Preference Eligible Veterans*—In evaluating experience, an examining office must credit a preference eligible's armed forces service as an extension of the work performed immediately prior to the service, or on the basis of the actual duties performed in the service, or as a combination of both, whichever would most benefit the preference eligible veteran.

• *Physical Qualifications*—In determining qualifications, agencies must waive a medical standard or physical requirement when there is sufficient evidence that the employee or applicant, with or without reasonable accommodation, can perform the essential duties of the position without endangering the health and safety of the individual or others.

• *Disqualification of Preference Eligible Veterans*—A preference eligible veteran can be eliminated from consideration only if the examining office sustains the agency's objection to the preference eligible for adequate reason. These reasons include medical disqualification, suitability disqualification, or other reasons considered by OPM or an agency under delegated examining authority to be disqualifying. Special provisions apply to disabled veterans with a compensable service-connected disability of 30 percent or more.

• *Nepotism*—Nepotism rules do not prohibit the appointment of a preference eligible veteran whose name is within reach for selection on an appropriate certificate of eligible veterans when an alternative selection cannot be made without passing over the eligible veteran and selecting an individual who is not preference eligible.

• *Excepted Service Employment*—The Veterans' Preference Act requires an appointing authority in the executive branch to select from among qualified applicants for appointment to excepted service vacancies in the same manner and under the same conditions required for the competitive service.

• *Reserved Positions*—Appointments to positions of guards, elevator operators, messengers, and custodians are restricted to preference eligible veterans when they are available.

• *Enforcement*—OPM enforces policies on veterans' preference in the competitive service while individual agencies are generally responsible for enforcement of preference rights in the excepted service.

VRA Appointments

Under Veterans Readjustment Appointment authority, agencies can appoint eligible veterans without competition to positions at any grade level through GS-11 or equivalent. VRA appointees are hired under excepted appointments to positions that are otherwise in the competitive service. After two years of satisfactory service, the agency must convert the veteran to career or career-conditional appointment.

To be eligible for a VRA appointment, a veteran must: have served in the armed forces on active duty (not active duty for training or inactive duty as a Reservist) for more than 180 days, any part of which occurred after August 4, 1964 (or February 28, 1961, for those who actually served in the Republic of Vietnam) and received other than a dishonorable discharge.

The 180-day requirement does not apply to veterans who were discharged or released from active duty because of a service-connected disability, or members of the Reserve or National Guard ordered to active duty for war or a campaign or expedition for which a campaign badge is authorized.

Military service is considered qualifying for positions at GS-3 and below. For higher positions, the appointee must meet the qualification requirements, but the agency may waive any written test requirement. If a test is required, a designated agency examiner may administer the test noncompetitively.

In general, veterans must apply within 10 years of their last discharge or separation, although no time limits apply to a veteran with a 30 percent or more service-connected disability.

Ordinarily, an agency may simply appoint any VRA eligible who meets the qualifications for the position without having to announce the job or rate and rank applicants. However, if an agency has two or more VRA candidates and one or more is a preference eligible, the agency must apply veterans' preference. An agency must consider all VRA candidates on file who are qualified for the position and could reasonably expect to be considered for the opportunity.

A VRA appointee may be promoted, demoted, reassigned, or transferred in the same way as a career employee. The time in grade requirement applies to the promotion of VRAs. If a VRA-eligible employee is qualified for a higher grade, an agency may, at its discretion, give the employee a new VRA appointment at a higher grade up through GS-11 (or equivalent) without regard to time in grade.

Agencies must establish a training or education program for any VRA appointee who has less than 15 years of education. This program should meet the needs of both the agency and the employee.

Agencies may make a noncompetitive temporary or term appointment based on an individual's eligibility for VRA appointment. The temporary or term appointment must be at the grades authorized for VRA appointment but is not a VRA appointment itself and does not lead to conversion to career-conditional.

Special Authority for Disabled Veterans

An agency may give a noncompetitive temporary appointment of more than 60 days or a term appointment to any veteran retired from active military service with a disability rating of 30 percent or more or who is rated by the Department of Veterans Affairs within the preceding year as having a compensable service-connected disability of 30 percent or more.

There is no grade level limitation for this authority, but the appointee must meet all qualification requirements, including any written test requirement. The agency may convert the employee, without a break in service, to a career or career-conditional appointment at any time during the employee's temporary or term appointment.

Further, disabled veterans eligible for training under the VA vocational rehabilitation program may enroll for training or work experience at an agency under the terms of an agreement between the agency and VA. While enrolled in the VA program, the veteran is not a federal employee for most purposes.

If the training is intended to prepare the individual for eventual appointment in the agency rather than just provide work experience, the agency must ensure that the training will enable the veteran to meet the qualification requirements for the position.

Upon successful completion, the host agency and VA will give the veteran a certificate of training showing the occupational series and grade level of the position for which trained. The certificate allows any agency to appoint the veteran noncompetitively under a status quo appointment, which may be converted to career or career-conditional at any time.

RIFs and Job Restorations

RIF Rights and Protections

Veterans have certain advantages over nonveterans in a reduction in force (RIF). Also, special provisions apply in determining whether retired military members receive preference in RIFs and whether their military service is counted. Certain special rules apply to the excepted service.

Eligibility standards for veterans preference in RIFs generally are the same as those for appointments (other than a Veterans Readjustment Authority appointment.) However, to be considered a preference eligible, a retired member of a uniformed service must meet additional conditions that vary depending on the rank at which the individual retired from the uniformed service.

During RIFs, employees are ranked on retention registers for competitive levels based on tenure, veterans' preference, length of service, and performance. Within each tenure group, they are placed in a subgroup based on their veteran status: subgroup AD, those with a compensable service-connected disability of 30 percent or more; subgroup A, all other preference eligible veterans not in subgroup AD; or subgroup B, all employees not eligible for veterans' preference. Within each subgroup, employees are ranked in descending order by the length of their creditable federal civilian and military service, augmented by additional service according to the level of their performance ratings.

Because veterans are listed ahead of nonveterans within each tenure group, they often are the last to be affected by a RIF action.

Employees are not subject to a reduction in force while they are serving in the uniformed services and also have some protections after return from active duty. If they served for more than 180 days, they may not be separated by RIF for one year after their return. If they served for more than 30 but less than 181 days, they may not be separated by RIF for six months.

The superior standing of preference eligible veterans also gives them an advantage in being retained over other employees when bumping and retreating take place in a RIF. Also, while in general employees may retreat to a position no more than three grades or grade intervals lower than the positions from which they are released, a preference eligible with a compensable service-connected disability of 30 percent or more may retreat to a position up to five grades or grade intervals lower.

In reviewing the qualifications of a preference eligible to determine assignment rights in a RIF, the agency must waive physical qualification requirements as noted earlier. If the veteran involved has a 30 percent or more compensable disability, additional obligations apply. OPM must approve the sufficiency of the agency's reasons to medically disqualify a 30 percent or more compensably disabled veteran for assignment to another position in a RIF.

After a RIF, separated competitive service employees are listed on the agency's reemployment priority list. The agency generally may not hire from most outside sources when qualified employees are on the list. In hiring from the list, preference eligible veterans receive preference over other employees.

Job Restoration after Military Service

An employee, permanent or temporary, in an executive agency or the U.S. Postal Service who performs duty with a uniformed service generally is entitled to be restored to the position he or she would have attained had the employee not entered the uniformed service. This policy applies to active duty, active duty for training or inactive duty training service, whether voluntary or involuntary, provided the employee was released from the service under honorable conditions and served no more than a cumulative total of five years.

Employees in the intelligence agencies have substantially the same rights, but are covered under agency regulations and have different appeal rights.

While on duty with the uniformed services, the employee must be carried on leave without pay unless he or she requests separation. A separation under these circumstances does not affect restoration rights. Agencies must tell employees who enter the service about their entitlements, obligations, benefits, and appeal rights.

Agencies may not question the timing, frequency, duration, or nature of the uniformed service, but employees are obligated to try to minimize the agency's burden by giving their employer as much advance written notice as possible of any pending military duty.

Employees who served in the uniformed services less than 31 days (or who leave to take a fitness exam for service) must report back to work at the beginning of the next regularly scheduled work day after their completion of service and time for travel home. Those who served more than 30 but less than 181 days must apply for reemployment no later than 14 days after completion of service. Those who served more than 180 days have 90 days after completion of service to apply for restoration.

Agencies must reemploy them as soon as practicable, but no later than 30 days after receiving the application. Agencies have the right to ask for documentation showing the length and character of the employee's service and the timeliness of the application. In addition, the following general rules apply:

• *Positions to Which Restored*— Employees who served less than 91 days must be placed in the position for which qualified that they would have attained had their employment not been interrupted. If not qualified for such position after reasonable efforts by the agency to qualify the person, the employee is entitled to be placed in the position he or she left. Employees who served more than 90 days have essentially the same rights, except that the agency has the option of placing the employee in a position for which qualified of like seniority, status, and pay.

Employees with service-connected disabilities who are not qualified for the above must be reemployed in a position that most closely approximates the position they would have been entitled to, consistent with the circumstances in each case.

Employees who were under time-limited appointments finish the unexpired portion of their appointments upon their return.

• *Service Credit*—Upon restoration, employees are generally treated as though they had never left. This means that time spent in the uniformed services counts for seniority, within-grade increases, completion of probation, career tenure, retirement, and leave accrual. Employees do not earn sick or annual leave while off the rolls or in a nonpay status.

To receive civil service retirement credit for military service time, a deposit to the retirement fund usually is required. Only active, honorable military service is creditable for retirement purposes. The deposit normally is 7 percent of military basic pay (plus interest under certain conditions) for those under the Civil Service Retirement System and 3 percent for those under the Federal Employees Retire-ment System. However, these amounts may differ under certain circumstances.

• *OPM Placement*—If the employing agency is unable to reemploy an individual returning from duty with a uniformed service, OPM will order placement in another agency when: OPM determines that it is impossible or unreasonable for an agency in the executive branch (other than an intelligence agency) to reemploy the person; or an intelligence agency or an agency in the legislative or judicial branch notifies OPM that it is impossible or unreasonable to reemploy the person, and the person applies to OPM for placement assistance; or a noncareer National Guard technician who is not eligible for continued membership in the Guard for reasons beyond his or her control applies to OPM for placement assistance.

• *Employee Protections*—Employees are not subject to a reduction in force while they are serving in the uniformed services. Discrimination or reprisal against an applicant or employee because of his or her service in the uniformed services is prohibited.

Employees serving on active duty also are eligible for other benefits including paid military leave, continued federal health and life insurance coverage, and the opportunity to make up for contributions to the retirement thrift savings plan they missed because of their service.

Appeal Rights and Routes

Procedure Depends on Complaint

Appeal rights of preference eligible veterans vary according to the action being appealed.

• *Adverse Actions*—Preference eligible veterans have protections against adverse actions, including demotion, suspension for more than 14 days, furlough for 30 days or less, and removal. These protections include advance notice, a reasonable time to respond, representation by an attorney or other person, a final written decision, and an appeal right to the Merit Systems Protection Board.

The law provides adverse action rights to preference eligible veterans of any rank who are: under career or career-conditional appointment and not serving probation; under competitive service appointments other than a temporary appointment not to exceed one year or less and who have completed one year of continuous service; or under excepted appointment in an executive agency, the U.S. Postal Service, or the Postal Rate Commission and who have completed one year of current continuous service in the same or similar positions. The law exempts certain categories of excepted employees.

• **Reductions in Force**—An employee who has been furloughed, separated, or demoted by RIF action has the right to appeal the action to MSPB except when a negotiated procedure must be used. Assignment to a position at the employee's same grade or representative rate is not appealable. Appeals must be filed during the period beginning on the day after the effective date of the RIF action and ending 30 days after the effective date. Time limits for filing a grievance under a negotiated procedure are contained in the negotiated agreement.

• **Restoration after Uniformed Service**—Applicants or employees who believe that an agency has not complied with the law or with OPM regulations governing the restoration rights of employees who perform duty with the uniformed services may file a complaint with the Department of Labor's local Veterans' Employment and Training Service office or appeal directly to MSPB.

If a complaint is filed with the DOL, a representative will attempt to resolve the complaint with the agency. Employees who are not satisfied can ask the representative to present the case to the director of the local OPM service center, who will decide the issue on its merits and notify all parties within 30 days. Those dissatisfied with that decision have 20 days to ask for final review at a higher level of OPM.

• **Prohibited Personnel Practices**—It is illegal to take, direct, recommend, or approve a personnel action, or fail to do so, if the action violates veterans' preference. A person who believes a prohibited personnel practice has occurred may file a complaint with the Office of Special Counsel.

A veteran who believes his or her rights or benefits were denied may present a complaint to the local OPM service center or to the OPM Office of Merit Systems Oversight and Effectiveness, Washington, DC 20415. This is in addition to the individual's formal appeal rights.

• **VRA Appointees**—During their first year of employment, VRA appointees have the same limited appeal rights as competitive service probationers, but otherwise they have the appeal rights of excepted service employees. This means that VRA employees who are preference eligible veterans have adverse action protections after one year. VRA appointees who are not preference eligible veterans do not get this protection until they have completed two years of current continuous employment in the same or similar position.

Veterans Groups

• **American Ex-Prisoners of War,** National headquarters, 3201 E. Pioneer Parkway, Suite 40, Arlington, TX 76010-5396. Phone (817) 649-2979, Fax (817) 649-0109, Clydie J. Morgan, Nat. Adjutant, Internet: *www.axpow.com*

• **American Legion, National Economic Commission.** 1608 K Street, NW, Washington, DC 20006. Phone (202) 861-2700. Internet: *www.legion.org*

• **AMVETS.** National Hqs. 4647 Forbes Boulevard, Lanham, MD 20706-4380. David E. Woodbury, Exec. Dir. National Executive Director. Phone (301) 459-9600, Fax (301) 459-7924. Internet: *www.amvets. org*

• **Blinded Veterans Association (BVA).** 477 H Street, NW, Washington, DC 20001. Thomas Miller, Exec. Dir. Phone (800) 669-7079, (202) 371-8880. E-mail: *bva@bva.org*

• **Catholic War Veterans, USA, Inc.** 441 North Lee Street, Alexandria, VA 22314. Phone (703) 549-3622, Fax (703) 684-5196.

• **Disabled American Veterans.** National Service & Legislative Headquarters, 807 Maine Avenue, SW, Washington, DC 20024. Arthur H. Wilson, Natl. Adjt. Phone (202) 554-3501 Internet: *www.dav.org*

• **Jewish War Veterans of the USA.** 1811 R Street, NW, Washington, DC 20009. Phone (202) 265-6280. Internet: *www.penfed.org/jwv/home.htm*

• **Military Order of the Purple Heart.** 5413-B Backlick Rd., Springfield, VA 22151. Phone (703) 642-5360, Fax (703) 642-2054. Internet: *www. purpleheart.org*

• **National Association for Uniformed Services/Society of Military Widows.** 5535 Hempstead Way, Springfield, VA 22151. Maj. Gen. Richard D. Murray, USAF (Ret.) Pres.; Phone (703) 750-1342. Internet: *www.naus.org*

• **Paralyzed Veterans of America.** 801 18th Street, NW, Washington, DC 20006. Gordon Mansfield, Exec. Dir. Phone (800) 424-8200.

• **U.S. Navy Cruiser Sailors Association.** 55 Donna Terrace, Taunton, MA 02780. Ronald J. Maciejowski, (U.S.S. Worcester CL-144) Sec. Phone (508) 824-0789.

• **Veterans of Foreign Wars.** 200 Maryland Avenue, NE, Washington, DC 20002. William Smith, Dir. of Public Affairs. Phone (202) 543-2239. Internet: *www.vfw.org*

Part 2

Dispute
and Appeal
Processes

CHAPTER THIRTEEN

Grievances

Grievances are a means of resolving workplace disputes outside the formal appeals channels established by administrative agencies like the Merit Systems Protection Board. Although the term "grievance" is most commonly associated with unionized settings, a federal employee need not belong to a union bargaining unit to be covered by a grievance procedure. Another category of grievances involves an administrative grievance procedure—a nonunion dispute-resolution channel available in most agencies.

Each type of grievance system has its own eligibility rules, scope of coverage, and required steps or procedures. Also, grievance procedures vary from agency to agency and even sometimes from site to site. That's because agencies have great discretion over use of their administrative grievance procedures, and negotiated grievance procedures vary widely among the several thousand federal-sector contracts now in effect between management and unions. The following information lays out the general principles that tend to govern each type of system; be sure to check agency policies and any applicable contracts for specifics.

—— Administrative Grievance Procedures ——

System Basics

Agency administrative grievance systems are designed to provide a forum for internal review and resolution of employment-related disputes and issues. Agencies always have had a great deal of latitude in the design of their programs. Until 1995, the Office of Personnel Management oversaw these types of grievance programs and issued centralized rules for carrying them out. In that year, however, OPM abolished its controls, leaving it fully up to individual agencies to set up and run their own administrative grievance systems.

While agency programs generally follow the outlines of the old centralized rules, agencies are free to modify or even eliminate procedures depending on their needs. One common change has been to incorporate a greater use of alternative dispute resolution techniques into the administrative grievance process.

Agencies commonly try to settle administrative grievances filed by employees. Settlements can occur at any stage of the process.

Rights to file an administrative grievance usually apply regardless of a worker's appointment status (e.g., competitive or excepted service, temporary or career) and normally are available only to employees who are not in union bargaining units. However, bargaining unit workers are allowed to use administrative grievance procedures where there is no contract or if the contract excludes the matter at hand. Also, bargaining unit employees in some places are covered by the administrative grievance procedure by virtue of an agreement of both management and labor.

Types of employees commonly excluded from coverage of these systems include noncitizens appointed to civil service jobs under various authorities, "Title 38" medical personnel, members of the foreign service who are covered by the foreign service grievance system, and other employee categories that the agency deems appropriate to exclude.

Also, the intelligence and law enforcement agencies, as well as government corporations, including the U.S. Postal Service, normally do not provide formal administrative grievance procedures or offer only highly restricted ones (in the postal service, the large majority of employees are covered by negotiated grievance procedures).

Administrative grievance procedures may be available to former employees if a remedy can be granted to them that is consistent with law.

Issues Covered

Common examples of issues posed in administrative grievances include unwanted reassignments, challenges to performance ratings, challenges to the application of the agency's staffing policies, denial of training requests, and minor disciplinary matters not appealable under other systems.

Standard exceptions to administrative grievance coverage are: matters not subject to the control of agency management, such as standard salary and benefit levels; the content of established agency regulations and policy; a matter on which the employee is entitled to file a grievance under a negotiated procedure or an

appeal to an appeals agency; nonselection for promotion or failure to receive a noncompetitive promotion; a preliminary warning notice of an action which, if taken, would be covered under the grievance system; the performance evaluation, job rating, or other action taken with respect to a senior executive service member; the substance of performance standards and/or statements of work objectives; the granting of, or failure to grant, various awards or pay or bonuses under merit pay systems or the SES evaluation system; the payment or failure to pay a recruitment or relocation bonus, retention allowance, or supervisory differential; the failure to request or grant an exception to dual compensation restrictions; and the termination of a time-limited excepted appointment and other limited appointments.

Because of the wide discretion agencies have over their administrative grievances, employees should check their own agency's policies to see if they are eligible to bring such a complaint in a given situation and if so, what they must do. This information can be found in agency policy statements and regulations, or in less formal materials such as pamphlets and brochures. Normally this information is available at personnel offices.

Typical Features

In general, an administrative grievance procedure is designed to give employees a reasonable opportunity to present the matter and receive fair consideration. This may or may not involve formal hearings or other means of obtaining and assessing information pertaining to the dispute at hand.

Common elements of administrative grievance programs are:

• Employees are guaranteed a reasonable processing time, freedom from restraint or reprisal, the right to be represented, and the right to official time to present the grievance, both for themselves and their representative (if they are used and are employed by the agency). Entitlement to official time generally applies only if the individuals involved would otherwise have been on duty, and normally does not apply to time spent preparing a grievance.

• There usually is some type of fact-finding process, although agencies have discretion over how to use fact-finding procedures, both in general as well as in a given case. If a fact-finder is used, that person normally is not someone who has been involved in the grievance. Fact-finders may hold hearings, informal discussions, or group meetings, and may have the authority to make or recommend a decision or merely determine the facts behind a dispute.

• Employees generally may bring grievances either as individuals or as members of a group. In some cases, similar grievances by several employees may be combined by management in order to have one decision rendered. An agency may set additional standards for accepting and processing group grievances—requiring, for example, that all members of a group be part of the same organizational unit.

The process of pursuing an administrative grievance varies greatly from one agency to the next. In general, an employee must comply with appropriate time limits, furnish sufficient detail to identify the matter being grieved, and specify the relief being requested. Relief can only be personal and cannot involve a request for discipline or other action against another employee or manager.

Agencies may impose specific time frames for various steps that must be observed both by the employee bringing a grievance and by the agency officials responsible for deciding it. Normally, if an employee submits a grievance in writing, a written file will be kept and a written decision will be issued that will include a report of the findings and the reasons for the decision. Often, agencies will keep written files and will issue written decisions on oral grievances as well.

The decision usually must be made by either an official at a higher organizational level than any employee involved in the grievance or by a designated official, such as a fact-finder, who is authorized to make a final decision. Generally, an official who previously was involved in the matter may not be the decision-maker.

The agency's decision is final. There is no further review procedure available for parties that are unhappy with the results of an administrative grievance. However, pursuing an administrative grievance normally does not remove an individual's option to challenge an agency action through other routes.

Negotiated Grievance Procedures

System Basics

The right to use a union grievance procedure is limited to employees covered by the contract. Thus, an employee must be part of a local's bargaining unit to take advantage of the protections under a negotiated grievance procedure.

The coverage of the contract applies on the basis of bargaining unit membership, not dues-paying status.

So does the duty of the union to represent an employee. Thus, many federal employees are eligible to use negotiated grievance procedures, even though they are unaware of it. Some workers mistakenly believe they must be dues-paying union members to be eligible for grievance rights, while others are unaware that they even are in a bargaining unit.

Although about 60 percent of executive branch employees are in bargaining units, a much smaller percentage typically pay union dues—the average is about 20-25 percent of unit employees, although there is wide variation. In the U.S. Postal Service, on the other hand, about 90 percent of employees are covered by bargaining units, and more than 90 percent of those workers are dues-paying members.

Unless the contract specifically prohibits it, former employees of a unit whose claims were grievable when they arose continue to have access to negotiated grievance procedures.

Unlike most forms of personnel appeals, a negotiated grievance is most commonly brought by someone other than the individual directly affected. Employees covered by such procedures do have the right to bring such complaints on their own, without the support or involvement of the union. More often, though, negotiated grievances are brought by the union—often a steward or other local official—rather than by an individual employee.

There are many reasons for this. Unions take seriously their duty—and opportunity—to represent employees in negotiated grievances, which are a main vehicle for the union to carry out its rights and obligations under its contract. The union also may view a given individual's situation as a potential precedent for other bargaining unit members and thus may want to get an agency practice stopped or changed quickly. From the individual's viewpoint, union representation provides a depth of experience and resources that go beyond the reach of most individuals—not to mention potential savings in out-of-pocket expenses from hiring a representative.

Often, a decision to file a grievance under a negotiated procedure forecloses an employee's option of challenging the same action through other routes, such as the Merit Systems Protection Board. However, the rules in this area can be complicated and vary according to the employee's career status, the nature of the dispute, and the employing agency. Employees should make sure they know the potential consequences of filing a grievance on any other appeal rights they may possess.

Grievances also may be filed by management against a union, although not against an individual.

Scope and Steps

The Civil Service Reform Act was in part designed to encourage union involvement in the federal government. Thus, its definition of what may be grieved under a negotiated contract is broad. It allows grievances on any matter relating to the employment of workers, any claimed violation, misinterpretation, or misapplication of a law or regulation affecting conditions of employment, or any claimed breach of a collective bargaining agreement.

Specific exceptions are: prohibited personnel practices; retirement and insurance disputes; suspensions or removals for national security reasons; any examination, certification, or appointment; and the classification of any position that does not result in an employee's reduction in pay or grade.

Under the Reform Act, contracts must provide for negotiated grievance procedures, ending in a binding arbitration step. But there is a wide variety in what negotiated grievance procedures actually cover, since contracts differ depending on what unions and management have bargained for in various agencies and sites. Normally, applicable contracts can be viewed at the agency's labor relations office or the union local's office.

The first step in the typical negotiated grievance process calls for a meeting between the employee and a local union representative. The union official may interview the employee—as well as others—in an effort to gather facts and other pertinent information. This may require that the employee sign a complaint form and grant permission for the union to see personnel records that otherwise would be unavailable.

At that point, the union may decide not to pursue the matter. If so, employees generally have the right to continue on their own. In such situations, however, the union has the right to send a representative to any grievance proceeding.

Most grievances proceed through several steps, each of which tends to be more formal than the last. Depending on how many levels are available, the process can take from several days to several months.

A typical early step might involve a simple oral or written presentation to the employee's immediate supervisor. From there the matter might be taken to a higher level management representative—often a second-level supervisor—and at this stage, a written presentation of the grievance usually is required. A possible further step is to raise the issue with a still higher agency official, such as a senior manager or executive. In these later stages, other agency employees may be called on to appear as witnesses.

At these meetings, usually the union representative (or in some cases, the employee) will present the worker's case, citing facts and the union's interpretation of laws, rules, and the contract. The matter might be settled on the spot, or management might opt to respond formally within a specified time frame.

If management's position remains unacceptable in the union's eyes, binding arbitration can be invoked. The arbitrator will be chosen from a list provided by organizations such as the American Arbitration Association or the Federal Mediation and Conciliation Service. The arbitrator will issue a decision that contains findings of fact and law, and will order a remedy if a violation is found. The remedy could include canceling the personnel decision that led to the grievance, with an award of back pay and benefits where appropriate, or otherwise reversing or mitigating manage-ment's decision in some way.

Only the union or the agency can invoke arbitration and only they can appeal the arbitrator's decision to the Federal Labor Relations Authority. This is done by filing "exceptions" to the decision within 30 days. FLRA's decision can in turn be appealed to the regional U.S. Court of Appeals, but only if an unfair labor practice is involved.

Procedural Pointers

Keep in mind that the union can back out of the case at any point. Unions sometimes stop short of invoking arbitration out of concern for the dollar and time costs involved and the potential consequences of a negative decision on the union or on other grievances involving similar issues. Also, the union might decide that the employee would fare better in another forum and try to end the case before it proceeds far enough that the employee loses the right to appeal elsewhere. Generally decisions to not pursue—or stop pursuing—a case are made at the union's local level.

Some unions have formal procedures for justifying those decisions to the employee. For example, the union might set up a meeting between the grieving employee and the steward or other union officials to discuss the findings of the union's investigation and applicable case precedents. In such cases, the employee might have the right to a review of the decision by the union's chief steward, executive board, or other leadership.

If the union ends its involvement, the employee can continue pursuing the grievance (although an individual cannot invoke arbitration). Those dissatisfied with their union representation can file an unfair labor practice complaint with FLRA. Generally, in such cases, employees must prove that the union's decision was arbitrary, discriminatory, or in bad faith.

Mediation and other forms of alternative dispute resolution might be used during the grievance process. These techniques are especially common where labor and management have formed a partnership or other cooperative arrangements.

CHAPTER FOURTEEN

Settlement Agreements

In recent years, it has become more and more common for employees and agencies to negotiate a settlement of their disputes, rather than pursue them all the way through a formal appeals procedure. Each of the major appeals agencies has programs in place that are designed to encourage settlement discussions and agreements.

For both sides, settling a case holds the promise of several potential benefits. First and foremost, the time, cost, and energy (for everyone involved) of pursuing a formal appeals procedure is saved. These savings can be significant. Moreover, another potential savings comes in the form of salvaging whatever may still exist in terms of a positive relationship between the employee and the supervisor or the agency in general. Pushing a dispute through the formal process almost always produces long-term hard feelings, no matter what the result.

It's also important to remember that many employees who win formal appeals find themselves back at the same desk, still working for the same person who proposed the action that was overturned. While perhaps legal points have been scored in the formal appeals process, in the aftermath, relations between the two sides usually are strained or tense—or worse—often permanently. The employee might find that a formal victory is a costly one, which results in retention of the job but reduced, or nonexistent, chances for advancement.

Advantages of Settlements

Potential Sources of Satisfaction

Settlements of job disputes typically reduce the level of ill feelings inherent in most disagreements. Supervisors often are eager to settle because defending a formal action requires setting aside other job duties, putting together documentation, meeting with agency lawyers, being responsible for an unbudgeted expense, and other difficulties. Many supervisors also believe the agency doesn't fully support their positions in formal appeals, which usually increases their willingness to settle rather than "go to the mats."

For both sides, settlements reduce the risk of coming out on the "losing" end. Despite what employees or the agency might believe going into an appeal, there is seldom anything resembling a "guaranteed victory" that comes before an appellate agency. Even a quick review of case history will reveal a long path in which both sides ended up losing cases they fully expected to win due to an unnoticed provision of the law, an error in following required procedures, a missing or inaccessible key document, unexpected testimony from a witness, or any of a number of similar "surprises."

Many an employee has rejected an offer of "half a loaf"—or more—in settlement discussions, pushed the case through to the end, and wound up not only with nothing from the agency, but also a large legal bill and months or years of wasted time and effort. Likewise, many a supervisor has found that a decision committing the agency to fight to the end produced costly, disruptive, embarrassing, and even career-limiting results.

Another advantage of settlements is that they enable parties to decide what issues are most important to them and what solutions they can live with, rather than having a remedy imposed by an appellate agency, arbitrator or court. This flexibility may allow them to craft solutions that would be outside the normal authority of a formal appeals channel to impose. (However, settlement agreements cannot make employees eligible for benefits for which they are not otherwise entitled by law.)

Settlements require a willingness by both sides to cooperate and meet each other, if not exactly halfway, then somewhere between the positions they hold going in. The earlier that settlement talks begin, the more likely they are to produce a compromise. While settlements can be reached at any stage, including as far down the process as awaiting a decision by the full Merit Systems Protection Board, once a dispute gets rolling through the legal process, it can be difficult to stop.

Because they are talks designed to achieve a compromise, settlement discussions often end up focusing on a course of action that neither side anticipated going in. Thus, a certain amount of flexibility—and creativity— is a big boost to the process.

Contract and Compromise

A settlement creates an enforceable contract between the employee and the employing agency. In a settlement, sides commit themselves to a course of action. The penalty for failing to follow that course might be spelled out in the agreement, or the other side's original position might be imposed. A reviewing or enforcing court or agency will weigh any alleged breaches of such an agreement under principles of contract law, rather than under the laws commonly governing federal employee appeal rights. Settlements are one of the few situations where federal employment creates an enforceable contract between an individual and the government.

Often a settlement's compromise calls for cancellation or suspension of an agency's proposed disciplinary action, but usually only with certain conditions attached—for example, the employee must meet strict requirements on productivity, attendance, or other standards that were the basis of the proposed discipline. In return, the agency also might promise to provide certain types of training or other accommodations, and such agreements frequently provide for removal from the employee's records of any references to the issue, either immediately or after a certain time period.

A subcategory of settlement agreements is the "last-chance agreement," whose name is self-explanatory: the settlement represents the last chance provided the employee to stave off serious discipline, which usually is specified as removal. Once such an agreement becomes effective, infractions that otherwise might be considered minor and be dealt with leniently, if standing alone, could trigger maximum penalties if the employee is viewed as failing to live up to the settlement's terms.

Additional Benefits

Sometimes both sides see that the agency's position is so strong that it almost assuredly would result in management's winning an appeal. Even in such cases, employees might profit from entering into settlement discussions. For example, a worker might be allowed to resign voluntarily rather than being removed, and the agency might promise either to purge the employee's records of information on the proposed removal, or at least agree not to provide any negative information to a potential future employer.

It works in the other direction as well. Management might come to realize that it "overreached" in its proposed disciplinary action and might wish to reduce a proposed penalty to one that it believes would be upheld as reasonable if appealed. A settlement could allow management to meet its goal of putting employees on notice that their performance or conduct is unacceptable while laying the groundwork for possible severe action in the future if an individual doesn't improve.

Possible Reservations

This is not to say that a settlement is the best course of action in all cases. Either side might consider it preferable or more advantageous to go through the full appeals process—even at the risk of losing—than accept the terms that the other side insists upon. Management might be concerned about damage to workplace morale—or even accomplishment of the agency's mission—if a settlement would result in the continued employment of someone the agency—and possibly co-workers—considers incompetent or disruptive.

In some cases, employees also might have legitimate reasons not to agree to a settlement. Some charges are indeed worth fighting, especially if they would unfairly create a paper trail that could make it difficult to gain future employment with the government—or anywhere else, for that matter. Many settlement agreements require that employees give up their appeal rights in the matter. Since access to various appeal rights is one of the advantages a federal job has over other types of employment, an individual might be well-advised to think hard before agreeing to such a provision.

Also, a settlement agreement calling for the cancellation of an agency action does not necessarily require the award of back pay and benefits. In contrast, such compensation could be awarded if the employee successfully challenged the action, and gained court or agency agreement that the disciplinary action should be canceled.

Breaches of Agreement

When a settlement is reached and an appeal already has been filed, the appeal normally is withdrawn and can only be reinstated if the agency breaches the agreement. Waivers of appeal rights can be overturned if the employee proves that the agency failed to comply with a material provision of the agreement—regardless of the agency's motive (i.e., regardless of whether the agency was acting in good faith or arbitrarily or capriciously).

The party asserting a breach of a settlement agreement has the burden of proving such a claim. It is not necessary to show that a prohibited personnel practice occurred to prove that a settlement was breached. Instead, employees must show that the agency's actions amounted to an unjustified and substantial deprivation of their rights as the incumbent of the position. In such cases, allegations of harassment and retaliation may be relevant to a decision on whether the agency complied in good faith with a settlement's terms.

If a settlement is breached, the party that did not breach the agreement has the option of going forward with the original claim. This might arise, for example, if an agreement calls for the employee to resign, but the worker subsequently refuses to tender a resignation. In such a case, the agency could go ahead with a proposed removal on grounds that the agreement constituted the employee's resignation.

Settlement agreements can be disavowed, although such circumstances are rare. The parties generally are bound to what they put in writing, except in rare circumstances. For example, an employee might be able to show that the parties never fully agreed on the meaning of the terms of the agreement. In such a situation, even if the agency was complying with the actual written terms of the agreement, a court or reviewing agency may find that the settlement agreement should be invalidated because there was a mutual mistake as to what each side promised to do.

Similarly, there also have been cases where workers were found innocent of breaching a settlement agreement because of their confusion about exactly what the agreement meant or required them to do.

Rulings Review

• An agreement that provides that it is a full and final settlement of all matters in the appeal constitutes a waiver of the right to move for payment of attorneys' fees. (Paderick v. Office of Personnel Management, 54 MSPR 456, 1992)

• An employee who claimed that he lost another job because the agency breached an agreement by responding improperly to an employment inquiry must show that he otherwise would have secured that employment. (Holmes v. Dept. of Veterans Affairs, 57 MSPR 115, 1993)

• Where a settlement agreement specifies that all information pertaining to the dispute will be expunged, the agency may not keep a "paper trail" of documents showing the proposed action and its termination. (Dial v. Dept. of the Army, 56 MSPR 617, 1993)

• The parties' conduct after they enter into an agreement may be relevant to an interpretation of the terms of the agreement, and the terms of a second agreement would be highly relevant to the interpretation of the first, where both deal with the same general topic and there was no indication of any intent to modify the first agreement. (McDavid v. Army, 58 MSPR 673, 1993)

• A claim of coercion by one's own representative provides no basis for overturning a settlement that is otherwise fair. Nor does an employee's failure to fully understand the agreement render it involuntary. (Jackson v. Army, 59 MSPR 242, 1993)

• The Merit Systems Protection Board lacks jurisdiction over an otherwise appealable suspension imposed under a settlement agreement because in that case the suspension is a voluntary action, unless there is language in the agreement specifically preserving a right to appeal to the Board. (Mays v. U.S. Postal Service, 995 F.2d 1056, Fed. Cir. 1993)

• Because the Back Pay Act sets a limit on back pay for all federal employment cases to which it applies, a settlement agreement may not go beyond that law's provisions for back pay. (Stipp v. Dept. of the Army, 61 MSPR 415, 1994)

• A party may challenge the validity of a settlement before the Merit Systems Protection Board, even if it is not entered into the record for enforcement. (Wade v. Dept. of Veterans Affairs, 61 MSPR 580, 1994)

• A discrimination allegation in a petition for enforcement of a settlement agreement does not establish mixed case status, and mixed case appeal rights do not apply in such a case. (King v. Reid, 59 F.3d 1215, Fed. Cir. 1995)

• An agency breaches a settlement agreement when it fails to comply with any material provision. When a material breach is shown, the Merit Systems Protection Board may not enforce any waiver of appeal rights contained in the agreement. (Link v. Department of the Treasury, 51 F.3d 1577, Fed. Cir. 1995)

• It is not necessary to show a prohibited personnel action in order to establish a breach of contract by the agency. The employee must show that the agency's actions amounted to an unjustified and substantial deprivation of his or her rights. (Kuykendall v. DVA, 68 MSPR 314, 1995)

• A settlement should be construed to give effect to all of its terms and should be read in context. The breach of a settlement term is not material if it would not significantly deprive a party of the benefit it reasonably expected from the agreement, and such a breach would provide no basis on which to set aside the agreement. (Corsiglia v. U.S. Postal Service, 69 MSPR 5, 1995)

• A settlement agreement must be lawful on its face; it may not provide for penalties that are outside the scope of law. (Special Counsel v. Reckard, 69 MSPR 130, 1995)

• Settlement agreements should be interpreted in light of the significant goals the parties sought to achieve, and an agency action that complies with those goals, even if it doesn't follow the agreement's specific language, doesn't amount to a breach of the contract. (Komiskey v. Army, 70 MSPR 607, 1996)

• Where a misunderstanding between the parties goes to the heart of the agreement and not just to a particular term, the entire agreement may be set aside. However, one party may waive the misunderstanding and enforce the contract in accordance with the understanding of the other. (Gullette v. U.S. Postal Service, 70 MSPR 569, 1996)

• Unless the parties show that they intended otherwise, when they use a legal term of art in a settlement, that term should be applied according to its regulatory or statutory definition. For example, a reference to back pay normally would be interpreted according to the Back Pay Act. (Kellihan v. Navy, 72 MSPR 47, 1996)

• The Merit Systems Protection Board has jurisdiction over a petition for enforcement of a settlement where, even though the aspect of the agreement that is the subject of the petition would not be independently appealable to the Board, the agreement's language specifies that the employee may seek compliance with the Board's final decision with respect to any aspect of the agreement. (Manley v. Department of the Air Force, 91 F.3d 117, Fed. Cir. 1996)

• A settlement agreement providing that an employee will voluntarily resign is a valid basis for an agency to refuse to allow the withdrawal of a resignation. The agency's refusal to permit withdrawal of the resignation does not make the resignation involuntary, and therefore within the Merit Systems Protection Board's jurisdiction. (Tretchick v. Department of Transportation, 109 F.3d 749, Fed. Cir. 1997)

• The U.S. Court of Appeals for the Federal Circuit held that where a settlement agreement between an employee and an agency contains some ambiguity, the agreement should be interpreted according to "the intent of the parties at the time the agreement was made" and that interpretation can be extended to "perfecting that which was flawed."(Hosey v. ICC, 132 F.3d 53, Fed. Cir., 1997)

• An employee is bound by the terms of an oral settlement agreement, even if the employee later refuses to sign a written version of the agreement, so long as the written version accurately reflects the oral agreement's terms, the U.S. Court of Appeals for the Federal Circuit decided. The court said that its own precedent and general contract law governing settlements indicate that a settlement exists once the parties reach oral agreement. (Thornton v. U.S. Postal Service, Fed. Cir., No. 97-3437, 1998)

• The U.S. Court of Appeals for the Federal Circuit held that an employee breached a settlement agreement by withdrawing a disability retirement application, but that the agency may have violated the agreement by failing to carry out its duties to pursue such an application. The court told the Merit Systems Protection Board to reopen the case. (Harris v. Dept. of Veterans Affairs, Fed. Cir., No. 98-3051, 1998)

• The Merit Systems Protection Board does not have jurisdiction over a settlement agreement that was not officially entered into the record before the Board, according to the U.S. Court of Appeals for the Federal Circuit. The court upheld MSPB's rejection of the employee's contention that the agreement was invalid because the postal service "had no intention of honoring" it. (Coleman v. USPS, Fed. Cir., No. 98-3089, 1998)

• An employee who entered into a settlement agreement after proposed discipline for alleged attendance problems was on sufficient notice that any future infractions could result in dismissal, the U.S. Court of Appeals for the Federal Circuit held, agreeing with a hearing officer that the worker's challenges to three of the six charges were "inconsequential to the outcome." (Braswell v. U.S. Postal Service, Fed. Cir., No. 98-3142, 1998)

• A federal agency violated its settlement agreement with a former employee by implying that he had something other than the clean employment record specified in the terms of the agreement, the U.S. Court of Appeals for the Federal Circuit ruled. The court added that such "wipe the slate clean" agreements are often the source of continuing problems for both employees and their former agencies and expressed its concern about the tendency of agencies to enter into settlement agreements that allow an unsatisfactory employee to resign in exchange for a "personnel record clear of charges and adverse actions." (Pagan v. Dept. of Veterans Affairs, 170 F.3d 1368, Fed. Cir., 1999)

CHAPTER FIFTEEN

Alternative Dispute Resolution

The term "alternative dispute resolution" covers a variety of techniques, which typically involve a neutral third party and provide assistance through a range of formal to informal dispute-resolution methods. Some ADR methods—arbitration and mediation in particular—date back to the early 1900s, while others are of more recent vintage. Originally, ADR was used mostly to resolve disputes involving employees covered by collective bargaining agreements. More recently, agencies have increasingly made use of ADR methods to resolve disputes involving non-bargaining unit employees as well.

The Administrative Dispute Resolution Act of 1990 required federal agencies to develop ADR policies and allowed them to use the procedures established under those policies in almost any type of dispute in which they become involved. An October 1, 1993, executive order (No. 12871) required agencies to train employees in consensual methods of dispute resolution, and was followed by the Administrative Dispute Resolution Act of 1996, which permanently reauthorized the 1990 act. Subsequently, a May 1, 1998, presidential memo directed agencies to promote greater use of a wide variety of ADR techniques, including mediation, arbitration, early neutral evaluation, agency ombudsmen, and other alternative methods.

Objectives and Methods

Purposes and Goals

Over the past few years, ADR has become increasingly popular as a means of avoiding more formal processes. It offers both individuals and agencies a way to save the time, dollar, and other costs typically expended on the administrative redress system or lawsuits. There also is a growing belief that ADR techniques represent a constructive alternative to what is typically an adversarial process by offering a "win-win" solution.

ADR most commonly is used to resolve equal employment opportunity complaints, personnel grievances, and labor-management issues. Agencies also use the techniques in other areas, such as procurement, enforcement, and program-related disputes.

Almost all agencies offer some form of ADR, although some agencies use it more aggressively than others, and the methods employed can vary from site to site. The Federal Mediation and Conciliation Service provides various ADR services to agencies. Depending on the nature of the dispute and the process followed, such techniques may result in formal settlement agreements (see separate chapter).

Among agencies, the primary reason for making ADR available has been to avoid the costs—especially those involving time and organizational efficiency—associated with the formal appeals or complaint system. The prospect of having to deal with the formal system's lengthy and complex processes also can have a damaging, long-term impact, since it can—and does—affect the willingness of federal managers to deal with employees' conduct or performance issues.

For individual employees, ADR techniques offer a route to head off disciplinary action or obtain a faster solution to a problem. The appeals agencies handling federal employment disputes commonly say many formal complaints reflect basic communications problems in the workplace. Such issues often end up in the formal processes as a result of employees' perceptions that there is no other forum available to air general workplace concerns.

Another factor in the widening use of ADR practices has been a recognition that traditional methods of dispute resolution do not always identify and resolve the underlying issues. Interest-based dispute resolution, which is the basis for many ADR techniques, focuses on determining both parties' underlying interests and working to resolve the conflict at a more basic level.

ADR can serve a purpose merely by giving employees an opportunity to be heard. Employees get a "day in court" where they can air a problem that otherwise might fester until it turned into a formal dispute. Meanwhile, management becomes more aware of the causes of workplace disputes, of the policies or decisions that led to the complaint, and of concerns and feelings that otherwise might not be apparent. And both sides can benefit by ADR's greater likelihood of preserving a working relationship and avoiding the hostility and acrimony that formal appeals often generate.

The regulations governing matters appealable to the Equal Employment Opportunity Commission encourage the parties to use ADR techniques. In fact, EEOC's November 1999 rule revisions require federal agencies to establish or make available an ADR process to help complainants achieve early, informal resolution of their discrimination charges.

ADR techniques also are widely used in labor-management partnership councils that are designed to promote cooperative working relationships and to avoid disputes by improving communications and understanding. Agencies have begun using interest-based bargaining and assisted negotiations to deal with difficult issues in the partnership councils or in formal contract negotiations. Agencies now use ADR methods to supplement formal grievance procedures under collective bargaining agreements as well.

Although ADR is now widely used as a tool for resolving disputes, it is not appropriate in all cases—for example, situations marked by violence or severe sexual harassment. ADR also is considered inappropriate when a formal decision is required for precedential value, the matter in dispute has significant policy implications, or the parties consider it important to produce a full record.

Also, before engaging in alternative dispute resolution, employees should examine the effect it might have on their other appeal rights. In certain situations, using an ADR channel may close off appeals routes that otherwise would be open.

Major ADR Methods

• *Arbitration* – Arbitration involves the presentation of a dispute to an impartial individual or panel for a decision. Typically, the parties have the ability to decide who will serve as their arbitrator. A common understanding in all cases is that the parties will be bound by the decision, rather than simply treating it as a recommendation, unless they specifically agree that the arbitration decision will be non-binding.

Some agencies have set up expedited arbitration processes that call for strict time limits, no formal transcripts or briefs, limits on the number of witnesses, and similar arrangements designed to save time or money. Often, such procedures feature early deadlines on all stages of the process, a strict time limit on the hearing itself, and a length limit on the arbitrator's report. These less formal arbitration processes are considered especially useful for less serious grievances.

A binding arbitration process is mandated by law as part of the federal labor-management program. In their collective bargaining agreements, the parties negotiate the terms and conditions under which arbitrators are used, including the procedures for their selection. These arbitral decisions generally have the force of law, but do not act as a legal precedent.

Non-binding arbitration commonly is used when the parties want to have a third party involved, but want to retain more control over the decision making process than is allowed under binding arbitration.

Arbitration has not traditionally been available to federal employees seeking redress outside the terms of collective bargain agreements. The Administrative Dispute Resolution Acts of 1990 and 1996 allow federal agencies to use arbitration if all the parties consent to its use, as long as the agency does not require any participant to consent to arbitration as a condition of entering into a contract or obtaining a benefit. The 1996 Act also requires that before using binding arbitration, the agency consult with the Department of Justice on its appropriateness. The Act also requires that the arbitrator interpret and apply relevant statutory and regulatory requirements, legal procedures, and policy directives.

Mediated arbitration is a variation in which a neutral party mediates the dispute until the parties reach an impasse. Once impasse is reached, either that arbitrator or another one issues a binding decision on the remaining issues in dispute.

• ***Conciliation***—Conciliation focuses on building a positive relationship between the parties, and typically involves a third party who may (or may not) be neutral to the parties' interests. A conciliator may help establish communication, clarify misperceptions, calm emotions, and build the trust needed for cooperative problem-solving.

Techniques include providing a neutral meeting place, carrying initial messages between the parties, checking perceptions of the parties to determine whether they are mistaken, and encouraging the parties to work together. The goal is to promote a spirit of "openness" among the parties, thereby enabling them to begin dialogues, know each other better, build positive perceptions, and enhance trust.

Conciliation often is used as part of other methods, such as facilitation or mediation.

• ***Cooperative Problem Solving***— Usually an informal process that does not employ the services of a third party, this technique is used when the parties agree to work together to resolve an issue. It often is the procedure of first resort when the parties recognize that a problem exists that could worsen if allowed to go unrecognized and unresolved. It is most commonly used when a conflict is not highly polarized and the parties have not taken hard-line positions.

A variation is interest-based problem solving, a technique designed to separate the people from the problem, explore their interests to define the issues clearly, and raise possibilities for resolving the issues.

Both of these techniques are commonly used in labor-management partnerships and other cooperative efforts, although they also can be used whenever parties are seeking to reach an agreement.

• *Dispute Panels*—These generally take the form of an informal process that leaves the parties with wide discretion over how the panel is used. The panels use one or more impartial individuals who provide assistance with clarifying misperceptions, filling in information gaps, resolving differences over facts, and suggesting ways for the parties to reconcile their differences.

The panel's recommendations may be procedural or substantive, depending on its delegated authority. A panel's factual analysis and suggestions may be used in other processes.

• *Dispute Prevention*—Many agencies have established programs designed to head off disputes by concentrating on work environment improvements, better communications, and more cooperation at all levels. Such programs often include "quality of worklife" efforts that may provide for direct employee-management discussions on matters that traditionally are reserved for formal bargaining and that encourage employees to apply their skills and experience to problems of work quality and productivity.

Many agencies also offer training to managers, personnel experts, counselors and others who commonly become involved in personnel disputes, aimed at improving their skills in such areas as mediation, communication, conciliation and other ADR techniques.

Dispute prevention efforts also are common features of local labor-management partnership programs.

• *Facilitation*—The goal of facilitation is to improve the flow of information between parties to a dispute. A facilitator typically does not become as involved in substantive issues, focusing primarily on the communication process involved in resolving a dispute.

A facilitator generally works with all of the participants at once and, while remaining neutral on the substance of the dispute, provides advice and recommendations as to how they can move through the problem-solving steps. Facilitation is considered most effective when emotional levels are relatively low and when the parties face a common predicament, but are not firmly set in their views and continue to trust each other.

• *Factfinding*—The role of a factfinder is to investigate and identify the facts underlying a dispute, not to resolve issues. Factfinders, who often have technical expertise on the subject matter of the dispute, evaluate a situation through personal and telephone interviews, meetings, conferences (which may produce a transcript), and informal investigations. The rationale is that the opinion of a trusted and neutral observer will carry weight with the parties as they move toward resolving a dispute.

Factfinders generally do not decide policy issues. Typically, they file a report on their findings and may be authorized to issue an assessment or a non-binding recommendation as to how a dispute might be resolved.

Where such recommendations are not accepted, the report on the facts commonly is used in further discussions or, potentially, in formal appeals.

• *Mediation*—A mediator is a neutral third party who helps the parties resolve the issues between themselves. The mediator has no decision-making authority, but takes an active role in discussions by helping to define the issues, while encouraging communication and offering options for settlement. Mediation is most commonly used when the parties hold firmly to their positions and have either reached an impasse or not even been able to begin a productive discussion.

Although mediation is typically associated with formalized bargaining settings, its use has been increasing in recent years in other dispute arenas, notably in cases involving alleged discrimination.

Mediators make recommendations that are primarily procedural, but at times may involve substantive options as a means of encouraging the parties to find a solution. Mediators work with the parties both jointly and individually to explore options and develop proposals that might move them closer to resolution. Depending on the parties' desires and the preferences of the mediator, a mediator's role in forging the details of an agreement can vary from virtually nonexistent to heavily involved.

• *Ombudsmen*— Ombudsmen are agency-designated neutral officials who serve as informal counselors, mediators, or fact-finders to help resolve work disputes. An ombudsman has no formal decision making authority; the power of ombudsmen lie in their ability to persuade the parties to accept their recommendations. Generally, an employee who doesn't accept the proposed solution of an ombudsman is free to pursue a remedy in other forums.

Ombudsmen also are points of contact within an agency that employees may seek out to obtain answers to questions about work-related activities. Typically, an ombudsman might review an employee's situation and give advice about the options.

Ombudmen also may be used to handle complaints and disputes about employees from agency customers or clients.

• *Peer Review*—A "peer review" process gives an employee's co-workers (and usually management representatives) a role in resolving a workplace dispute, with the goal of resolving problems before they become formal complaints or grievances. Typically, these panels consist of colleagues and disinterested agency officials who volunteer for the duty and who are trained in listening, questioning, and problem-solving skills.

Peer review panels may consist of standing groups of individuals who are available to address disputes at any time, or they may be formed on an ad hoc basis through a designated selection process—for example, blind selection of a certain number of names from a pool.

Peer review panels collectively act in much the same way as an arbitrator, although they typically operate under short time limits. After investigating and considering the matter, the panel may issue a recommendation by a simple majority vote. The decision may or may not be binding on the parties, depending on the terms of the arrangement. If the recommendation is not binding on employees, they can seek relief through formal appeals routes.

ADR Programs
at Appellate Agencies

• **Merit Systems Protection Board**—MSPB hearing officers, formally called administrative judges, use a variety of ADR techniques in handling cases, including prehearing conferences, mediation, settlement negotiations, conciliation, facilitation, and, at times, "mini-trials" in which the parties present abbreviated summaries of their cases that give the hearing official a solid basis for settlement discussions. Usually, at least one prehearing conference for settlement and simplification of issues is required.

Other than the required prehearing conference, there is no mandated single or formal procedure for dispute resolution. Hearing officers have discretion to use whichever ADR techniques they consider appropriate for a particular case. However, the Board does formally favor settlements, and its procedures require hearing officers to focus the parties' attention on settlement possibilities.

Some MSPB regional and field offices designate one hearing officer to serve full-time as a settlement judge. Overall, about half of appeals to regional and field offices that are not dismissed for various technical reasons are settled.

MSPB also encourages settlements at the full Board level, which hears appeals of hearing officer decisions. Staff attorneys there work to identify cases that are appropriate for settlement; cases might also be referred for settlement attempts by Board members or at a party's request. Settlements are reached in about a fifth of cases where attempted at the Board level.

If the parties do not settle, the cases are assigned to other attorneys to prepare recommended decisions. The Board has a confidentiality policy designed to allow parties to openly discuss their cases with the settlement attorney without fear that information divulged might damage their cases if the matter is later referred for formal adjudication.

• **Equal Employment Opportunity Commission**—EEOC is placing more emphasis on resolving discrimination complaints informally at various stages of the discrimination complaint process. Under EEOC's new charge-processing rules that took effect in November 1999, federal agencies now are required to establish (or make available) an alternative dispute resolution program aimed at early, informal resolution of a complainant's discrimination charges. Agencies have the discretion, on a case-by-case basis, to refrain from offering ADR for certain types of "inappropriate" disputes (e.g., geographic restrictions on the availability of a pre-complaint ADR process). However, when ADR programs are offered, agencies generally must make them available during both the pre-complaint process and the formal complaint stage.

EEOC stresses that agencies are free to offer whatever ADR program is best suited to their needs, with the choices including mediation (the most frequently used), facilitation, fact-finding, early neutral evaluation, ombudsmen, settlement conferences, "minitrials," and peer review, as well as combinations of these techniques. Whatever technique is offered, agencies must take steps to ensure the fairness of the ADR initiative. Basically, this means that an agency must make sure its ADR program incorporates certain required "core principles," including voluntariness, neutrality, confidentiality, and enforceability. If an agency offers ADR, EEO counselors are required to inform aggrieved individuals of their right to choose traditional counseling or ADR participation (if offered) at the initial counseling session (or within a reasonable time thereafter). The 90-day ADR time limit begins to run from the complainant's first contact with the ADR contact person. If the time limit expires or the ADR process fails to produce a satisfactory resolution, the aggrieved person is entitled to a final interview with the EEO counselor and has the right to file a formal complaint. The terms of any resolution achieved through the ADR process must be set forth in writing and signed by both parties.

EEOC also is working to encourage agencies to train managers and supervisors on the use and advantages of ADR, and to give its administrative judges more authority to quickly resolve cases at the hearing stage. It is also experimenting with mandatory mediation in federal employee cases that are suitable for a hearing before an administrative judge. In addition, several agencies, most notably the U.S. Postal Service, are offering employees mediation as an alternative to pursuing formal discrimination complaints.

• *Federal Labor Relations Authority*—FLRA offers a program called the "Collaboration and Alternative Dispute Resolution Program," which targets each step of a labor-management dispute for possible ADR use, from investigation and prosecution to the adjudication of cases. The agency's general counsel uses several approaches to resolving unfair labor practice and representation disputes short of litigation. These include facilitation, intervention, training and education services delivered jointly to both the labor and management sides, interest-based bargaining, and relationship building. Such programs can be initiated by the general counsel's office at the regional level or by the parties.

FLRA's office of administrative law judges operates an unfair labor practice trial settlement project aimed at voluntary settlement of ULP cases. The project involves assigning a settlement attorney or a judge other than the trial judge to conduct settlement conference negotiations with the parties before formal proceedings.

The Federal Service Impasses Panel, an arm of FLRA that attempts to resolve bargaining deadlocks, uses formal and informal procedures to resolve impasses short of a written decision and order from the panel. These techniques include mediation, fact finding, and arbitration by panel or staff members or offered through private providers.

CHAPTER SIXTEEN

Merit Systems Protection Board

The Merit Systems Protection Board hears appeals of personnel actions brought by individual federal employees. It is an independent, quasi-judicial agency designed to be the guardian of the federal merit system.

MSPB was created by the 1978 Civil Service Reform Act. Its mission is to ensure that employees are protected against abuses by agency management, that employment decisions are made in accordance with law, and that the personnel system is kept free of prohibited personnel practices.

The Board also conducts studies of the merit systems to make sure they are free of prohibited personnel practices and issues reports on personnel issues. Significant actions of the Office of Personnel Management are reviewed by the MSPB to determine whether they are in accord with merit principles and are free of prohibited personnel practices.

The Board itself is a three-member body based in Washington, D.C., which is responsible for overseeing a network of regional offices and hearing officials—called administrative judges—who issue about 10,000 decisions on employee appeals annually. The Board itself issues about 2,000 decisions annually.

MSPB Rules and Procedures

Who's Covered

Nearly two million executive branch employees, as well as certain U.S. Postal Service employees, currently have appeal rights to the Board. Generally, eligible executive branch employees include those in the competitive service who have completed a probationary period and those in the excepted service (other than the postal service and certain designated agencies, mostly in law enforcement and national security) with at least two years of service.

Probationary employees have only limited appeal rights. They may ap-peal a termination based on political affiliation or marital status. They also may appeal a termination based on conditions that arose before employment if the dismissal is not in accordance with regulations.

Your rights to an MSPB appeal sometimes depend on the agency, your position, or the type of action involved. Certain classes of employees, such as political appointees, are excluded. Employees of specific agencies, such as the intelligence agencies and the General Accounting Office, are excluded with respect to certain actions.

Generally, employees who may appeal adverse actions, the largest category of cases brought to MSPB, include: employees in the competitive service who have completed a 1-year probationary period or trial period; veterans' preference-eligible employees with at least one year continuous employment in the same or similar positions outside the competitive service; Postal Service supervisors and managers, and Postal Service employees engaged in personnel work (other than those in non-confidential clerical positions), who have completed one year of continuous service in the same or similar positions; and excepted service employees, other than preference eligibles, who are not serving a probationary or trial period and who have completed two years continuous service in the same or similar positions in an executive agency.

Types of Appeals

For the Board to decide any appeal of a personnel action, it must have jurisdiction over not just the employee bringing the appeal, but also the type of adverse action suffered by the worker. Due to the overlapping nature of civil service law, there are several situations where the test of jurisdiction can be confusing.

One such situation could occur if you are a member of a union bargaining unit that has negotiated grievance procedures covering matters that can be appealed to MSPB. You normally must use the grievance route. If the agreement covers adverse actions and/or performance based actions, however, you may choose to go through the grievance procedure or to MSPB—but not both. You also have a choice when the grievance procedure covers an action appealable to the Board and you raise an issue of prohibited discrimination.

Another overlapping situation occurs when you allege discrimination in a case that is appealable to MSPB. The Board will hear such cases, including the discrimination charges that normally would be appealable only to the Equal Employment Opportunity Commission. If you are dissatisfied with MSPB's decision, you may ask the EEOC to review it (see "Mixed Cases" in EEOC chapter).

The majority of cases brought to MSPB involve adverse actions against employees. These include removals, suspensions of more than 14 days, reductions in grade or pay, and furloughs of 30 days or fewer. The rest of MSPB's workload largely includes appeals regarding performance-based removals or reductions in grade; denials of within-grade salary increases; reduction-in-force actions; determinations of suitability for a position by the Office of Personnel Management; an OPM denial of restoration or reemployment rights; OPM determinations in retirement matters; terminations of probationary employees under the circumstances described above; and removals from the Senior Executive Service for failure to be recertified.

Under the Whistleblower Protection Act of 1989, individual employees gained the right to appeal additional actions to MSPB in certain circumstances. They include actions that may be the subject of a prohibited personnel practice complaint to the Office of Special Counsel, such as appointments, promotions, details, transfers, reassignments, and decisions concerning pay, benefits, awards, education, and training. To appeal such actions to MSPB, employees must allege that the action was taken because of their whistleblowing, and they also must have filed a complaint with OSC and that Office must not have asked MSPB to order corrective action.

The Board also hears corrective and disciplinary actions brought by the Special Counsel against employees or agencies who are alleged to have committed prohibited personnel practices or to have violated certain civil service laws or rules. Along with its powers, the Board can issue stays of personnel actions as requested by the Special Counsel in prohibited personnel practice cases.

The Board also has jurisdiction over complaints relating to the employment and reemployment rights of employees who serve in the uniformed services. The Board can hear appeals of personnel actions that would not otherwise be appealable, if the employee alleges that the action resulted from discrimination based on military service.

MSPB has the authority to modify or overturn agency decisions, including putting the employee back in the status quo before the action was taken, with back pay and other benefits. In certain cases, it also can order stays of personnel actions before they become final. MSPB decisions are legally binding on agencies; MSPB has the authority to dock the salaries of federal officials who refuse to comply with its orders, although this is rarely even threatened. MSPB also can take disciplinary actions, for example for violations of the Hatch Act or prohibited personnel practices (see Office of Special Counsel chapter).

Appeal Deadlines

When an agency takes an appealable action against an employee, it must provide the individual with a notice of the time limits for filing an MSPB appeal, the address of the appropriate Board regional office for filing the appeal, a copy or access to a copy of the Board's regulations, a copy of the Board's appeal form, and a notice of any rights concerning an agency or negotiated grievance procedure.

An appeal must be filed in writing with the Board regional office serving the employee's area within 30 days of the effective date of the action or 30 days after receiving the agency's decision, whichever is later. Letters to MSPB headquarters or members of Congress and other such outside contacts are not considered formal notices of appeal, and may result in a case being dismissed as untimely filed.

In the case of whistleblower appeals where the employee has first filed a complaint with the Special Counsel, an appeal to the Board must be filed within 65 days of the date of notice from that office that it does not intend to seek corrective action. If 120 days have passed since the employee filed the complaint and the Special Counsel has not advised the employee that it will seek corrective action, the employee may appeal to the Board anytime thereafter.

The MSPB does provide an appeal form, but your appeal can be in any format as long as it is in writing and contains all the information specified in MSPB regulations. Any appeal must also have your signature or the signature of your representative, if you have designated one.

Certain types of cases are processed initially at Board headquarters rather than in a regional office. These include appeals from MSPB employees, appeals involving classified national security information, and petitions to review an arbitrator's award.

If you miss your deadline for filing any type of appeal, you may apply for a waiver by showing good reason for the delay and including supporting evidence. Granting such a waiver is up to the discretion of the administrative judge, however.

You may represent yourself or you may hire a private attorney, make use of union attorneys or representatives, or have other types of representatives.

When the Board regional office receives an appeal, it issues an order acknowledging receipt and raising any questions of timeliness or jurisdiction. The appeal is then assigned to an administrative judge. The agency has the right to respond within 20 days of the regional office's order. If no response is received by the Board within that time limit, the case may be decided on the basis of the information available.

Hearing Rights

Once jurisdiction and timeliness have been established, you have the right to a hearing on the merits of the complaint, but you may waive that right and ask that the case be decided on the basis of the written record. Both you and the agency will have an opportunity to participate in "discovery" proceedings (i.e., taking depositions and making information and document requests). A prehearing conference normally is held in which issues are defined and narrowed, stipulations to undisputed facts are obtained, and the possibility of settlement is discussed.

If a formal hearing is conducted, each party has the opportunity to call and cross-examine witnesses, present evidence, and make arguments to the administrative judge. Hearings are open to the public and are recorded by a court reporter, with copies of the record subsequently made available to the parties. You have the right to see relevant documents and other information before the hearing.

Burdens of Proof

The agency bears the burden of proving that it was justified in taking its action. Standards of proof vary according to the type of appeal. For example, in adverse action cases the standard is the "preponderance of the evidence," but a lesser "substantial evidence" standard applies to actions based on unacceptable performance. And in whistleblowing cases, once an employee shows that disclosures were a contributing factor in the agency decision, the agency must show by "clear and convincing" evidence that it would have made the same decision regardless of the whistleblowing.

If the agency meets its burden, in order to prevail you must show that there was "harmful error" in the agency's procedures, that the agency decision was based on a prohibited personnel practice, or that the decision was not in accordance with the law. You bear the burden of proving any affirmative defenses, such as contentions that discrimination or retaliation for whistleblowing motivated the personnel action.

Board Decisions

Once the record is closed, the administrative judge issues an initial decision. That decision may dismiss the appeal on various grounds, accept a settlement that has been agreed to by the parties, or affirm, reverse or mitigate the agency's action. The average time to process appeals at the regional office level is four months.

The initial decision becomes final unless one of the parties petitions the three-member Board for review within 35 days or the Board opens the case on its own motion. Petitions for review must be filed with the Office of the Clerk at MSPB headquarters.

A petition for review does not automatically mean that the three-member Board will hear your case. The Board accepts appeals only when it is clear that the initial decision was based on an erroneous interpretation of law or regulation, or that new and material evidence is available that was not available when the record was closed. When it accepts a case, the Board acts as an appeals court, reviewing the record and the legal motions and occasionally hearing oral arguments. The Board may affirm, reverse, or modify the initial decision, or may send the case back to the administrative judge for further consideration. The average processing time at Board headquarters of appeals of initial decisions is about six months.

If you win an initial decision that is appealed to the Board, you normally will be granted the relief that the decision specifies while the case is under review—"interim relief." This does not apply, however, if the administrative judge deems it inappropriate or if the decision requires that an employee be returned to the workplace and the agency determines that this would be "unduly disruptive." In such cases, the agency still would be required to provide such workers with any applicable pay and benefits.

The Board makes use of various alternative dispute resolution techniques that can result in cases being settled or dismissed at various stages of the process. Settlements reached at the initial decision stage are reviewed by the administrative judge, who determines if the agreement is legal, the parties freely entered into it, and it is fair to the employee. Agreements that are entered into the official record become the final resolution of the appeal, and MSPB retains jurisdiction to enforce the agreement. Parties also sometimes reach settlements that are not made part of the record, often with the case being voluntarily withdrawn. MSPB has no authority to enforce those agreements.

You may seek review of a final MSPB decision—either an initial de-

cision that has become final or a decision by the three-member Board— by appealing within 30 days to the U.S. Court of Appeals for the Federal Circuit. Cases involving certain types of discrimination may be appealed to a U.S. district court or the Equal Employment Opportunity Commission. In addition, the Office of Personnel Management may seek judicial review of a Board decision that it believes will have a substantial impact on civil service law, rule, or policy. No other agency may seek judicial review of a Board decision.

Contacting the MSPB

MSPB's headquarters is at 1615 M Street, N.W., 5th floor, Washington, D.C. 20419, phone (202) 653-7124 V/TDD (202) 653-8896, fax (202) 653-7130. MSPB's World Wide Web address is:

http://www.mspb.gov.

MSPB Regional Offices

Atlanta Regional Office
401 W. Peachtree Street, NW.
Suite 1050
Atlanta, GA 30308
 (404) 730-2751
Fax (404) 730-2767
Alabama, Florida, Georgia, Mississippi, South Carolina, and Tennessee

Central Regional Office
230 South Dearborn Street
Room 3100
Chicago, IL 60604
 (312) 353-2923
Fax (312) 886-4231
Illinois; Indiana; Iowa; Kansas City, Kansas; Kentucky; Michigan; Minnesota; Missouri; Ohio; and Wisconsin

Dallas Field Office
1100 Commerce Street
Room 6F20
Dallas, TX 75242
(214) 767-0555
Fax (214) 767-0102
Arkansas, Louisiana, Oklahoma, and Texas

Northeastern Regional Office
U.S. Customhouse, Room 501
Second & Chestnut Streets
Philadelphia, PA 19106
(215) 597-9960
Fax (215) 597-3456
Delaware, Maryland (except the counties of Montgomery and Prince George's), New Jersey (except the counties of Bergen, Essex, Hudson, and Union), Pennsylvania, and West Virginia

Boston Field Office
99 Summer Street
Suite 1810
Boston, MA 02110
(617) 424-5700
Fax (617) 424-5708
Connecticut, Maine, Massachusetts, New Hampshire, Rhode Island, and Vermont

New York Field Office
26 Federal Plaza
Room 3137A
New York, NY 10278
(212) 264-9372
Fax (212) 264-1417
New Jersey (counties of Bergen, Essex, Hudson, and Union), New York, Puerto Rico, and Virgin Islands

Washington Regional Office
5203 Leesburg Pike
Suite 1109
Falls Church, VA 22041
(703) 756-6250
Fax (703) 756-7112
Washington, DC, Maryland (counties of Montgomery and Prince George's), North Carolina, Virginia, and all overseas areas not otherwise covered

Western Regional Office
250 Montgomery Street
Suite 400, 4th Floor
San Francisco, CA 94104
(415) 705-2935
Fax (415) 705-2945
California and Nevada

Denver Field Office
12567 W. Cedar Drive
Suite 100
Lakewood, CO 80228
(303) 969-5101
Fax (303) 969-5109
Arizona, Colorado, Kansas (except Kansas City), Montana, Nebraska, New Mexico, North Dakota, South Dakota, Utah, and Wyoming

Seattle Field Office
915 Second Avenue
Room 1840
Seattle, WA 98174
(206) 220-7975
Fax (206) 220-7982
Alaska, Hawaii, Idaho, Oregon, Washington, and Pacific overseas areas

CHAPTER SEVENTEEN

Equal Employment Opportunity Commission

The Equal Employment Opportunity Commission was established by Title VII of the Civil Rights Act of 1964. The mission of the EEOC is to promote equal opportunity in employment for job applicants and employees. It does this through administrative and judicial enforcement of the federal civil rights laws. EEOC also provides education and technical assistance to federal agencies through seminars offered across the country.

Federal and postal employees are protected by the EEOC from discrimination because of race, color, gender, religion, national origin, age, or disability. EEOC further oversees and coordinates federal rules, practices and policies affecting equal employment opportunity.

— EEO Laws, Complaints, and Procedures —

EEOC Enforcement Authority

Key anti-discrimination laws enforced by the Equal Employment Opportunity Commission of interest to federal and postal workers are:

• *Title VII of the Civil Rights Act of 1964,* which prohibits employment discrimination based on race, color, religion, sex, or national origin.

• *Age Discrimination in Employment Act of 1967,* which protects employees 40 years of age or older by prohibiting age discrimination in hiring, discharge, pay, promotions and other terms and conditions of employment.

• *Equal Pay Act of 1963,* which protects men and women who perform substantially equal work in the same establishment from sex-based wage discrimination.

• *Section 501 of the Rehabilitation Act of 1973,* which prohibits federal sector employment discrimination against persons with disabilities.

EEOC also enforces the Americans with Disabilities Act of 1990 and the Civil Rights Act of 1991, which primarily affect employees of the private sector and of state and local government, but which also contain some provisions affecting federal and postal employees.

Additionally, federal employees who file a complaint, participate in an investigation of a complaint, or oppose a personnel practice made illegal by any of the above laws also are protected from retaliation for their actions by the EEOC.

Complaint Options

If you have a complaint regarding equal employment opportunity, you may be able to pursue a remedy in more than one way. Generally, federal and postal equal employment opportunity complaints are processed under regulations (29 C.F.R. part 1614) issued by the EEOC, and federal employees must exhaust the administrative process before pursuing their complaints in court.

However, postal workers who are covered under collective bargaining agreements and who allege discrimination have more redress opportunities than other federal workers covered under collective bargaining agreements. Unionized postal workers generally can take two courses of action concurrently: file a discrimination complaint under the federal employee discrimination complaint process and also file a grievance through procedures under the collective bargaining agreement. (The EEO complaint may be deferred pending resolution of the grievance, however.)

Executive branch employees who are covered under collective bargaining agreements must choose between the EEOC and grievance processes. The election is made by the filing of a formal complaint or the initiation of a written grievance, whichever comes first. If you file a written grievance first, you may not afterward file an EEO complaint on the same matter, even if the grievance does not raise allegations of discrimination. If an allegation is taken to arbitration under a collective bargaining agreement, the union may file exceptions to the arbitrator's decision with the Federal Labor Relations Authority.

Your appeal to EEOC can be based on: a final agency decision on the grievance; an arbitrator's decision; or an FLRA decision (on exceptions to an arbitrator's award). Such appeals are then processed in the same way as appeals from the agency EEO complaint procedure.

Special procedures apply to cases that include matters that are appealable to the Merit Systems Protection Board (see "Mixed Cases", page 155).

At all stages of the administrative process, you are entitled to be represented by a person of your choosing. However, the agency is not obligated to change work schedules, incur overtime costs, or pay travel expenses to facilitate your desire for a specific representative or to allow you and your representative to confer. In addition, a representative may be disqualified if that role would conflict with his or her official duties.

A discrimination complaint also may be brought on behalf of a class of employees, former employees, or applicants. Such a complaint may be brought by an individual acting in the interests of the group. The complaint will be certified as a class action if: the class is so large that a consolidated complaint of the members of the class is impractical; questions of fact are common to the class; the individual's claims are typical of the class claim; and the individual complaint will adequately protect the interests of the class. If the agency certifies it as a class complaint, the complaint proceeds through the appeals process, and members of the class may come forward to claim relief if the employing agency or the EEOC finds that discrimination has occurred.

Filing a Complaint

If you feel, as an employee or an applicant, that you have been discriminated against, the first step is to contact an equal employment opportunity counselor at the agency where the alleged discrimination took place. You should contact the EEO counselor within 45 days of the discriminatory action, the effective date of the personnel action involved, or the date you knew or should have known of a discriminatory event or personnel action.

Ordinarily, counseling must be completed within 30 days. The counseling period is designed to explore whether the complaint can be resolved without formal proceedings. If dissatisfied at the end of the counseling period, you have 15 days to file a complaint with the employing agency. The agency must acknowledge or reject the complaint. A complaint may be rejected for a variety of reasons, including your failure to follow proper procedures, failure to state a claim on which relief can be granted, or a determination that the same matters already have been decided or already are pending. Agency decisions to reject complaints can be appealed to EEOC within 30 days. The EEOC may determine that the dismissal was improper and remand the matter back to the agency.

If your agency does not reject the complaint, it must, within 180 days, conduct an investigation. An extension of not more than 90 days can be granted, but only by your written agreement. Agencies are allowed to use a variety of investigative techniques and dispute resolution methods. You and agency officials are expected to cooperate with an investigation. The investigator may draw an adverse inference from a refusal to cooperate.

At the conclusion of the investigation, you have 30 days to request either a hearing by an EEOC administrative judge or a final decision by the employing agency. If no hearing is requested, the final agency decision must be issued within 60 days from the end of the investigation.

If a hearing is requested, you will have an opportunity to conduct "discovery" (e.g., taking depositions from individuals involved and making document and information requests) before proceeding to a hearing by an administrative judge. The administra-tive judge must process the request for a hearing, issue findings of fact and conclusions of law, and issue a final decision, including any remedy, within 180 days. After the administrative judge's decision, agencies have 40 days to decide whether they will "fully implement" the AJ's ruling or appeal the decision to EEOC.

Complainants may appeal an agency's unfavorable implementation decision to the Commission within 30 days or file a suit in the local U.S. district court within 90 days. EEOC reviews the complaint file and all relevant written material and issues a written decision. If you are dissatisfied with a final EEOC decision, you may file a civil action in the local U.S. district court within 90 days of the decision.

You also may file a civil action 180 days after filing a complaint with the agency, if the agency has not issued a final decision, or 180 days after filing an appeal with the Commission if no decision has been issued. Filing a court action ends the administrative processing of a complaint.

Choice of Forum

At various points in the discrimination complaint process, federal emloyees may choose to file suit in federal district court, rather than proceeding through either the internal agency process or the EEOC's procedures. This present the employee, on several occasions, with a "choice of forum" consideration—i.e., a choice between using the court process or the administrative procedures.

There is no clear-cut answer as to which forum is the "best" arena for resolving a worker's EEO complaint. The answer usually depends on many variables, including: the availability of experienced, affordable legal counsel for a court battle, the case law of the jurisdiction where a court case may be tried, and who's likely to be the judge—and jury pool—in your locality.

Keep in mind that federal workers are entitled to proceed through the entire EEOC administrative process and *then* initiate a court action if they are dissatisfied with the EEOC result. However, this path requires exceptional patience (and possibly significant resources), since the EEOC process alone can take several years to complete.

Range of Remedies

Where corrective action is ordered by the Commission and the agency has exhausted its administrative appeals, the agency must carry out the corrective action within the time specified by the Commission's order. Remedies imposed by EEOC may include:

• posting a notice to all employees advising them of their rights under the laws EEOC enforces and their right to be free from retaliation;

• corrective or preventive actions taken to cure or correct the source of the identified discrimination;

• nondiscriminatory placement in the position the victim would have occupied if the discrimination had not occurred;

• compensatory damages (see "Damages" below);

• back pay (with interest where applicable), and lost benefits;

• stopping the specific discriminatory practices involved; and

• payment of reasonable attorney's fees and costs.

If EEOC finds that an agency has not complied with its decision of corrective action, it can issue a notice to the head of the agency to show cause for lack of compliance; refer the matter to the Office of Special Counsel for action; and notify you of the right to file a private lawsuit for judicial review of the agency's refusal to comply with the decision.

Complaints that are dismissed by the agency, withdrawn by you, or settled by the parties may not go through all the stages of the complaint process. Withdrawals and settlements may occur at any point before a final agency decision. For example, you may withdraw a complaint or an agency may pursue a settlement after reviewing investigation results. Likewise, you may withdraw a complaint or an agency may pursue a settlement based on facts raised during a hearing before an EEOC administrative judge. If an agency does not comply with the terms of a settlement agreement, however, the complaint may be reinstated.

What's Due in Damages?

Successful complainants in EEO actions may be entitled to an award of "compensatory damages" in addition to other forms of relief, such as reinstatement or reversal of a discriminatory personnel action, back pay, and an attorney's fees reimbursement. According to EEOC, a "compensatory damages" award is designed to make the victim whole for both past and future pecuniary losses, as well as nonpecuniary losses that have been directly or proximately caused by the agency's discriminatory conduct.

"Pecuniary losses" typically consist of the out-of-pocket expenses complainants have incurred as a result of the employer's unlawful actions, including such items as job-hunting and moving expenses, medical and psychiatric bills, physical therapy expenses, and other quantifiable expenditures by the individual. "Past" pecuniary losses are those costs incurred before the resolution of the complaint, while "future" pecuniary losses are those that are likely to be incurred following the resolution. "Non-pecuniary" losses are those that are not subject to precise quantification. The term covers damages for items such as emotional pain or suffering, inconvenience, mental anguish, loss of life's enjoyment, injuries to an individual's professional standing, character, reputation, or credit standing, and loss of health.

There is no "cap" on the amount of back pay and past pecuniary losses that can be awarded. However, there is a $300,000 cap on the total damages that can be awarded for non-pecuniary losses (e.g., past and future emotional distress) and future pecuniary losses.

Punitive damages are not available against the federal government.

Mixed Cases

A "mixed case" is a complaint based on an action that is appealable to the Merit Systems Protection Board and also includes one or more allegations of discrimination. An example of this type of case is the termination of a career employee, who suspects that management's decision may have been motivated, at leasst in part, by unlawful bias.

If a personnel action has been taken against you that is appealable to the Merit Systems Protection Board (see MSPB chapter) and you feel the action had discriminatory motives, you can file an EEO complaint with the agency or you can file an appeal with the MSPB.

If you file a complaint with the agency, it has 120 days to resolve the complaint. If the agency fails to meet this time limit, you may file an appeal with the MSPB at any time after the 120-day period. If your agency does issue a decision that you are unhappy

with, you may appeal the final agency decision to the MSPB within 30 days. You could also file suit at the appropriate U.S. district court within 30 days.

If you choose to appeal to the MSPB instead of going through the agency's EEO process, the Board will have jurisdiction over both the appealable action and the discrimination issue. Your appeal to the MSPB must be made within 30 days after the effective date of the agency's personnel action.

If you have filed a grievance under a negotiated grievance procedure, you may request the MSPB to review the final decision of the arbitrator within 35 days of the arbitrator's decision.

When discrimination is an issue in an appeal, the MSPB must decide both the discrimination issue and the appealable action within 120 days. If discrimination was not an issue until after the MSPB proceedings began, then the Board must decide all issues within 120 days after the discrimination issue was raised. However, the discrimination issue could be remanded back to the agency if the Board's administrative judge thinks it in the interest of justice and both parties agree. The remand order will specify how long (but not more than 120 days) the agency has to make a decision. When a discrimination issue has been returned to the agency, the MSPB processing of the appeal must be completed within 120 days after the agency action is completed and the case is returned to MSPB.

Following a final decision by MSPB in a mixed case, you may:
• accept the decision of the MSPB,
• file suit in the appropriate U.S. district court within 30 days of receipt of the MSPB's final decision,
• file a petition for review with the EEOC within 30 days, or

• file a petition for review of the appealable action only (not the discrimination issues) with the U.S. Court of Appeals for the Federal Circuit.

If you petition the EEOC to review the MSPB's discrimination decision, the Commission must determine whether it will consider the case within 30 days or else the MSPB decision becomes final. If the EEOC determines that it will review the decision, it must complete the process within 60 days and either concur in the MSPB decision or tell the Board its reasons for disagreeing with the decision.

If the EEOC disagrees with the MSPB decision on the discrimination issue, the Board has 30 days in which to concur in and adopt the EEOC decision or reaffirm its original decision with whatever revisions are considered necessary. If MSPB concurs with the EEOC ruling, that decision becomes final. However, any such decision may be appealed to the appropriate U.S. district court.

If the MSPB does not concur in the decision of the EEOC, the matter must immediately be referred to a "Special Panel" provided for by law. Composed of a chair appointed by the president, one member of the MSPB and one member of the EEOC, the Special Panel must issue a final decision in mixed cases no later than 45 days after the matter was referred by the MSPB. The decision of the Special Panel is final (although it may be appealed to the appropriate U.S. district court).

Contacting the EEOC

Information on all EEOC-enforced laws may be obtained by calling 1-800-669-EEOC. EEOC's toll-free TDD number is 1-800-800-3302. The Commission's World Wide Web site is *http://www.eeoc.gov.*

EEOC Headquarters
U.S. Equal Employment Opportunity Commission
1801 L Street, N.W.
Washington, D.C. 20507
Phone: (202) 663-4900;
TDD: (202) 663-4494

Field Offices
To be automatically connected with the nearest EEOC field office, call:
Phone: 1-800-669-4000;
TDD: 1-800-669-6820.

——————— EEOC Offices ———————

Albuquerque District Office
505 Marquette Street, N.W.
Suite 900
Albuquerque, NM 87102
Phone: 505-248-5201;
TDD: 505-248-5240

Atlanta District Office
100 Alabama Street, Suite 4R30,
Atlanta, GA 30303
Phone: 404-562-6800;
TDD: 404-562-6801

Baltimore District Office
City Crescent Building,
10 South Howard Street, 3rd Floor,
Baltimore, MD 21201
Phone: 410-962-3932;
TDD: 410-962-6065

Birmingham District Office
1900 3rd Avenue North, Suite 101,
Birmingham, AL 35203-2397
Phone: 205-731-1359;
TDD: 205-731-0095

Boston Area Office
1 Congress Street, 10th Floor,
Room 1001 Boston, MA 02114
Phone: 617-565-3200;
TDD: 617-565-3204

Buffalo Local Office
6 Fountain Plaza, Suite 350,
Buffalo, NY 14202
Phone: 716-846-4441;
TDD: 716-846-5923
Charlotte District Office
129 West Trade Street, Suite 400,
Charlotte, NC 28202
Phone: 704-344-6682;
TDD: 704-344-6684

Chicago District Office
500 West Madison Street,
Suite 2800,
 Chicago, IL 60661
Phone: 312-353-2713;
TDD: 312-353-2421

Cincinnati Area Office
525 Vine Street, Suite 810,
Cincinnati, OH 45202-3122
Phone: 513-684-2851;
TDD: 513-684-2074

Cleveland District Office
1660 West Second Street,
Suite 850,
 Cleveland, OH 44113-1454
Phone: 216-522-2001;
TDD: 216-522-8441

Dallas District Office
207 S. Houston Street, 3rd Floor,
Dallas, TX 75202-4726
Phone: 214-655-3355;
TDD: 214-655-3363

Denver District Office
303 E. 17th Avenue, Suite 510,
Denver, CO 80203
Phone: 303-866-1300;
TDD: 303-866-1950

Detroit District Office
477 Michigan Avenue, Room 865,
Detroit, MI 48226-9704
Phone: 313-226-7636;
TDD: 313-226-7599

El Paso Area Office
The Commons, Building C,
Suite 100,
 4171 N. Mesa Street,
El Paso, TX 79902
Phone: 915-534-6550;
TDD: 915-534-6545

Fresno Local Office
1265 West Shaw Avenue,
Suite 103,
Fresno, CA 93711
Phone: 209-487-5793;
TDD: 209-487-5837

Greensboro Local Office
801 Summit Avenue,
Greensboro, NC 27405-7813
Phone: 910-333-5174;
TDD: 910-333-5542

Greenville Local Office
Wachovia Building, Suite 530,
15 South Main Street,
Greenville, SC 29601
Phone: 803-241-4400;
 TDD: 803-241-4403

Honolulu Local Office
300 Ala Moana Boulevard,
Room 7123-A, P.O. Box 50082,
Honolulu, HI 96850-0051
Phone: 808-541-3120;
TDD: 808-541-3131

Houston District Office
1919 Smith Street, 7th Floor,
Houston, TX 77002
Phone: 713-209-3320;
TDD: 713-209-3367

Indianapolis District Office
101 W. Ohio Street, Suite 1900,
Indiana, IN 46204-4203
Phone: 317-226-7212;
TDD: 317-226-5162

Jackson Area Office
207 West Amite Street,
Jackson, MS 39201
Phone: 601-965-4537
TDD: 601-965-4915

Kansas City Area Office
400 State Avenue, Suite 905,
Kansas City, KS 66101
Phone: 913-551-5655;
TDD: 913-551-5657

Little Rock Area Office
425 West Capitol Avenue,
Suite 625,
Little Rock, AR 72201
Phone: 501-324-5060;
TDD: 501-324-5481

Los Angeles District Office
255 E. Temple, 4th Floor,
Los Angeles, CA 90012
Phone: 213-894-1000;
TDD: 213-894-1121

Louisville Area Office
600 Dr. Martin
Luther King Jr. Place,
Suite 268, Louisville, KY 40202
Phone: 502-582-6082;
TDD: 502-582-6285

Memphis District Office
1407 Union Avenue, Suite 521,
Memphis, TN 38104
Phone: 901-544-0115;
TDD: 901-544-0112

Miami District Office
One Biscayne Tower,
2 South Biscayne Boulevard,
Suite 2700,
Miami, FL 33131
Phone: 305-536-4491;
TDD: 305-536-5721

Milwaukee District Office
310 West Wisconsin Avenue,
Suite 800,
Milwaukee, WI 53203-2292
Phone: 414-297-1111;
TDD: 414-297-1115

Minneapolis Area Office
330 South Second Avenue,
Suite 430,
Minneapolis, MN 55401-2224
Phone: 612-335-4040;
TDD: 612-335-4045

Nashville Area Office
50 Vantage Way, Suite 202,
Nashville, TN 37228
Phone: 615-736-5820;
TDD: 615-736-5870

Newark Area Office
1 Newark Center, 21st Floor,
Newark, NJ 07102-5233
Phone: 201-645-6383;
TDD: 201-645-3004

New Orleans District Office
701 Loyola Avenue,
Suite 600, New Orleans, LA
70113-9936
Phone: 504-589-2329;
TDD: 504-589-2958

New York District Office
7 World Trade Center, 18th Floor,
New York, NY 10048-0948
Phone: 212-748-8500;
TDD: 212-748-8399

Norfolk Area Office
World Trade Center,
101 West Main Street, Suite 4300,
Norfolk, VA 23510
Phone: 804-441-3470;
TDD: 804-441-3578

Oakland Local Office
1301 Clay Street, Suite 1170-N,
Oakland, CA 94612-5217
Phone: 510-637-3230;
TDD: 510-637-3234

Oklahoma Area Office
210 Park Avenue,
Oklahoma City, OK 73102
Phone: 405-231-4911;
TDD: 405-231-5745

Philadelphia District Office
21 South 5th Street, 4th Floor,
Philadelphia, PA 19106
Phone: 215-451-5800;
TDD: 215-451-5814

Phoenix District Office
3300 N. Central Avenue,
Phoenix, AZ 85012-1848
Phone: 602-640-5000;
TDD: 602-640-5072

Pittsburgh Area Office
1001 Liberty Avenue, Suite 300,
Pittsburgh, PA 15222-4187
Phone: 412-644-3444;
TDD: 412-644-2720

Raleigh Area Office
1309 Annapolis Drive, .
Raleigh, NC 27608-2129
Phone: 919-856-4064;
TDD: 919-856-4296

Richmond Area Office
3600 West Broad Street,
Room 229,
Richmond, VA 23230
Phone: 804-278-4651;
TDD: 804-278-4654

San Antonio District Office
5410 Fredericksburg Road,
Suite 200,
San Antonio, TX 78229-3555
Phone: 210-229-4810;
TDD: 210-229-4858

San Diego Area Office
401 B Street, Suite 1550,
San Diego, CA 92101
Phone: 619-557-7235;
TDD: 619-557-7232

San Francisco District Office
901 Market Street, Suite 500,
San Francisco, CA 94103
Phone: 415-356-5100;
TDD: 415-356-5098

San Jose Local Office
96 North 3rd Street, Suite 200,
San Jose, CA 95112
Phone: 408-291-7352;
TDD: 408-291-7374

Savannah Local Office
410 Mall Boulevard, Suite G,
Savannah, GA 31406-4821
Phone: 912-652-4234;
TDD: 912-652-4439

Seattle District Office
Federal Office Building,
909 First Avenue, Suite 400,
Seattle, WA 98104-1061
Phone: 206-220-6883;
TDD: 206-220-6882

St. Louis District Office
Robert A. Young Building,
122 Spruce Street, Room 8100,
St. Louis, MO 63103
Phone: 314-539-7800;
TDD: 314-539-7803

Tampa Area Office
501 East Polk Street, 10th Floor,
Tampa, FL 33602
Phone: 813-228-2310;
TDD: 813-228-2003

Washington Field Office
1400 L Street, N.W., Suite 200,
Washington, D.C. 20005
Phone: 202-275-7377;
TDD: 202-275-7518

CHAPTER EIGHTEEN

Federal Labor Relations Authority

Labor-management relations in the federal government are governed by a complex mosaic of law, regulations, agreements, and procedures. For most employees the top level of authority is the Federal Labor Relations Authority. Its role is to interpret and enforce the federal labor-management relations statute, otherwise known as Title VII of the 1978 Civil Service Reform Act.

The statute protects the rights of executive branch employees to organize, bargain collectively, and participate through labor organizations in decisions affecting them. The FLRA also ensures compliance with the statutory rights and obligations of federal employees and the labor organizations that represent them in their dealings with federal agencies.

Entities within the FLRA are the Federal Service Impasses Panel, which provides assistance in resolving deadlocks reached in bargaining between labor and management, the Foreign Service Labor Relations Board, which oversees the labor management program for foreign service workers, and the Foreign Services Impasse Disputes Panel, which resolves bargaining deadlocks for those employees.

The FLRA also assists federal agencies and unions in understanding their rights and responsibilities under the law and helps them improve their relationships so they can resolve problems without formal intervention.

FLRA Rules and Procedures

Who's Covered

To be covered by the federal labor relations statute, you must be represented by a union. This is often subject to misunderstanding. Many federal employees believe they are covered by union protections when in fact they are not; for others, the opposite is true.

Federal union membership is generally available to employees of the executive branch, as well as the Library of Congress and the Government Printing Office.

An employee must be in a recog-nized bargaining unit—that is, must be in the group of employees covered by the union's representation rights—in order to be represented by a union. There are many sites within the government eligible to be organized into a bargaining unit, but for one reason or another no unit has been formed. Employees in such situations lack rights of representation that would otherwise be available to them if they were in a bargaining unit.

Employees covered by the statute have a right to form, join, or assist a labor organization or to refrain from such activity without fear of penalty or reprisal. The right includes acting for a labor organization in the capacity of a representative, and presenting the views of that organization before agency officials, the Congress, or other authorities.

Covered employees also have the right to engage in collective bargaining with respect to conditions of employment—meaning personnel policies and practices affecting their working conditions. Topics of such disputes can range from office amenities to use of alternative work schedules, promotions, and reassignments.

Excluded from union membership are non-citizens, members of the armed services, supervisors and management officials, certain employees who act in a confidential capacity to a superior involved in labor-management policy, certain personnel and professional employees, those engaged in intelligence, investigative or security work directly affecting national security, certain foreign service employees, and anyone who participates in a strike against the government.

Also excluded are employees of designated agencies including the General Accounting Office, Federal Bureau of Investigation, Central Intelligence Agency, National Security Agency, Tennessee Valley Authority, FLRA itself, and the Federal Service Impasses Panel.

For employees, FLRA's primary role is its power to resolve negotiability disputes, unfair labor practice complaints, and appeals of arbitration decisions. Other FLRA responsibilities include determining the appropriateness of bargaining units, supervising representation elections, and consultation rights with regard to internal agency policies and government-wide rules.

Role of the Labor Union

Unlike other forms of federal employee appeals, where the individual acts on his or her own behalf (possibly represented by an attorney or someone else), complaints under the labor-management statute are primarily brought by labor organizations that have won the right to represent a group of employees—often called a bargaining unit.

There is a difference between bargaining unit status and dues-paying status, although not for representation purposes. If you are in a bargaining unit, the union has a duty to represent you, even if you do not pay union dues. Most employees who are in bargaining units, in fact, are not dues-paying members. But employees who are not in a bargaining unit cannot choose to join a union.

Once a labor organization is recognized as the representative for a group of employees, it becomes entitled to act for them and negotiate collective bargaining agreements. Those agreements must contain a negotiated procedure for resolving grievances and provide that binding arbitration may be invoked if the grievance proceeding fails to resolve a dispute. Such grievances can be brought by a union—acting on its own behalf or on behalf of a bargaining unit member—or by an individual unit member or by management. Certain topics are excluded from grievance coverage (see Grievances chapter).

A union may choose not to file a grievance on your behalf or to withdraw from the process at any point. If that happens, you may pursue the grievance on your own but may not invoke arbitration. Thus, you have no direct line of appeal to the FLRA. You can, however, try to compel union representation by bringing before the FLRA an unfair labor practice complaint against the union, charging it with a failure to represent.

The union also has the right to be represented at any formal discussion between agency officials and bargaining unit employees or their representatives concerning any grievance, personnel policy, or practice or condition of employment. Further, the union has the right to be represented if you are examined during the course of an investigation and you reasonably believe that the examination might result in disciplinary action and you request union representation. Unions also must be given advance notice of proposed changes to conditions of employment and an opportunity to bargain over those that are negotiable.

The rights of a union do not preclude you from being represented by an attorney or other person of your own choosing in any grievance or appeal action, except in the case of grievance or appeal procedures negotiated under the statute. Nor do they prohibit you from exercising any grievance or appeal rights established by law or rule, except in the case of mandatory grievance or appeal procedures negotiated between the union and management. An aggrieved employee generally has the option of using either an appeals procedure set by statute or a grievance procedure created by contract, but not both.

Types of Appeals

• *Arbitration Appeals*—If you are a bargaining unit member and have a workplace grievance, your contract outlines the steps you must follow to pursue your grievance. Formal settlements or other types of agreements may occur at any step in the process. If the final decision on a grievance is negative, the union — not you as an individual — may invoke binding arbitration. Binding arbitration is conducted by a private-sector arbitrator whose services are paid for by the union and/or agency. The parties to the contract—the union or management but not an individual employee—can appeal an arbitrator's decision to FLRA by filing "exceptions" within 30 days of the decision. If no appeal is filed during that period, the arbitrator's award is final and binding.

The FLRA's review of an arbitrator's award is limited. Certain arbitrator awards, including those concerning unacceptable performance, reductions in grade, and reductions in pay, are not reviewable by the FLRA. Reviewable arbitration awards involve, for example, disputes over shift assignments or restrictions on the use of leave. The FLRA may affirm, modify, or reverse the arbitrator's award in whole or in part. Unless an unfair labor practice is involved, the FLRA's decision is final and binding and may not be appealed to any court.

• *Unfair Labor Practices*— If either labor or management fails to perform their obligations to each other, an unfair labor practice charge may be filed (see box on next page). A charge may also be filed if either labor or management interferes with the rights each has been given under the statute. Employees may also file charges against labor or management. In practice, the vast majority of such charges are filed by unions against management.

Unfair labor practice charges must be filed with the appropriate FLRA regional office within six months from the date the alleged unfair practice occurred. The regional office investigates the allegations and may seek sworn testimony, documents, or statements. The regional director can also ask the general counsel to issue subpoenas. After the investigation, the union may decide to withdraw the

Unfair Labor Practices

The underlying concept of unfair labor practices is that unions and management must refrain from infringing upon each other's basic rights, as well as from violating the basic rights of employees.

For management, it is an unfair labor practice:

• To interfere with, restrain, or coerce any employee in the exercise by the employee of any right under 5 U.S.C. Chapter 71 (prohibited interference by an agency with the rights of federal employees to organize, form, join, or assist a labor organization, to bargain collectively, or to refrain from any of these activities constitutes a violation of this subsection);

• To encourage or discourage membership in any labor organization by discrimination in connection with hiring, tenure, promotion, or other conditions of employment;

• To sponsor, control, or otherwise assist any labor organization other than to furnish, upon request, customary and routine services and facilities, if the services and facilities are also furnished on an impartial basis to other labor organizations having equivalent status;

• To discipline or otherwise discriminate against an employee because the employee has filed a complaint, affidavit, or petition, or has given any information or testimony under Chapter 71;

• To refuse to consult or negotiate in good faith with a labor organization as required by the Chapter (This section protects many of the different rights of an exclusive representative, such as the right to bargain collectively and in good faith over conditions of employment, the right to be the sole representative for its appropriate unit of employees, and the right to be notified of proposed changes in conditions of employment.);

• To fail or refuse to cooperate in impasse procedures and impasse decisions as required by the Chapter;

• To enforce any rule or regulation (other than a rule or regulation implementing 5 U.S.C. section 2302), which is in conflict with any applicable collective bargaining agreement if the agreement was in effect before the date the rule or regulation was prescribed; or

• To otherwise fail or refuse to comply with any provision of the Chapter (5 U.S.C 7116(a)).

For unions, it is an unfair labor practice:

• To interfere with, restrain, or coerce any employee in the exercise by the employee of any right under 5 U.S.C. Chapter 71;

• To cause or attempt to cause an agency to discriminate against any employee in the exercise by the employee of any right under 5 U.S.C. Chapter 71;

• To coerce, discipline, fine, or attempt to coerce a member of the labor organization as punishment, reprisal, or for the purpose of hindering or impeding the member's work performance or productivity as an employee or the discharge of a member's duties as an employee;

• To discriminate against an employee with regard to the terms or conditions of membership in the labor organization on the basis of race, color, creed, national origin, sex, age, preferential or non-preferential civil service status, political affiliation, marital status, or disability;

• To refuse to consult or negotiate in good faith with an agency as required under 5 U.S.C. Chapter 71 (This includes the union's responsibility to approach negotiations with a sincere resolve to reach agreement and to be represented by duly authorized representatives.);

• To fail or refuse to cooperate in impasse procedures and impasse decisions as required under 5 U.S.C. Chapter 71 (This is identical to the agency requirement.);

• To call, participate in, or "condone" a strike, work stoppage, or slowdown, or picketing of an agency in a labor-management dispute if such picketing interferes with an agency's operations, or

• To otherwise fail or refuse to comply with any provision of 5 U.S.C. chapter 71 (5 U.S.C. 7116(b)).

complaint, or the regional director could refuse to issue a complaint. If a complaint is not issued, you can appeal that decision within 25 days to the general counsel. The general counsel may grant an appeal if the regional director's decision was based on incomplete or untrue information or there is no FLRA precedent on the legal issue in the case.

If the regional director issues the complaint, a recommendation is then made to FLRA's Office of the General Counsel—the investigative and prosecutorial component of the FLRA. The General Counsel investigates and settles or prosecutes all unfair labor practice complaints filed with the FLRA and brings complaints before an administrative law judge.

The law judge's decision may be appealed to the FLRA by any party. On appeal, the FLRA may affirm, modify, or reverse the judge's decision and recommended order in whole or in part. The FLRA's decision may be appealed to the appropriate federal court of appeals.

• *Negotiability Appeals*—These appeals arise where the union and management disagree over a matter proposed for bargaining. They must be filed with FLRA's national office within 15 days after the agency notifies the union of its position that a matter raised in bargaining is not negotiable.

Examples of these disputes include whether an agency has a duty to bargain over the work environment or reduction in force procedures. Only unions (not agencies or individuals) may file negotiability appeals with the FLRA. After reviewing the case, the FLRA issues a decision and order stating whether the agency has a duty to bargain. The FLRA's decision may be appealed to the appropriate federal court of appeal.

Disputes about what is negotiable may also be resolved in the unfair labor practice process.

• *Bargaining Impasses*—During the collective bargaining process, when an agency and union do not reach agreement on issues, they may seek mediation assistance and then a decision by the Federal Service Impasses Panel. Cases brought to the Panel involve, for example, impasses in negotiations over reorganization-related proposals such as the selection procedures used to relocate employees and procedures available for employees to request reconsideration of transfers.

After an investigation and determination is made concerning jurisdiction, the Panel has authority to recommend a variety of informal and formal procedures to resolve the impasse. The final action by the Panel is binding on the parties for the term of the collective bargaining agreement unless they both agree otherwise. The Panel's decision may not be appealed to any court.

• *Representation Issues*—FLRA resolves a variety of issues related to questions of union representation of employees. These issues include, for example, conducting elections to determine if the employees desire to be represented, making decisions about who can be in a bargaining unit, and determining the impact of reorganizations on the scope of existing bargaining units.

An agency or union (or an individual in rare circumstances) may file representation petitions with regional offices. After a petition is filed, the regional office notifies any labor organization, agency or activity that may be affected by issues raised in the petition and investigates the representation issues and any challenges to the petition. A regional director may issue a decision or a direction of election.

A regional director's decision and

order may be appealed to the FLRA. FLRA review of representation cases is limited. FLRA may affirm, modify, or reverse the regional director's decision and order in whole or in part. The FLRA's decision is final and may not be appealed to any court.

Appeal Process

Parties wishing to challenge FLRA final orders that are appealable generally can appeal in the U.S. Court of Appeals for the circuit in which the party resides or in the U.S. Court of Appeals for the District of Columbia. Arbitration awards on discipline for poor performance or misconduct may be appealed to the U.S. Court of Appeals for the Federal Circuit on the same basis as if the award were the final decision of the Merit Systems Protection Board.

Contacting FLRA

For unfair labor practice charges and complaints, contact the FLRA regional office covering your geographic area. For appeals to the general counsel of dismissals of unfair labor practices, contact the Office of the General Counsel at (202) 482-6680. For trials by administrative law judges, contact the Office of Admin-istrative Law Judges at (202) 482-6630. For appeals to the Authority from administrative law judge decisions, contact the Office of Case Control at (202) 482-6540.

For general questions about representation issues, contact the FLRA regional office covering your geographic area. For appeals to the Authority of representation decisions and orders, contact the Office of Case Control at (202) 482-6540.

For appeals ("exceptions") to the Authority from arbitrator's decisions and orders, contact the Office of Case Control at (202) 482-6540.

For bargaining impasses, contact the Federal Service Impasses Panel at (202) 482-6670.

For negotiation appeals, contact the Office of Case Control at (202) 482-6540.

For duty to bargain and unfair labor practice disputes, contact the FLRA regional office covering your geographic area.

For copies of FLRA publications or general questions about the FLRA, contact the Information Resources Management Division at (202) 482-6550.

FLRA's World Wide Web address is *http://www.flra.gov.*

FLRA Regional Offices

Atlanta Region
Marquis Two Tower, Suite 701
285 Peachtree Center Avenue
Atlanta, GA 30303-1270
Telephone: (404) 331-5300
FAX: (404) 331-5280
Alabama, Florida, Georgia, Mississippi, North Carolina, South Carolina, Tennessee, Virgin Islands, Puerto Rico

Boston Region
99 Summer Street, Suite 1500
Boston, MA 02110-1200
Telephone: (617) 424-5731
FAX: (617) 424-5743
Connecticut, Maine, Massachusetts, New Hampshire, New Jersey, New York, Pennsylvania, Rhode Island, Vermont

Chicago Region
55 West Monroe, Suite 1150
Chicago, IL 60603-9729
Telephone: (312) 353-6306
FAX: (312) 886-5977
Illinois, Indiana, Iowa, Kentucky, Michigan, Minnesota, North Dakota,Ohio, Tennessee, Wisconsin and all land and water areas east of the continents of North and South America to long. 90 degrees E., except the Virgin Islands, Panama, Puerto Rico and coastal islands.

Dallas Region
Federal Office Building
525 Griffin Street, Suite 926, LB 107   (limited jurisdiction)
Dallas, TX 75202-1906
Telephone: (214) 767-4996
FAX: (214) 767-0156
Arkansas, Louisiana, New Mexico, Oklahoma, Texas, Panama

Denver Region
1244 Speer Blvd., Suite 100
Denver, CO 80204-3581
Telephone: (303) 844-5224
FAX: (303) 844-2774
Arizona, Colorado, Idaho, Kansas, Missouri, Montana, Nebraska, Nevada, South Dakota, Utah, Wyoming

San Francisco Region
901 Market Street, Suite 220
San Francisco, CA 94103-1791
Telephone: (415) 356-5000
FAX: (415) 356-5017
Alaska, California, Hawaii, Oregon, Washington, and all land and water areas west of the continents of North and South America (except coastal islands) to long. 90 degrees E.

Washington, D.C. Region
1255 22nd Street, N.W., Suite 400
Washington, D.C. 20037-1206
Telephone: (202) 653-8500
FAX: (202) 653-5091
Deleware, District of Columbia, Maryland, Virginia, West Virginia

CHAPTER NINETEEN

Office of Personnel Management

The Office of Personnel Management is the federal government's main personnel agency. Headquartered in Washington, D.C., the agency has regional offices throughout the country. OPM performs a wide variety of duties to support agency personnel services and administers the government's retirement systems, along with the life and health insurance programs.

OPM also provides employment information to the public. In conjunction with that duty, it has responsibility for administering the merit system for the federal government. This includes recruiting, examining, and promoting people based on their knowledge and skills, rather than non-merit issues such as gender, age, ethnicity, or political influence.

OPM's Authority and Procedures

Scope of Appeals

Generally, OPM hears appeals regarding job status, benefits decisions, and some monetary issues. Under those major areas, however, the following issues are *not* appealable to OPM, although they may be reviewable under administrative or negotiated grievance procedures:

• the accuracy of the official position description, including the inclusion or exclusion of a major duty;

• an assignment or detail out of the scope of normally performed duties;

• the accuracy, consistency, or use of agency supplemental classification guides;

• the title of the position, unless the title reflects a qualification requirement or authorized area of specialization or the title is authorized in an OPM classification standard guide;

• the class, grade, or pay system of a position to which the employee is not officially assigned;

• a proposed classification decision;

• the class, grade, or pay system of a position to which an employee is detailed or promoted on a time-limited basis for less than two years;

• the classification of a position based on position-to-position comparisons and not standards;

• the accuracy of grade level criteria in an OPM guide or standard.

Job Status Disputes

Job status disputes include classification issues, termination of grade or pay retention—sometimes called saved pay or grade—and questions regarding examination ratings.

• *Classification Issues*—A general schedule employee may appeal his or her official position classification at any time. Generally, you appeal a job classification if you have been promoted, demoted or otherwise moved. You may also appeal inclusion or exclusion from the General Schedule, occupational series, grade, or position title.

If your position is reclassified to a lower grade base in whole or in part, you should receive prompt, written notice from your agency, even if you are eligible for retained pay or grade. The notice should inform you of your right to appeal the classification decision. You may appeal the decision to the agency if the agency has an established appeal system and is authorized to review the classification decision (the notice will tell you). If not, you appeal directly to OPM.

If you are reclassified to a lower grade and pay and are not entitled to retained pay or grade, you can seek a retroactive adjustment through an appeal. The appeal must be filed within 15 calendar days of receiving notice of the action or within 15 days of the action itself, whichever is later.

You may also request an OPM decision on the appropriate occupational series or grade of the employee's official position.

An employee may appeal a classification by writing directly to OPM's Classification Appeals Office, 1900 E Street, NW, Washington, DC 20415. Your appeal must be in writing and should include the following:

• your name, mailing address, and office telephone number;

• your department or agency, with complete mailing address, and your exact location within the agency;

• your current position title, pay plan, occupational series, and grade;

• requested pay plan, position title, occupational series, and grade;

• copy of the official position description, if available, along with a statement concerning its accuracy;

• reason why you believe the position is erroneously classified; and

• name, address and business telephone number of your representative, if you have one.

You may use a representative to help prepare and present a classification appeal. However, your agency can prohibit your choice from acting as representative if his or her activities would cause a conflict of interest, if he or she cannot be released from their duties because of the priority needs of the government, or if such a release would be too costly to the government.

You can also appeal by forwarding the appeal through the employing agency. If you go through your agency, the agency must forward your appeal to OPM within 60 days if:

• the agency is not authorized to act on the appeal;

• the agency has not decided the appeal within the established time limits; or

• the employee has directed the appeal to OPM and the agency's written decision is not favorable.

The agency, when forwarding your appeal or when requested by OPM, must furnish all relevant facts concerning the position and its reasons for the decision. Both you and your agency may submit relevant information to OPM at any time following the filing of an appeal.

Once OPM receives your appeal it will send an acknowledgement letter to you or your representative and to your agency. OPM will review the particulars of your case and may request further information from you or your agency. OPM may conduct an on-site review of the position. After OPM completes its review, it will issue a decision—called a classification certificate.

An OPM decision is final unless OPM decides to reconsider it at its own discretion. The decision is binding on all administrative, payroll, and other offices. Agencies must review their own classification decisions for identical, similar, or related positions to assure consistency with OPM's decision.

• **Termination of Grade or Pay Retention**—Grade or pay retention benefits accrue to employees placed in lower grade positions because of a reduction in force. The benefits generally last for two years after which an employee will be placed in the proper grade. Generally, you will keep the higher rate of pay if it exceeds the rate of pay for the new grade—up to a cap. The retained rate may not exceed 150 percent of the top rate of the grade to which you are reduced.

During this period, the agency may terminate your benefits if you refuse a "reasonable offer" of another position of equal or greater grade or pay than that of your retained grade or pay. In general, a "reasonable offer" must be in writing and must include an official position description. The position must be of a tenure equal to or greater than that of the position creating the retention benefit, and should have a work schedule of no less time. Finally, the position offered should be in the same commuting area unless you are subject to a mobility agreement or an agency policy requiring employee mobility.

The offer should inform you that a failure to accept the position will cause your grade or pay retention benefit to end. If you feel the offer was not reasonable and, after declining the offer, your benefits are terminated, you may appeal to OPM. If you are a member of a bargaining unit, there may be a negotiated grievance process for an appeal.

An appeal must be filed with OPM within 20 calendar days after you are notified that your grade or pay retention benefits have been cancelled. The appeal must include information identifying you and the organization involved and must state the reasons why you feel the offer was not reasonable.

OPM may conduct any investiga-tion or hearing it determines necessary to learn the facts, including requiring the agency to provide needed information. OPM's decision could require corrective action by the agency, including retroactive or prospective restoration of grade or pay retention benefits.

OPM's decisions are final. It may, at its discretion, reconsider a decision when new information is presented in writing that establishes reasonable doubt about the original decision. The request to reconsider must show that the information was not readily available when the decision was issued and must be submitted within 30 calendar days of the original decision.

Eligibility for grade or pay retention also may be lost for other reasons, including a break in service or demotion for cause or at the employee's request.

• **Examination Ratings**—Applicants for certain federal positions receive ratings based on hiring factors, including written performance tests. People who take these tests are assigned ratings by the examination office.

You may appeal an examination decision or the rejection of an application either by OPM or an agency with examining authority. Your appeal will go to the examining office, but it will be reviewed by someone other than the rater who made the original decision. The request for reconsideration should be in writing and should state why the original decision was not proper.

If you are unhappy with the first review, you may request a second review. The second request should also be sent to the examining office but will be forwarded to a higher level.

There is no set time period for requesting a review other than a general policy that applicants who object to their ratings should act promptly.

The filing of a request for reconsideration doesn't affect any other rights you, as an applicant, may have under the law.

Life and Health Disputes

Federal employees enjoy a host of employment-related benefits including life, health, and retirement benefit coverage. OPM is charged with running and maintaining these programs and this is where you go if you experience problems in these benefit areas.

• *Life Insurance*—Active employees and former spouses who are not receiving annuities are entitled to reconsideration of an initial agency decision to deny them enrollment in one or more life insurance coverages or the opportunity to change coverage. The reconsideration process applies only to enrollment issues.

OPM makes initial decisions for annuitants and for former spouses who are receiving annuities. An initial decision—one that is given in writing—should state the right to an independent level of review. The only time an initial decision is not eligible for reconsideration is when it is made at the highest level of review within OPM.

A request for reconsideration must be made in writing, must include your name, address, date of birth, Social Security number, reason for the request, and, if applicable, the retirement claim number. If you are an active employee, your request for reconsideration should be made to your agency. Retiree requests for consideration should be made to:

OPM,
Retirement Operations Center
Reconsideration Staff
Boyers, PA 16017-0001

Your request should be made within 30 days from the date of the written decision. That time limit may be extended if you can show that you were not notified of the deadline or were not otherwise aware of it, or that circumstances beyond your control prevented a timely filing.

After reconsideration, the agency or OPM must issue a final decision in writing that fully sets forth the findings and conclusions. If you are still unhappy with the final decision, you may file suit in the appropriate federal district court or in the United States Court of Claims.

• *Health Insurance*—Decisions on enrollments in the Federal Employees Health Benefits Program are made by the employing agency for active employees and by OPM for retirees. All decisions can be reconsidered unless they were made at the highest level of review within OPM. These decisions should give you the appropriate address for filing a request for reconsideration.

If you want to request a reconsideration of an enrollment decision, your request must be made in writing and must include your name, address, date of birth, Social Security number, name of the carrier, reason for the request, and, if applicable, the retirement claim number. The reconsideration review must be made at or above the level at which the initial decision was rendered.

You should file your request within 30 days of the date of the written decision. That time limit may be extended if you can show that you were not notified of the deadline and were not otherwise aware of it, or that circumstances beyond your control prevented a timely filing.

After reconsideration, the agency or OPM will issue a final decision, in writing, that fully sets forth the findings and conclusions.

If you are denied health insurance coverage, you must first contest that decision with the insurance carrier. Enrollees have six months to ask the carrier to reconsider a denial of all or part of requested coverage. Your request for reconsideration must be in writing and must give the reasons, in terms of applicable brochure provisions, that the denied coverage should have been approved. The carrier then has 30 days to affirm the denial in writing, pay the bill, provide the requested service, or request additional information from you or the health care provider. If additional information is requested, the carrier has 30 days from receiving that information to make a decision. That decision must give specific and detailed reasons for a denial and must notify the individual of the right to request a review by OPM.

After a final decision from the carrier—or a refusal to respond within the time limits—you may ask (within 90 days) for a review by the Office of Insurance Programs, Insurance Review Decisions, at OPM headquarters. The request for OPM review must include a copy of the denial notice, as well as documents to support your position. OPM may request additional information from you and/or the carrier, obtain advice from an independent physician, or may make its decision solely on the information you provided.

OPM normally issues its decision within 90 days after receipt of the request for review. OPM may reopen its review if it receives evidence that was unavailable at the time of the original decision.

You must exhaust both the carrier and OPM review processes before seeking judicial review. A suit to compel enrollment must be brought against the employing office that made the enrollment decision. You may sue OPM in federal district court

to force payment of disputed benefits, no later than the end of the third calendar year after the year in which the claim arose.

Retirement Benefit Disputes

OPM decides basic retirement issues ranging from eligibility for benefits to payment levels, as well as special provisions such as termination of benefits and collection of debts owed to the retirement system for various reasons. An initial decision concerning these issues is made in writing and will state the retiree's right to reconsideration at a higher level of review within OPM. A request for reconsideration must be made in writing, must include your name, address, date of birth, and claim number, if applicable, and must state the basis for the request.

OPM must receive the request within 30 calendar days of its initial decision. That time limit may be extended if you can show that you were not notified of the deadline and were not otherwise aware of it, or that circumstances beyond your control prevented a timely filing.

On reconsideration, OPM issues a final decision in writing that sets forth the findings and conclusions of the reconsideration and provides notice of appeal rights to the Merit Systems Protection Board.

When a decision in favor of one applicant would affect another, such as cases of competing claimants for survivor benefit designations, all parties concerned will be notified of the decision and those adversely affected will be given an opportunity to request reconsideration.

A decision initially rendered at the highest level of review within OPM is not subject to reconsideration and may be appealed directly to MSPB. MSPB decisions may be appealed to the U.S. Court of Appeals for the Federal Circuit.

Special provisions apply to OPM decisions on the various prohibitions on payments of annuities. In those cases, you have 30 days from receiving notice of intent to withhold payment of the annuity to request a hearing before an OPM hearing examiner. The examiner may have witnesses testify under oath and may require legal briefs or other documents to be filed. The officer will make a written initial decision, which can be appealed within OPM for a final decision before a possible appeal to MSPB.

In cases involving collection of debts — either as a lump-sum or under an offset schedule — OPM will inform you in writing of the reason for and the amount of debt, the date on which the payment is due, policies on interest, penalties, and administrative charges, and available arrangements if payment in full would create a financial hardship. You have 30 days from that notice to request reconsideration, waiver and/or compromise. OPM's decision on such requests can be appealed to MSPB. An appeal to MSPB can stop collection of the debt in cases involving denial of a requested waiver.

Contacting OPM

The general address and phone number for OPM is Office of Personnel Management, 1900 E St., N.W., Washington, D.C. 20415, (202) 606-1800. OPM's web site is *http://www.opm.gov.*

OPM Atlanta Oversight Division
75 Spring Street, SW, Suite 972
Atlanta, GA 30303-9763
(404) 331-3451
Alabama, Florida, Georgia, Mississippi, North Carolina, South Carolina,

Tennessee, Virginia (except as noted under the Washington, DC Oversight Division)

OPM Chicago Oversight Division
230 S. Dearborn Street, DPN 30-6
Chicago, IL 60604-1687
(312) 353-0387
Illinois, Indiana, Iowa, Kansas, Kentucky, Minnesota, Missouri, Nebraska, North Dakota, Ohio, South Dakota, West Virginia, Wisconsin

OPM Dallas Oversight Office
1100 Commerce Street, Room 4C22
Dallas, TX 75242-9968
(214) 767-0561
Arizona, Arkansas, Colorado, Louisiana, Montana, New Mexico, Oklahoma, Texas, Utah, Wyoming

OPM Philadelphia Oversight Division
600 Arch Street, Room 3400
Philadelphia, PA 19106-1596
(215) 597-9797
Connecticut, Delaware, Maryland (except as noted under the Washington, DC Oversight Division), Massachusetts, New Hampshire, New Jersey, New York, Pennsylvania, Rhode Island, Vermont, Puerto Rico, Virgin Islands

OPM San Francisco Oversight Division
120 Howard Street, Room 760
San Francisco, CA 94105-0001
(415) 281-7050
Alaska, California, Hawaii, Idaho, Nevada, Oregon, Washington, Pacific Ocean Area

OPM Washington D.C. Oversight Division
1900 E Street, NW
Washington, DC 20415-0001
(202) 606-2990
The District of Columbia, in Maryland: counties of Charles, Montgomery, and Prince Georges; in Virginia: counties

of Arlington, Fairfax, King George, Loudoun, Prince William, and Stafford, the cities of: Alexandria, FairFax, Falls Church, Manassas, and Manassas Park; and overseas areas not included above

CHAPTER TWENTY

Office of Special Counsel

The Office of Special Counsel (OSC) is an independent federal investigative and prosecutorial agency. OSC's enforcement authority includes the investigation of alleged prohibited personnel practices and Hatch Act political activity violations. It also litigates cases arising out of these investigations before the Merit Systems Protection Board (MSPB).

OSC's main responsibilities are:

• investigating alleged prohibited personnel practices, especially reprisal for whistleblowing, and other activities prohibited by civil service law, rule, or regulation, and pursuing corrective or disciplinary action when warranted;

• interpreting and enforcing Hatch Act prohibitions on political activity by federal, postal, state, and local employees; and

• operating a whistleblower disclosure hotline for federal employees to report wrongdoing in government.

———— OSC Authority and Procedures ————

Prohibited Personnel Practices

The Civil Service Reform Act outlines a series of personnel practices that, if taken, undermine the federal merit system and thus are prohibited by the Act. The ban on these practices is designed to protect current or former federal employees or applicants in most positions in most agencies. The restrictions apply to federal officials who can take, direct others to take, recommend, or approve any personnel action, such as an appointment, promotion, reassignment, suspension, removal, or other action.

The OSC receives and investigates allegations that prohibited personnel practices have occurred, and seeks action if a violation is found.

The 11 prohibited personnel practices are:

• unlawful discrimination;

• solicitation or consideration of improper background references;

• coercion of political activity;

• obstruction of the right to compete;

• influencing withdrawal of applicants from competition;

• unauthorized preferences;

• nepotism;

• reprisal for whistleblowing;

• reprisal for the exercise of an appeal right, or cooperation with the OSC or an agency Inspector General's office;

• discrimination based on non-job related conduct; and

• violation of laws or regulations implementing or concerning merit system principles.

Coverage and Complaints

Employees who fall under the protection of the OSC include most current or former employees or federal job applicants in the executive branch, the Administrative Office of the U.S. Courts, or the Government Printing Office. Exceptions include employees of government corporations, most intelligence agencies, the General Accounting Office, U.S. Postal Service, Postal Rate Commission, and Federal Bureau of Investigation.

Usually, it is through federal employee requests for help that the OSC hears allegations that a prohibited personnel practice has been, or is soon to be, executed. You can report an alleged prohibited personnel practice at any time and without the aid of an attorney. OSC needs certain information to proceed. You can use an OSC complaint form or provide the following information: name and address of the complainant and specific office involved, the job title, grade and employment status of the affected employee or employees, information on the alleged violations of personnel laws or rules, and a statement of facts providing evidence of violations and a description of the actions and events being reported.

OSC does not give advisory opinions (except in Hatch Act matters), but it will clarify its authority and advise you of information it needs to take action.

How OSC Handles Charges

Allegations are sent to OSC's complaints examining unit for initial examination. You will receive a letter from OSC acknowledging your request that it look into a matter. The letter will identify the OSC examiner assigned to your request. The examiner may contact you to ensure that the allegations are clearly understood. Examiners look into all matters received to the extent needed to determine whether they warrant further investigation.

OSC has authority to issue subpoenas for documents or for the attendance and testimony of witnesses and may require employees or other persons to give testimony under oath, sign written statements, or respond formally to written questions.

If the matter consists of certain allegations of discrimination (based on age, race, religion, color, national origin, disability or sex), OSC normally defers to procedures in federal agencies and the Equal Employment Opportunity Commission.

Information contained in a request may be sent to the OSC disclosure unit for possible transmittal to the agency head, if the information is a whistleblower disclosure. The OSC does not disclose the identity of the requester without his or her consent.

After the examination stage, the matter will be closed if the information does not indicate a violation within OSC's jurisdiction, or if the matter is resolved with corrective action by the agency involved. The examining unit sends you a letter reporting on the OSC's findings, and provides you with an opportunity to comment before a case is closed.

If the examination shows a potentially valid claim, the matter will be sent to OSC's investigation division for field investigation. The field investigation results are reviewed by the OSC prosecution division. The prosecutors are looking for any violation of law, rule or regulation and to see if the matter warrants corrective or disciplinary action.

OSC representatives may have discussions at any stage of a pending matter with the agency involved, in an effort to negotiate corrective action acceptable to all parties before starting litigation at the MSPB.

If the evidence is insufficient to establish a violation, the prosecution division sends you a letter, reporting the OSC's findings and providing you an opportunity to comment. If an investigation discloses a violation of any law, rule, or regulation not within the OSC's jurisdiction, the Special Counsel reports its findings to the agency head concerned. OSC reports evidence of possible criminal violations identified during an investigation to the Department of Justice.

Relief and Penalties

Forms of relief (or penalties) OSC action may result in include:

• A stay of any personnel action if the available evidence provides reasonable grounds to believe that a personnel action was taken, or is to be taken, as the result of a prohibited personnel practice.

• Relief designed to make you whole if OSC's review indicates that corrective action is warranted. Corrective action may be sought through negotiation with the agency involved, or if that fails, through litigation against the agency before the MSPB.

• Disciplinary action against an employee who has committed a violation within its jurisdiction. Disciplinary action may be taken by the employee's agency (with OSC's prior consent), or by OSC in a prosecution before the MSPB. Individuals found by the MSPB to have committed a prohibited personnel practice are subject to removal, reduction in grade, debarment from federal employment for up to five years, suspension, reprimand, or fines of up to $1,000.

Officials who willfully refuse to comply with an MSPB order can be the subject of a further complaint.

Current or former federal employees and applicants for employment who have filed a matter with the OSC alleging actual or threatened reprisal for whistleblowing may have their allegation heard by the MSPB as an "individual right of action" if OSC closes the matter after investigation, or if OSC does not seek corrective action within 120 days from receiving the complaint. If such an appeal is filed, MSPB may not take into account OSC's decision to terminate an investigation of a whistleblowing complaint without seeking corrective action.

The Special Counsel may participate in most proceedings before the MSPB. But it may not intervene in certain proceedings, including individual right of action cases, without the consent of the employee.

Hatch Act Enforcement

Under the 1939 Hatch Act, executive branch and postal employees and certain state and local government employees are restricted in their ability to participate in political activities. Congress amended the Hatch Act in 1993 to allow most federal and postal employees to take a more active part in political activities or campaigns.

However, certain federal agencies, primarily those involving national security and law enforcement, and certain categories of employees, such as career senior executive service employees and administrative law judges, continue to be covered by the original, broader restrictions. Meanwhile, there are partial exemptions from the Hatch Act for those living in certain designated communities where most voters are federal or postal employees.

OSC receives and investigates complaints of Hatch Act violations. It may issue a warning letter to the employee involved in less serious cases and will prosecute violations before the MSPB where it believes that is warranted. Violations of the Hatch Act are punishable by penalties ranging from a 30-day suspension without pay to removal.

OSC also issues advisory opinions to those seeking advice about what activities are permitted under the Hatch Act. Individuals may request such advice orally or in writing, including by e-mail.

Whistleblower Disclosure Hotline

OSC provides a channel through which current and former federal employees (and applicants for employment) can disclose evidence of a violation of law, rule, or regulation, gross mismanagement, gross waste of funds, abuse of authority, or a substantial and specific danger to public health or safety. OSC guarantees confidentiality to the discloser.

The Special Counsel is authorized to order an agency head to investigate and report on the information disclosed. After any such investigation, the Special Counsel is required to send the agency's report, with any comments by you (as the source of the disclosure), to the President, Congress, and the Comptroller General.

After reviewing the information you provide, the OSC may determine that there is not a substantial likelihood that the information shows the type of wrongdoing required to formally deem the disclosure an act of whistleblowing. In such cases, the Special Counsel may, with your consent, send the information to the head of the agency, who must report to the Special Counsel on any action taken or to be taken. The information provided by the agency head is given to you.

If OSC does not send information disclosed by you to an agency head, OSC returns the information and any accompanying documents to you. OSC will tell you why the information has not been referred to the agency and advise you of any other available disclosure channels.

Other OSC Responsibilities

The Uniformed Services Employment and Reemployment Rights Act of 1994 gave OSC authority to investigate and prosecute cases involving the denial of employment or reemployment rights to veterans and reservists seeking to return to the federal workplace after active duty with the armed services. OSC can, after Labor Department review of the matter, represent a veteran or reservist before MSPB, and potentially on appeal to the U.S. Court of Appeals for the Federal Circuit.

Also, OSC is authorized to investigate: activities prohibited by any civil service law, rule, or regulation; allegations of arbitrary or capricious withholding of information under the Freedom of Information Act; and involvement by any employee in any prohibited discrimination found by a court or administrative authority to have occurred in the course of a personnel action.

The Special Counsel also supports efforts to educate federal employees about their rights and remedies in connection with prohibited personnel practices, and about the rights and restrictions of the Hatch Act.

Contacting OSC

Requests for assistance in connection with allegations of prohibited personnel practices, as well as requests for the appropriate forms, should be directed to the OSC Officer of the Week at: Complaints Examining Unit, U.S. Office of Special Counsel, 1730 M Street, N.W., Suite 300, Washington, D.C. 20036-4505. Tel: (800) 872-9855 (TDD-equipped), (202) 653-7188 (TDD-equipped)

Inquiries about the Hatch Act may be made in writing or by telephone to: Hatch Act Unit, U.S. Office of Special Counsel, 1730 M Street, N.W.,

Suite 300, Washington, D.C. 20036-4505. Tel: (800) 85-HATCH or (800) 854-2824, (202) 653-7143. Requests for Hatch Act advisory opinions may be made by e-mail to: hatchact@osc.gov

Disclosures of violations of law, rule, or regulation, gross mismanagement, gross waste of funds, abuse of authority, or a danger to public health or safety may be reported in confidence to (and the appropriate form requested from): Disclosure Unit, U.S. Office of Special Counsel, 1730 M Street, N.W., Suite 300, Washington, D.C. 20036-4505. Tel: (800) 572-2249, (202) 653-9125.

Questions from federal agencies about obtaining copies of the OSC informational program guide for federal agencies on diskette should be directed to: U.S. Office of Special Counsel, 1730 M Street, N.W., Suite 300, Washington, D.C. 20036-4505. Tel: (202) 653-9485 Fax: (202) 653-5161.

OSC's World Wide Web address is *http://www.osc.gov.*

Part 3

Appendices

I. OBTAINING DECISIONS

It is always a good idea to obtain a copy of the original decision, especially if the research is being done in preparation for a formal appeal. Administrative bodies and courts will only accept legal arguments taken directly from the earlier, presidential decisions. For a copy of a decision, contact the court or agency, providing the identifying number, date and case title.

Federal courts have varying policies regarding charges for copies of opinions. Most assess a fee of a few dollars, but as this changes from time to time and from place to place, it is best to contact the clerk of that court first to ascertain its policy.

A court clerk's office may only maintain copies of decisions going back a certain period of time. For decisions no longer on file, the requester usually will have to research the case in one of the compilations that are available in law libraries, agency libraries and other places where legal research resources are kept.

Some court decisions may not appear in such compilations because they were "unpublished" rulings. These decisions have the same force of law as "published" decisions but they are not considered precedential in nature because they break no new legal ground. To obtain copies of the full decisions, contact the courts that issued them. Also note that decisions can be overturned on appeal. Thus, a particular decision you might find could later have been reversed. This is a good reason to do research in legal compilations.

Compilations of the decisions of administrative agencies usually also are available in law libraries, agency libraries and other places where legal research resources are kept. The decisions also are generally available directly from the agencies that issued them.

Federal employees can obtain individual copies of rulings on employment disputes by contacting the deciding agencies and providing the case title and number. The decisions generally are provided free of charge by the agencies unless a large number of copies is being requested. The agencies do not provide copies of court rulings on their decisions, however. Those must be obtained from the individual courts.

Decisions of the Merit Systems Protection Board or its regional hearing officials can be obtained from MSPB's Office of the Clerk, 1615 M Street, NW, Washington, DC 20419, phone (202) 653-7200. Copies of MSPB reports can be obtained from the Office of Policy and Evaluation, same address as above, phone (202) 653-8900.

For decisions of the Federal Labor Relations Authority and the Federal Service Impasses Panel, an arm of FLRA, contact FLRA's Office of Information Resources and Research Services, 607 14th St., NW, Washington, DC 20424, phone (202) 482-6550 (FLRA) or (202) 482-6670 (FSIP).

For a copy of an EEOC decision contact Personnet at (800) 320-4555 or visit their home page at http:www.personnet.com.

Administrative agencies generally assess no charge if only one copy is being requested and the decision is not unusually lengthy. The Equal Employment Opportunity Commission is an exception, charging a per-page fee for all opinions. Fee policies may change over time. Contact the agencies for information on the potential cost of a given decision.

Both the courts and the administrative bodies routinely provide copies of final decisions only. A specific request must be made to obtain legal briefs, supporting evidence or other background material on a case. Usually this will entail a charge per page copied. And such information may not be readily available, especially for older cases.

Should briefs and other papers not be available through the court or administrative body, they may still be available through the law firm that handled the case. Many rulings give the attorney's names at the beginning on a title page or at the end in a list of those to whom the decision was sent. However, a law firm may have a policy of not providing such papers, or may charge for duplicating.

——— How To Get Copies of Decisions ———

Administrative Agencies	
Name	**Address**
Merit Systems Protection Board	Office of the Clerk, MSPB 1615 M Street N.W. Washington, D.C. 20419 (202) 653-7200
Federal Labor Relations Authority and the Federal Service Impasses Panel	Office of Information Resources and Research Services 607 14th Street N.W. Washington, D.C. 20424 (202) 482-6550 (FLRA) (202) 482-6670 (FSIP)
Comptroller General	GAO Headquarters Room 1000 441 G Street N.W. Washington, D.C. 20548
Equal Employment Opportunity Commission	Information Handling Service 15 Inverness Way Englewood, CO 80150 (800) 525-7052 Commerce Clearing House Customer Service 4025 W. Peterson Ave. Chicago, IL 60646 (800) 449-9525 Bureau of National Affairs 1231 25th Street N.W. Washington, D.C. 20037 (800) 372-1033
Labor Agreement Information Retrieval Service (LAIRS)	LAIRS Section Office of Personnel Mgmt. Room 7429 1900 E Street N.W. Washington, D.C. 20415 (202) 606-2940

II. FEDERAL COURTS

United States Supreme Court	
Name	**Address**
Supreme Court of the United States (Address correspondence to "Clerk of Court")	One First Street N.W. Washington, D.C. 20543

United States Courts of Appeals		
Court of Appeals	**Districts Included in Circuit**	**Postal Address**
Federal Circuit	United States	Washington, D.C. 20439
District of Columbia	District of Columbia	Washington, D.C. 20001
First Circuit	Maine Massachusetts New Hampshire Rhode Island Puerto Rico	Boston, MA 02109
Second Circuit	Connecticut New York Vermont	New York, NY 10007
Third Circuit	Delaware New Jersey Pennsylvania Virgin Islands	Philadelphia, PA 19106
Fourth Circuit	Maryland North Carolina South Carolina Virginia West Virginia	Richmond, VA 23219
Fifth Circuit	Louisiana Mississippi Texas	New Orleans, LA 70130

United States Courts of Appeals

Court of Appeals	Districts Included in Circuit	Postal Address
Sixth Circuit	Kentucky Michigan Tennessee	Cincinnati, OH 45202
Seventh Circuit	Illinois Indiana Wisconsin	Chicago, IL 60604
Eighth Circuit	Arkansas Iowa Minnesota Missouri Nebraska North Dakota South Dakota	St. Louis, MO 63101
Ninth Circuit	Alaska Arizona California Hawaii Idaho Montana Nevada Oregon Washington Guam N. Mariana Islands	San Francisco, CA 94101
Tenth Circuit	Colorado Kansas New Mexico Oklahoma Utah Wyoming	Denver, CO 80294
Eleventh Circuit	Alabama Florida Georgia	Atlanta, GA 30303

III. GLOSSARY OF LEGAL TERMS

(Editor's Note: The following glossary of commonly used legal terms was prepared by the Administrative Office of the U.S. Courts. While not all of the listed terms have a direct bearing on most federal workers' job-related disputes (e.g., "acquittal," "grand jury," "voir dire," etc.), in certain situations, federal employees may find themselves involved in legal actions that require them to be familiar with such words or phrases.)

A

acquittal
Judgment that a criminal defendant has not been proved guilty beyond a reasonable doubt. In other words, a verdict of "not guilty."

affidavit
A written statement of facts confirmed by the oath of the party making it, before a notary or officer having authority to administer oaths.

affirmed
In the practice of the court of appeals, it means that the court of appeals has concluded that the lower court decision is correct and will stand as rendered by the lower court.

answer
The formal written statement by a defendant responding to a civil complaint and setting forth the grounds for his defense.

appeal
A request made after a trial by a party that has lost on one or more issues that a higher court (appellate court) review the trial court's decision to determine if it was correct. To make such a request is "to appeal" or "to take an appeal." One who appeals is called the "appellant;" the other party is the "appellee."

appellate
About appeals; an appellate court has the power to review the judgment of a lower court (trial court) or tribunal. For example, the U.S. circuit courts of appeals review the decisions of the U.S. district courts.

arraignment
A proceeding in which an individual who is accused of committing a crime is brought into court, told of the charges, and asked to plead guilty or not guilty.

B

bail
Security given for the release of a criminal defendant or witness from legal custody (usually in the form of money) to secure his appearance on the day and time set by the court.

bankruptcy
A legal process by which persons or businesses that cannot pay their debts can seek the assistance of the court in getting a fresh start. Under the protection of the bankruptcy court, debtors may discharge their debts, usually by paying a portion of each debt. Bankruptcy judges preside over these proceedings.

bench trial
Trial without a jury in which a judge decides which party prevails.

brief
A written statement submitted by each party in a case that explains why the court should decide the case, or particular issues in a case, in that party's favor.

C

chambers
A judge's office, typically including work space for the judge's law clerks and secretary.

capital offense
A crime punishable by death.

case law
The law as reflected in the written decisions of the courts.

chief judge
The judge who has primary responsibility for the administration of a court; chief judges are determined by seniority.

clerk of court
An officer appointed by the judges of the court to assist in managing the flow of cases through the court, maintain court records, handle financial matters, and provide other administrative support to the court.

common law
The legal system that originated in England and is now in use in the United States that relies on the articulation of legal principles in a historical succession of judicial decisions. Common law principles can be changed by legislation.

complaint
A written statement filed by the plaintiff that initiates a civil case, stating the wrongs allegedly committed by the defendant and requesting relief from the court.

contract
An agreement between two or more persons that creates an obligation to do or not to do a particular thing.

conviction
A judgment of guilt against a criminal defendant.

counsel
Legal advice; a term also used to refer to the lawyers in a case.

court
Government entity authorized to resolve legal disputes. Judges sometimes use "court" to refer to themselves in the third person, as in "the court has read the briefs."

court reporter
A person who makes a word-for-word record of what is said in court, generally by using a stenographic machine, shorthand or audio recording, and then produces a transcript of the proceedings upon request.

D

damages
Money paid by defendants to successful plaintiffs in civil cases to compensate the plaintiffs for their injuries.

default judgment
A judgment rendered in favor of the plaintiff because of the defendant's failure to answer or appear to contest the plaintiff's claim.

defendant
In a civil case, the person or organization against whom the plaintiff brings suit; in a criminal case, the person accused of the crime.

deposition
An oral statement made before an officer authorized by law to administer oaths. Such statements are often taken to examine potential witnesses, to obtain discovery, or to be used later in trial. See discovery.

discovery
The process by which lawyers learn about their opponent's case in preparation for trial. Typical tools of discovery include depositions, interrogatories,requests for admissions, and requests for documents. All of these devices help the lawyer learn the relevant facts and collect and examine any relevant documents or other materials.

docket
A log containing the complete history of each case in the form of brief chronological entries summarizing the court proceedings.

E

en banc
"In the bench" or "as a full bench." Refers to court sessions with the entire membership of a court participating rather than the usual number. U.S. circuit courts of appeals usually sit in panels of three judges, but all the judges in the court may decide certain matters together. They are then said to be sitting "en banc" (occasionally spelled "in banc").

equitable
Pertaining to civil suits in "equity" rather than in "law." In English legal history, the courts of "law" could order the payment of damages and could afford no other remedy. See damages. A separate court of "equity" could order someone to do something or to cease to do something. See, e.g., injunction. In American jurisprudence, the federal courts have both legal and equitable power, but the distinction is still an important one. For example, a trial by jury is normally available in "law" cases but not in "equity" cases.

evidence
Information presented in testimony or in documents that is used to persuade the fact finder (judge or jury) to decide the case in favor of one side or the other.

F

federal public defender
An attorney employed by the federal courts on a full-time basis to provide legal defense to defendants who are unable to afford counsel. The judiciary administers the federal defender program pursuant to the Criminal Justice Act.

federal question jurisdiction
Jurisdiction given to federal courts in cases involving the interpretation and application of the U.S. Constitution, acts of Congress, and treaties.

felony
A serious crime carrying a penalty of more than a year in prison. See also misdemeanor.

file
To place a paper in the official custody of the clerk of court to enter into the files or records of a case.

G

grand jury
A body of 16-23 citizens who listen to evidence of criminal allegations, which is presented by the prosecutors, and determine whether there is probable cause to believe an individual committed an offense. See also indictment and U.S. attorney.

H

habeas corpus
A writ (court order) that is usually used to bring a prisoner before the court to determine the legality of his imprisonment. Someone imprisoned in state court proceedings can file a petition in federal court for a "writ of habeas corpus," seeking to have the federal court review whether the state has violated his or her rights under the U.S. Constitution. Federal prisoners can file habeas petitions as well. A writ of habeas corpus may also be used to bring a person in custody before the court to give testimony or to be prosecuted.

hearsay
Statements by a witness who did not see or hear the incident in question but heard about it from someone else. Hearsay is usually not admissible as evidence in court.

I

impeachment
1. The process of calling a witness's testimony into doubt. For example, if the attorney can show that the witness may have fabricated portions of his testimony, the witness is said to be "impeached;"
2. The constitutional process whereby the House of Representatives may "impeach" (accuse of misconduct) high officers of the federal government, who are then tried by the Senate.

indictment
The formal charge issued by a grand jury stating that there is enough evidence that the defendant committed the crime to justify having a trial; it is used primarily for felonies. See also information.

in forma pauperis
"In the manner of a pauper." Permission given by the court to a person to file a case without payment of the required court fees because the person cannot pay them.

information
A formal accusation by a government attorney that the defendant committed a misdemeanor. See also indictment.

injunction
A court order prohibiting a defendant from performing a specific act, or compelling a defendant to perform a specific act.

interrogatories
Written questions sent by one party in a lawsuit to an opposing party as part of pretrial discovery in civil cases. The party receiving the interrogatories is required to answer them in writing under oath.

issue
1. The disputed point between parties in a lawsuit;
2. To send out officially, as in a court issuing an order.

J

judge
An official of the judicial branch with authority to decide lawsuits brought before courts. Used generically, the term judge may also refer to all judicial officers, including Supreme Court justices.

judgment
The official decision of a court finally resolving the dispute between the parties to the lawsuit.

jurisdiction
1. The legal authority of a court to hear and decide a case;
2. The geographic area over which the court has authority to decide cases.

jury
The group of persons selected to hear the evidence in a trial and render a verdict on matters of fact. See also grand jury.

jury instructions
A judge's directions to the jury before it begins deliberations regarding the factual questions it must answer and the legal rules that it must apply.

jurisprudence
The study of law and the structure of the legal system.

L

lawsuit
A legal action started by a plaintiff against a defendant based on a complaint that the defendant failed to perform a legal duty which resulted in harm to the plaintiff.

litigation
A case, controversy, or lawsuit. Participants (plaintiffs and defendants) in lawsuits are called litigants.

M

magistrate judge
A judicial officer of a district court who conducts initial proceedings in criminal cases, decides criminal misdemeanor cases, conducts many pretrial civil and criminal matters on behalf of district judges, and decides civil cases with the consent of the parties.

misdemeanor
An offense punishable by one year of imprisonment or less. See also felony.

mistrial
An invalid trial, caused by fundamental error. When a mistrial is declared, the trial must start again with the selection of a new jury.

motion
A request by a litigant to a judge for a decision on an issue relating to the case.

N

nolo contendere
No contest. A plea of nolo contendere has the same effect as a plea of guilty, as far as the criminal sentence is concerned, but may not be considered as an admission of guilt for any other purpose.

O

opinion
A judge's written explanation of the decision of the court. Because a case may be heard by three or more judges in the court of appeals, the opinion in appellate decisions can take several forms. If all the judges completely agree on the result, one judge will write the opinion for all. If all the judges do not agree, the formal decision will be based upon the view of the majority, and one member of the majority will write the opinion. The judges who did not agree with the majority may write separately in dissenting or concurring opinions to present their views. A dissenting opinion disagrees with the majority opinion because of the reasoning and/or the principles of law the majority used to decide the case. A concurring opinion agrees with the decision of the majority opinion, but offers further comment or clarification or even an entirely different reason for reaching the same result. Only the majority opinion can serve as binding precedent in future cases. See also precedent.

oral argument
An opportunity for lawyers to summarize their position before the court and also to answer the judges' questions.

P

panel
1. In appellate cases, a group of judges (usually three) assigned to decide the case;
2. In the jury selection process, the group of potential jurors;
3. The list of attorneys who are both available and qualified to serve as court-appointed counsel for criminal defendants who cannot afford their own counsel.

party
One of the litigants. At the trial level, the parties are typically referred to as the plaintiff and defendant. On appeal, they are known as the appellant and appellee, or, in some cases involving administrative agencies, as the petitioner and respondent.

petit jury (or trial jury)
A group of citizens who hear the evidence presented by both sides at trial and deter-mine the facts in dispute. Federal criminal juries consist of 12 persons. Federal civil juries consist of at least six persons. See also jury and grand jury.

petty offense
A federal misdemeanor punishable by six months or less in prison.

plaintiff
The person who files the complaint in a civil lawsuit.

plea
In a criminal case, the defendant's statement pleading "guilty" or "not guilty" in answer to the charges. See also nolo contendere.

pleadings
Written statements filed with the court which describe a party's legal or factual assertions about the case.

precedent
A court decision in an earlier case with facts and legal issues similar to a dispute currently before a court. Judges will generally "follow precedent"— meaning that they use the principles established in earlier cases to decide new cases that have similar facts and raise similar legal issues. A judge will disregard precedent if a party can show that the earlier case was wrongly decided, or that it differed in some significant way from the current case.

procedure
The rules for conducting a lawsuit; there are rules of civil procedure, criminal procedure, evidence, bankruptcy, and appellate procedure.

presentence report
A report prepared by a court's probation officer, after a person has been convicted of an offense, summarizing for the court the background information needed to determine the appropriate sentence.

pretrial conference
A meeting of the judge and lawyers to plan the trial, to discuss which matters should be presented to the jury, to review proposed evidence and witnesses, and to set a trial schedule. Typically, the judge and the parties also discuss the possibility of settlement of the case.

pretrial services
A department of the district court that conducts an investigation of a criminal defendant's background in order to help a judge decide whether to release the defendant into the community before trial.

probation
1. A sentencing alternative to imprisonment in which the court releases convicted defendants under supervision of a probation officer, who makes certain that the defendant follows certain rules (e.g., gets a job, gets drug counseling, etc.);
2. A department of the court that prepares a presentence report.

probation officer
Officers of the probation office of a court. Probation officer duties include conducting presentence investigations, preparing presentence reports on convicted defendants, and supervising released defendants.

pro per
A slang expression sometimes used to refer to a pro se litigant. It is a corruption of the Latin phrase "in propria persona."

pro se
A Latin term meaning "on one's own behalf "; in courts, it refers to persons who present their own cases without lawyers.

prosecute
To charge someone with a crime. A prosecutor tries a criminal case on behalf of the government.

R

record
A written account of the proceedings in a case, including all pleadings, evidence, and exhibits submitted in the course of the case.

remand
The act of an appellate court sending a case to a lower court for further proceedings.

reverse
The act of an appellate court setting aside the decision of a trial court. A reversal is often accompanied by a remand to the lower court for further proceedings.

S

sentence
The punishment ordered by a court for a defendant convicted of a crime.

sentencing guidelines
A set of rules and principles established by the United States Sentencing Commission that trial judges use to determine the sentence for a convicted defendant.

service of process
The delivery of writs or summonses to the appropriate party.

settlement
Parties to a lawsuit resolve their dispute without having a trial. Settlements often involve the payment of compensation by one party in at least partial satisfaction of the other party's claims, but usually do not include the admission of fault.

sequester
To separate. Sometimes juries are sequestered from outside influences during their deliberations.

statute
A law passed by a legislature.

statute of limitations
A law that sets the deadline by which parties must file suit to enforce their rights. For example, if a state has a five-year statute of limitations for breaches of contract, and John breached a contract with Susan on January 1, 1995, Susan must file her lawsuit by January 1, 2000. If the deadline passes, the "statute of limitations has run" and the party may be prohibited from bringing a lawsuit; i.e. the claim is "time-barred." Sometimes a party's attempt to assert his or her rights will "toll" the statute of limitations, giving the party additional time to file suit.

subpoena
A command, issued under authority of a court or other authorized government entity, to a witness to appear and give testimony.

subpoena duces tecum
A command to a witness to appear and produce documents.

summary judgment
A decision made on the basis of statements and evidence presented for the record without a trial. It is used when it is not necessary to resolve any factual disputes in the case. Summary judgment is granted when—on the undisputed facts in the record—one party is entitled to judgment as a matter of law.

T

temporary restraining order
Prohibits a person from taking an action that is likely to cause irreparable harm. This differs from an injunction in that it may be granted immediately, without notice to the opposing party, and without a hearing. It is intended to last only until a hearing can be held. Sometimes referred to as a "T.R.O."

testimony
Evidence presented orally by witnesses during trials or before grand juries.

toll
See statute of limitations.

tort
A civil wrong or breach of a duty to another person. The "victim" of a tort may be entitled to sue for the harm suffered. Victims of crimes may also sue in tort for the wrongs done to them. Most tort cases are handled in state court, except when the tort occurs on federal property (e.g., a military base), when the government is the defendant, or when there is diversity of citizenship between the parties.

transcript
A written, word-for-word record of what was said, either in a proceeding such as a trial, or during some other formal conversation, such as a hearing or oral deposition.

trustee
In a bankruptcy case, a person appointed to represent the interests of the bankruptcy estate and the unsecured creditors. The trustee's responsibilities may include liquidating the property of the estate, making distributions to creditors, and bringing actions against creditors or the debtor to recover property of the bankruptcy estate.

U

uphold
The appellate court agrees with the lower court decision and allows it to stand. See affirmed.

U.S. Attorney
A lawyer appointed by the President in each judicial district to prosecute and defend cases for the federal government. The U.S. Attorney employs a staff of Assistant U.S. Attorneys who appear as the government's attorneys in individual cases.

V

venue
The geographical location in which a case is tried.

verdict
The decision of a trial jury or a judge that determines the guilt or innocence of a criminal defendant, or that determines the final outcome of a civil case.

voir dire
The process by which judges and lawyers select a trial jury from among those eligible to serve, by questioning them to make certain that they would fairly decide the case. "Voir dire" is a phrase meaning "to speak the truth."

W

warrant
A written order authorizing official action by law enforcement officials, usually directing them to arrest the individual named in the warrant. A search warrant orders that a specific location be searched for items, which if found, can be used in court as evidence.

witness
A person called upon by either side in a lawsuit to give testimony before the court or jury.

writ
A formal written command or order, issued by the court, requiring the performance of a specific act.

writ of certiorari
An order issued by the U.S. Supreme Court directing the lower court to transmit records for a case which it will hear on appeal.